# My Case
# Unpacked

## Lois M. Ainger

First published in the United Kingdom by
Lois M. Ainger

**British Library Cataloguing in Publication Data.**

Ainger, Lois M.
  My Case Unpacked
  I. Title
  942.342082092

ISBN 0-9525238-0-9

Typeset in 10/11½ pt New Baskerville.
Origination by
Alan Sutton Publishing Ltd, Stroud, Gloucestershire.
Printed in Great Britain by
The Guernsey Press, Guernsey.

Map on front cover reproduced from Philip's New School
Atlas of Comparative Geography by permission of George Philip

# Contents

With gratitude
to
**Margaret, David and Paul**
who so generously
gave me their childhood
and have now become
my friends

# Preface

I have greatly enjoyed talking of old times and gathering information for this book. It is now finished, but the story will never be complete. There will always be more to say and new perspectives to explore. The saga evolves, depending on the point of approach and the degree of involvement. It has a life of its own. I am part of that process, although the scenes I have described are in the past. They depict where many of us have come from. The experiences of our early years live on, whatever we make of them at later stages.

I was already collecting reminiscences of childhood, when, many years ago, I was asked to consider writing the story of the Girls' Intermediate School during the period of its evacuation from Guernsey to Rochdale (1940–5). I was there and the world was at war. I soon found that my descriptions of the school's activities and of our industrial surroundings were not conveying the ethos and dilemmas of those times. I would need to be more personal and reflect the thoughts and feelings of those involved. The task loomed large and I put it to one side, because of heavy work commitments.

Years passed and I retired. My thoughts focused on the suitcase which I had carried with me as an evacuee and the memories returned. I approached others and, with their help, compiled this story. For our generation, the process of growing up was sharply sectioned into three: before, during and after the war. These demarcations chopped our lives into segments, but the emotional experiences of evacuees cannot be understood without reference to all that preceded and followed on. In the long term, processes of healing and integration were needed. The scope of this story, which, at first, was centred on the war years, has been widened to take this into account.

I have included some reflection of the pain and misgivings, as well as the confidence and hope, which coloured our lives. I gave up early attempts to be detached and impartial and have not given a balanced picture of anyone, least of all of myself. Many of us, in the war years, had the tendencies of teenagers to be critical, brash, dismissive, dependent, idealistic, enthusiastic, trusting, arrogant and full of doubts. I have allowed some of these traits to show, but we must now acknowledge the worth and generosity of the adults who stood their ground and took responsibility for us: parents, relations, billeting hosts and hostesses, local authorities, friends, voluntary workers and many others.

Mostly, we lived by the norms and expectations of the day; we were constrained by influences which have lost much of their impetus and were fired by ideals no longer so dynamic. Whatever it was that gave rise to shame or pride is now construed in a different way. We were of that time. Today, we have new hopes and visions to energise and send us forward and a renewed sense of God's purposes.

In trying to recapture the scenes of the 1930s and 1940s, I hope I have presented in microcosm, a significant step in the evolution of Guernsey's social and cultural life. The emphasis was once on preserving the self-sufficient elements of a small rural community. Modes of relating were expressed uniquely in the tonal variations of the patois. One could tell from the inflection in someone's voice just where the one addressed stood in a complex network of interrelationships. It is impossible within the scope of this book to recreate a sense of that particular way of belonging or to do justice to that close-knit island community. Some will remember it and approach my book with inside knowledge. The anglicising process was undoubtedly hastened by the war and there are many interpretations of what has happened since.

For readers outside the island, I have given occasional references to geographical detail and the local context, so that a better understanding of the story can be achieved.

The chapters are headed with lines from the songs we knew in those days. Some evoke vivid memories of the dank and darkened atmosphere of the air raid shelters.

I have made every effort to check factual details, but apologise for any inaccuracies and misrepresentations and for not accommodating all the divergent evaluations of people and events. I have integrated many viewpoints, but the responsibility for this presentation is mine and for the way I have used the anecdotes and information provided by others.

I acknowledge with warm thanks the valuable contribution of those who have lent me resource materials such as letters, diaries, extracts from newspapers, reports and various memorabilia. A few have since died and others, in some cases, are frail and elderly.

I owe much to those in my immediate family circle and am very grateful for the continuous backing of my sons, David and Paul and of my son-in-law, Duncan. Margaret, my daughter, has given much valued help with the shaping of the script and her comments on detail have been most useful and perceptive. All four have their own strong attachments to Guernsey. I thank my Robin cousins, Ruth Crozier, Jean De Garis and Marion Dorey for their warm personal support and encouragement. Other relations have contributed reminiscences and background information. Without them all, my efforts would have flagged!

Those who taught at the Girls' Intermediate School, while I was there, have, over the years, been most cooperative and resourceful: Bessie Clayton, F. Emily Hartwell (née Sayer), Ella Mahy, Elsie Naftel, Norah Roughton and Elizabeth Stewart.

Many of the following participated in discussions, wrote of their experiences or supplied resource material:

Monica Ball, Frances Bateson, Frances Billington (née Hemming), Alan Bisson, Joan Bisson (née Adams), Olive and Cecil Brouard, Audrey Clover (née Courts), Margaret Colognoli, Kathleen Cowling (née Cochrane), Gwen Creed (née Damarell), Jean Dilcock (née Bellot), Angèle and Roy Dorey, Lily Foxen, Jane Giles, Bob and Margaret Gill (née Palmer), Peter Girard, Pat Holmes (née Pontin), Winifred Keating, Mary Knight, Kathleen Lainé (née Frampton), Donald le Blancq, Rose Legg (née Colognoli), Doreen Mooney (née Nicholson), Beryl Moore, Marjorie and Edward Naftel, Dan Nicolle, Delma Noyon (née Torode), Audrey Oliver (née Hamel), Kathleen Patten (née Buckley), Anetta Quinn (née Crabtree), Hazel Rabey (née Maplesden), Ruth Reddall (née Gaudion), Yvonne Robilliard, Alice Roughton, Anne Roussel, Marjorie Tostevin (née Brehaut), Maud Thorn (née Bewey), Jean Vidamour, Pat Wild (née Hartland).

The list is far from comprehensive and would need to include more one-time pupils of the Boys' and Girls' Intermediate Schools, the Elizabeth College and the Ladies' College, a few staff members and Old Girls of the Rochdale Municipal High School for Girls, residents of Rochdale, Gt. Hucklow and Summerseat, friends in Dunstable and scattered parts of the UK, the staff of the Rochdale and Dunstable Public Libraries, members of La Société Guernesiaise, the Guernsey Society and the Priaulx Library in St. Peter Port. Thanks are also due to Hugh Lenfestey (Guernsey Archives Service) for taking a personal interest in my project, to Susan Laker who looked up records of Methodism and to various members of the Methodist Church, mainly in the Forest. Many others sat by their telephones for long conversations or read sections of the script.

The typing has been undertaken by Marjorie Field, a valued Dunstable friend. I thank her most warmly for her encouragement and unfailing cheerfulness.

Christopher Sackett and the staff of the Guernsey Press and of Alan Sutton Publishing Limited have all worked hard to launch this publication.

I am deeply grateful to you all for sharing your insights and contributing so much to the recording of this story.

Lois M. Ainger (née Brehaut)<br>
Dunstable<br>
1995

# Chapter I

## *'Now You Ought to Meet Our Family'*

I want to tell you about my suitcase. Once it was strong and sturdy. For many years, I clutched it in my dreams and rushed to catch a moving train or boat, which would not wait. I woke up running.

In June 1940, the case was new and I was twelve. It held all I could carry when I was pitchforked from my home in the Channel Islands. We were nine months into the Second World War. German armies had raced through Europe and reached the coast of France. In Guernsey, we could hear the gunfire rumble over miles of water. The cows grazed on in normal unconcern, while chilling waves of fear swept up our beaches. Invasion threatened.

Shocked into action, the authorities arranged for mass evacuation. Abruptly, thousands of us were lifted from our familiar Guernsey surroundings and set down in unknown territory. I landed among the cotton mills of industrial Lancashire. The Germans occupied the islands and, like many others, I was cut off from my parents. They had stayed behind. My world was split and I was torn apart, with the Channel as divider, slicing past from present.

As I struggled to find my bearings outside my own known boundaries and guidelines, I depended on the suitcase. It held all I had . . . the things I needed for the moment. But more, it linked me with the past and reassured me as I faced the future. With case in hand, I stood prepared for what might happen. It spanned my world, now sectioned into disparate parts to south and north, each coloured with a different set of expectations. The case connected 'what is gone', with 'now' and 'later'. It was a token of my self in transit.

Decades have passed, and when, again, I forage in my attic for this creaking suitcase, I find, bereft, its worn out carcase like a tired old horse that's done its work and manages with scant attention. I rummage through its relegated contents.

Ah! Here's the Liquorice Allsorts box which holds some Southport shells and a little yellow tin of wizened shrapnel. A folded piece of stiff black leather with a rusty zip can once again be coaxed into the shape that held my gas mask. Some fluffy feathers, snuggling in their paper sachet, have far outstripped the owners of the bird they warmed. That small grey disc, which rolls behind a wad of letters, is a brooch with stylised leaves still curling out of beaten pewter – a token from my billet of that tacit bargain struck: provision in return for good behaviour. A purse of tapestry brings memories of the wrinkled hands that made it and, limping lamely on their tired elastic, are pearly segments of a bracelet I was given. Is that Peel's tower in silhouette high over Holcombe Moor? My clear bright sketch belies the banks of smoke which were the dreary toll of being in work. Some small red crosses top the cryptic messages from home and here are poems of the First World War. I mouth again the ones I knew by heart . . . 'The laughter of unclouded years and every sad and lovely thing'. . . . And in my battered Bible is the pale blue marker with its silvered bell still ringing out its age-old invitation to eternity: COME UNTO ME.

I turn now to the closely written pages of my crumbling diaries, and re-read the entries. Beneath the surface jottings, I can burrow for the mood and rhythm of each passing day. Then, slowly, through the blandness and intentional camouflage, I see a girl emerging. That girl was me? She comes as a surprise.

At first the images are blurred and indistinct, an amateur's attempt to capture incident and movement, while hiding the emotion. But I can bring them into sharper focus and zoom in on dormant detail. So more will come to light. I'm touching something real, but not liking all I see. Is that the person I have been? Did all that really happen?

This case of childhood debris holds more by far than I'd imagined. I must unpack it and arrange the clutter of discarded things to tell their story and convey their meaning, how they were used and stood for what I valued. I see that case today as travelling-home, my self in progress, en route and making headway on a journey.

Others who left their island homes in haste will share their memories. We'll all be young again and vulnerable: bit-players on a wartime stage, each with our own unique perspective on the others and the space between them. But we are viewers too. We see our parts enacted from the vantage balcony of years. We are both actors and reactors. I use this dual way of viewing and it is mine, reflected in the selections I have made, the questionings and interpretations and, to some extent, the gaps.

The story must begin with the life that had been mine till that memorable day in 1940 and with a portrait of the girl I left behind in my parents' memory. . . .

\* \* \* \* \*

Find me, at the age of seven, somersaulting down the length of a field larger than a football pitch. As I roll on at breakneck speed with my face tucked into the dark folds of my dress, voices above me guide my progress. "To the left!" shouts Brian. "Careful!" shrieks Jean, as she sees me heading for a cowpat. Then, as I blindly hurtle into another arc, correcting hands come down to straighten my course. Overhead, Ruth maintains a steady count of the rolls . . . 89, 90, 91, 92. . . . On and on I go, till my feet touch the hedge on the far side of the field. I have arrived, breathless and a little dizzy. And now it's someone else's turn. We all run back to the starting point and as I pick dried stalks and fragments from my tangled ringlets, I take the role of marshal: "Ready, steady, go!"

Soon we are swinging from the wooden supports of our water-tank. This round landmark, high as a house, squats over our field, Le Petit Manoir. Then as we cartwheel under the adjacent windmill, we upturn its mighty latticed framework in the handstand and see it pierce the sky beyond. The iron crisscross bars become a perch for spying on marauders. Ignoring the 'dares', we seldom shin far up its forbidden ladder for fear of being observed from a distance or falling to a dizzy death onto the craning heads below.

Abruptly, a petrol engine clanks into action to work the pump for the well water when the level in the tank is low and the windmill flagging. Snake-like hoses festoon the nearby green-house and the water soaks freely to the roots of fine tomatoes. The long rows of plants, trapped in arches under their roof of glass stretch into the distance, away to the farthest end of the field. Prancing inside along the hardened avenues holds little interest, unless the rats are active. We keep a close watch on the traps and report any sightings. Sometimes a workman creeps up with a garden fork, intent on spiking them into the ground. When it gets too hot under glass, we run outside and scamper to the top of a hedge and pick one of our number to face us from the ground below and pull us forward into flight. With arms waving wildly to propel us further, we choose contorted angles for the landing and freeze into an impassive pose to impress the others. The first one to move or laugh becomes the puller and we end up collapsed in helpless giggling heaps.

Suddenly we are racing towards an old wrecked car, roofless and long-abandoned. Brian, my brother, is often the bus driver. He sits in rusty splendour in his skeleton seat, knocking aside the dangling cables with his knees, and wiping rancid lubricant from his short grey trousers. The passengers take their seats among the

jutting springs and tickly horsehair and swing their legs into the
weeds protruding through the broken chassis. "And how is your
rheumatism today, Mrs. Rabey?" one asks politely. "Not so good,
Mrs. Tostevin." "What kind of fish did you get in the market this
morning?" "Isn't the mackerel expensive? It's wicked." When we
have travelled to Pleinmont and distant parts of the island, we are
glad to hear the Forest church clock striking five. Clutching the
wilting bunches of buttercups, vetch and clover, we scurry indoors
for our tea. Heaped slices of bread, spread with salty Guernsey
butter, nestle in deep yellow brightness on the curling pattern of
a blue and white plate. "Lord, bless this food to our use. Amen."
my father mutters. Before long, the bowls of jelly, stewed plums
and custard are emptied and we are tucking into the swiss roll
invariably bought for such family treats.

The scraping of my father's chair signals the time for our
cousins, Ruth and Jean, to return to their home at Les Fontaines
in the Câtel parish, where their parents, my Aunty Adele and
Uncle Arthur, have a guest house in a cluster of old and beautiful
brown granite buildings. "Cheerio!" "So long!" they call as they
bundle into my father's car which heads slowly up our yard. It's a
two mile journey, taking twenty minutes through the twisting
lanes. Safely home, Ruth and Jean explain why a sandal buckle is
hanging loose and a tooth has fallen out.

At Rue des Landes, Brian and I slip back into the house. The
day for us is ending. I salvage all the wild flowers I can and
arrange them carefully into fish paste pots and jam jars kept
specially for the purpose in an enormous pine cupboard which
had come from the childhood home of my father's mother, Gran,
from Milestone. Little stray insects are flicked onto the red
cemented floor, destined, as I think, to find their own instinctive
way towards the door. Oddments of dead leaves and petals are
flung into the slop bucket ready to be tipped on to the rotting
rubbish heap the following day.

Then it is time to notice the green knees and stained elbows and
to remove the socks, whose heels have slipped into rumpled ridges
inside our sandals. A chipped enamel bowl is filled with hot water
from the kettle. Strenuous rubbing with Lifebuoy soap leaves limbs
and joints a tingling pink. The worst of the day's grime has been
removed by my mother. Still warm from the day's exertions and
excitement, Brian and I troop up the stairs to our beds.

On his return, my father strides into the office he has made in
the house and reaches for the ledger on the heavy metal safe. He
sits at a trestle table and opens the workshop entry book. His

papers are arranged on the thick red pile of the patterned curtain which covers the uneven boards. Then he begins the day's accounts. Besides growing tomatoes for export, he carries on the family carpentry and building business and serves the neighbourhood as undertaker.

Two hours later, when the last of the bills has been tucked inside a manila envelope, he joins my mother, who is quietly sitting in the living room darning his grey hand-knitted socks. He lowers the slatted back of his chair for comfort and settles himself on its corduroy padding. He is quickly immersed in the local paper, homing in on items which are the stuff of his daily business: the state of nearby property and deaths. . . . "Nobody will want to buy that run-down old place at Le Bigard. They ought to have the roof repaired." "Did you see that Henri le Page is gone? What's to become of old Alice? She won't go and live with her son, that's for sure. His wife will see to that."

A gentle wheezing breaks the silence. He glances down at the tortoiseshell cat which he barely tolerates, but himself had brought from Sark to please his children. She sleeps on at his feet, encased in old felt slippers and shares with them the benefits of a homely rug. The elderly mother of a customer had cut into strips the patched relics of my father's old black suit and combined them with red and grey flecked rags, coaxed into a sackcloth backing. She had been rewarded with a few shillings to relieve her poverty. The floor is covered with lino and the walls are panelled with interlocking planks of knotted pine, varnished to a bronze and honeyed glow. The resin coming from the holes, where the knots have loosened, can be fingered out and tastes acrid. A workman was praised for his imitation graining on the doors and window sill, which is deep-set into the thick old granite walls. In the mornings, the sun streams in through a small sash window and warms a pile of newspapers on which the cat purrs her contentment.

Dangling from the ceiling is a long sticky band of flypaper, coiling slightly like the unrolled film of a camera. The earthly remains of some thirty assorted flies and daddy-longlegs cover its glutinous surface. The buzzing wings of survivors give up the effort to free their legs from its lethal hold.

As always, on the stroke of ten, my father gets up to locate the key of the clock among the scattered farthings and pencils on the mantelpiece. Having wound it and checked the doors and windows, he makes his way up to bed.

* * * * *

The traditional nine-window Guernsey farmhouse where we lived was built of dark grey granite and stood with its gable to the road. There was a lawn and apple tree in front. In the days before houses were given individual names, it became known as Rue des Landes from the road which passed through former wasteland on the highest part of the island. It had been in the family since 1910 when my grandfather, Frederick Martel Brehaut, acquired it from the Guernsey Banking Company. They had siezed it from Paul Breton when he ran into grave financial difficulties. My grandfather quickly took the opportunity to add this small holding of several fields, greenhouses and buildings to his adjoining property at Milestone where he lived. The stone which marks four miles from town is still to be seen, set into the granite wall along the road.

He did not live to see the wedding of my father, Bazil Priaulx Brehaut, to my mother, Miriam Louise Robin, in 1926. They settled down at Rue des Landes, which had come to my father. In readiness, he had worked on extensive renovations himself. The front room to the left of the central porch with its blue and red decorative panes, had previously served as the local Telephone Exchange, to which people brought one penny and had their calls put through. He transformed it into a dining room. Mahogany furniture was installed. A large sideboard was matched with an extending table, whose six extra leaves were housed in a corner cabinet. The downstairs area to the right of the porch was cleared of cliff furze, once heaped there to fuel the old black range at the back of the house. The bulk of it had been stored in the loft over the first floor directly above and was forked down a chute to ground level. Now the loft was sealed off and the chute removed. The downstairs room was turned into a neat, carpeted parlour for use on Sundays and on special days. Wedding presents and dishes inherited from my mother's relations displayed the family's standing.

In another wave of renovations in 1935, 'la lavrie', the stone-flagged scullery area at the back, was extended and its floor cemented over. The indoor pump, which had provided cool water from the well underneath the house, was removed. At one end, a kitchen sink with taps appeared. Another section was partitioned off to form my father's office. Gas and electricity were laid on and the paraffin lamps and candle-holders were put away. Above, a bathroom and two bedrooms for the children were built on. Brian and I were allowed to choose the colour of our walls. I plumped for blue and he decided on yellow, because he was very fond of custard. In the living room, the old black range was replaced by a modern grate flanked by an oven faced with mottled tiles in fawn. A kettle boiled on the fire, now fuelled with anthracite.

The old stable in the yard housed farm implements, ploughs and carts, mostly owned by the neighbours. The barn, whose lintel bore the date 1680, had a newer adjunct, which was leased to a butcher and later a grocer. This shop had once been a village store and Post Office and retained the chute built into the front wall to receive people's letters. There was no separate pillar box. The pigs which had been reared in the granite sties were sold and taken away. Brian and I had often leaned over the walls and dropped handfuls of grass on to their backs to test out their reactions.

During those years, my father worked hard to foster his business. He took pride in his achievements. Brian and I frequently followed him to his workshop at Milestone and kicked through the wooden shavings or, more helpfully, tidied up the boxes of nails.

So often did we watch a coffin being assembled that we knew exactly how it was done from start to finish. I still remember. All the preparations for a funeral were an everyday experience. If printed invitation cards were ordered, my mother addressed the envelopes. When the day came, we peeped between the drawn curtains of the bedroom windows at home and watched the slow procession of mourners filing past the house on its way from the home of the deceased to the Forest Church behind us. At its head was the rector and my father wearing his black top hat and tail-coat. He walked with deliberate steps, and the jaunty swinging of his walking stick revealed him in his element. There followed the coffin, borne on the shoulders of the bereaved men of the family. It gained a last resplendence from its fine pall of purple velvet overlaid with golden braid and tassels. There was always an added poignancy when the small black pall was in use. Another baby had died. As we scanned the faces of the mourners who trailed solemnly behind, firm adult hands behind us prevented us from waving.

On wet afternoons, we raided a heavy swatch of out-dated wallpaper samples. It was kept in a battered pine desk, which was the cherished handiwork of my Milestone grandfather. We cut out flowers from the patterned borders and stuck them on to larger pages with a paste of flour and water and a 'brush' made of newspaper tied to a pencil.

Lily, who came on weekdays to help with the housework, brightened things up with her cheerful singing,

> *Underneath the spreading chestnut tree,*
> *There she said she'd marry me.*

In another song, there was a mysterious piece of crockery called 'the FA cup' which seemed worth shouting about and, taking a trip to the Wild West, we induced the old 'carbered' wagon to roll along, roll along. Even when I found it was 'covered', I had no idea what it was or why it was always so relentlessly on the move.

On windy days, we begged Lily to help us make a kite with bamboo and brown paper. Donald le Blancq, the carpentry apprentice, released its wriggling frame into the sky and, running up the field, we flew it till it fluttered and dipped to an ungainly end.

A frequent visitor to the house was Gran from Milestone. She brought us tracing books and pencils on her way back from town. To make her welcome, we fetched the wicker chair that was her favourite and plumped the patchwork cushion for her to sit on. She was invariably dressed in black and wore a band of fox fur draped loosely over one shoulder. Its pointed snout was secured to its swinging tail by a silken tassel and hook under the opposite arm. I was allowed to cajole its beady eyes into greater prominence and besport myself in style, enwrapped in this fascinating creature. Then, wearing her black toque which was trimmed with blue and green feathers, I paraded to the kitchen with all the grandeur of Queen Mary, whose choice of hats had set this fashion. An umbrella, used in the manner of royalty, completed my majestic outfit. As Gran rose to go, drifting traces of perfume lingered, leaving us with a pervasive sense of unnamed sadness.

In the stillness of the nearby Forest churchyard with its twinkling daisies and dandelions, were the graves of the family members. Gran had lost four of her six children, when they were in the prime of life, all victims of tuberculosis. The stones, already covered with lichen, recorded the shortened span of their lives:

| Winna May Mauger | 1922, aged 19 |
| Eunice Marie | 1924, aged 25 |
| Harold John | 1930, aged 23 |
| Frederick Graham | 1934, aged 37 |

Here also was buried my grandfather, Frederick, who died in 1925 at the age of 64, unable, it was said, to recover from grief over the death of his daughters. Winna, his youngest girl, had been the first to die. She was looking forward to marrying Ambrose Mahy, who happened to be a cousin of my mother's. After her death, her sister, Eunice, became engaged to him, but the young couple each succumbed to the illness and they both died before the marriage could be celebrated. The sisters' untimely deaths from TB occurred in the run up to my parents' marriage and led them both to wonder if my father would survive. Long afterwards, the cause of the trouble was ascribed to an infection in the milk of the Milestone cows. Nothing was known about this at the time. My father subsequently maintained that he escaped because of his strong dislike of milk. Fredena, the eldest in the family, shared this distaste, but, perhaps because she had moved away when she married, she was less susceptible. The two brothers, Fred and Harold, went on living at Milestone and died a few years later.

Gran spent many years looking after one or the other of her children as they lay coughing for long nights and days in a marquee set up for them in a Milestone field, so that they could gain maximum benefit from the fresh air the doctors recommended. No drugs were at hand to effect a cure.

As children, we heard about the musical attainments of our grandfather, who was a chapel organist, and of our dead aunts and uncles. They were held up as models. (The girls always cleaned their shoes on a Saturday.) When I could, I slipped quietly to the graveyard and traced their grooved names in the stone with my finger. The church spire with its trusted clock and glinting weather vane capped the dark silhouette of oak, elm and sycamore which were grouped around the old granite houses and cottages of le Bourg. The age-old church, with its history rooted in the twelfth century, presided, immutable and reassuring, over those rural scenes of my early childhood.

## Chapter II

### *'A Garden of Roses for You and for Me'*

My first days at school were overshadowed by a great handicap. I couldn't speak the language. I was in a small private school for young children and only English was spoken. All the conversation at home was in the island patois, Guernsey French, which resembled a dialect still used in parts of Normandy.

Each of the Channel Islands had its own patois, hardly understood in the others. Within Guernsey itself, there were marked variations. These arose from the days when people rarely left the parishes surrounding their birthplace and never travelled the nine mile stretch, which forms the longest side of this small triangular island, only half the size of Sheffield. Footpaths were precarious and often too narrow for carts and there was little motivation to improve them. People were self-sufficient in their own localities. For centuries, intermingling was very limited between the higher parishes in the west (with which the Forest is grouped) and the lower parishes of the north and east where the town of St. Peter Port is situated.

Between these two sections of the island, there evolved marked differences in the pronunciation of vowel sounds, intonation and vocabulary. As soon as someone spoke, you could tell which part of the island they came from. Even as a child, I knew these differences were geographical and could broadly locate the speaker's parish. Although my mother and father were born only four or five miles apart, they differed widely in their accents, my father coming from the higher parishes (Haut Pas) and my mother from the low (Bas Pas). These differences also suggested variations in life style. Those in the west were often considered uncouth and earthy, well-rooted in the ways of the peasantry and less cultivated than their fellows in the north and east, who had easier access to town and the more advanced educational facilities it provided and were more likely to be exposed to influences from outside the island and reflect English social conventions and attitudes. Earlier, the Huguenot settlers from France had also left their mark there. Island habits, thought patterns and prejudices were, however, deep-rooted and modifications were slow in coming.

Many people lived in great poverty and depended on the demand for casual labour, fluctuating though that was. In broad terms, the impoverished country people worked as labourers on the farms and in the greenhouses and spoke the patois; their counterparts in the town areas of St. Sampson's and St. Peter Port drifted to the quarries and to the docks and spoke in English.

The elderly retained an old-style patois vocabulary often approximating to standard (or 'good') French, but were forced to use English words when there was no Guernsey equivalent for 'new' features of transport, such as *car, lorry, plane, tram, driver, pilot, airport, bike* and *van*. An English word was also used for 'modern' items of home life: *tap, stove, 'phone, wireless, letter-box, sandwich, electricity* and *gas*. My parents' generation, in addition, frequently incorporated a whole range of English descriptive words and colloquialisms: *My word!, happy, decent, nice, out of the blue, OK, skipper*. (My father was always 'skip' to his employees.) They also added patois verb endings to actions which could only be expressed by English words: *cycle, 'phone* and *post* for example.

When I was a small child, English was the language used in schools and offices, in many of the town shops, in the newspapers and in some official announcements. Formal Standard French was used in all legal contracts and in the documentation of island government business. Old people read their Bibles in French and attended French church services. Besides reading the language, they could also speak it, but their grasp of English might be tenuous. Some had never been to France or England and proudly refused to go. (In short, if you were from what was considered a well-grounded family, then familiarity with French was a visible sign of it.)

Since the patois could not be written (except by Frenchifying it almost out of recognition) it was essential for islanders to master a language that could. As ties with England had strengthened over the years, so English came to predominate over French and became the language most used for outside communication. Its importance increased. The patois was given the status of the vernacular and dismissed as 'not good enough'. It was seen as useless to those who wanted to 'get on', rated as socially inferior, downgraded and disregarded. This trend was already well under way when war broke out in 1939.

My father had grown up with all three languages and could speak them fluently. My mother knew and could read all three, but was not a fluent speaker in French.

As I had received little preparation in English before I went to my first school, a small private one at Eastleigh House in the Forest, I was embarrassed when I didn't know how to speak to the other children and must have appeared shy and withdrawn. I had been taught the basic '*Yes*', '*No*', '*Please*' and '*Thankyou*' and understood something of what was said, but hesitated to launch out myself. I sat quietly at a table and listened, watched and absorbed. When I tried out a few words, I suffered acutely from the taunts of an aggressive boy, who ridiculed my small mistakes. I decided to translate and formulate a sentence completely from start to finish in my own mind before speaking. That way I would not risk the shame of getting stuck half way through or of inadvertently using a patois word in an English sentence. I learned that this was not allowed although it was quite alright to use English words in patois. Before opening my mouth, I had to decide which words would do and juggle them into a sequence different from the one I'd thought in. The sentence structure was not the same. All this hardly made for spontaneous chatting!

No sooner was I fairly fluent in English and could read quite passably, then I was saddled with the misery of learning French. I disliked the school proprietor's attempts to teach me from a difficult grammar book, but enjoyed the other activities which the full-time teacher, Miss Baker, organised. Although she understood my language problems, there was little she could do to help, as she could not speak the patois herself and thus tide me over the early emotional adjustments.

When I was seven, the school was closed. By that time, Brian, nearly two years my junior, had started. We were both transferred to town and joined that section of the Girls' Intermediate School which took in young children of both sexes. In those days, it was mainly fee-paying pupils who were admitted. At a later stage, the boys were moved up to the Boys' Intermediate School, housed in a separate building nearby, and the girls continued through till they reached school-leaving age. (Eventually the schools combined to form the grammar school and lost the younger element.)

Now that I was bilingual, I settled down well and over the years, I made good progress and was sometimes elected form captain. I began, at last, to enjoy reading and was excited when my father bought *The Book of Ten Thousand Things* edited by Arthur Mee and the ten-volume set of the *Children's Encyclopaedia*. These had stories and information about the stars, the tides, animal habits, volcanoes, works of art and historical figures with a teasing sprinkle of puzzles, riddles and ideas for things to make and do. Here lay the answers to many questions that my parents could not adequately deal with: Why do birds migrate? Who were the Vikings? Where does sugar come from?

Singing in the packed school hall roused a latent esprit de

corps, which Miss Roughton, the headmistress was at pains to foster. At the weekly practice, we made it our 'first avow'd intent, to be a pilgrim' and with a mixture of amusement, disparagement and zeal we raised the roof with:

*Glad hearts adventuring*
*The way is wide*
*Valour and faith shall shield*
*The pilgrim's side.*
*Constant and undismayed*
*Your journey passed*
*Across the hills of time*
*Home lies at last . . .*
　　*Glad hearts adventuring*
　　*The City of God dawns far*
　　*Brothers, take to the trail again*
　　*Sisters, follow the star!*

Although in those years my mother went through troubled periods, she found she could settle if she lived her life quietly by a familiar routine which suited her. As she recovered, I did not worry so much about her and the weight was lifted.

In December 1936, my younger brother, John, was born. He grew into a lively and lovable toddler. I greatly enjoyed blowing soap bubbles at his bath-times and invented bedtime stories for his amusement. "Once there was a cartload of people going out on a picnic. . . ." All the relations were named, one by one, and stuffed in, destined for improbable adventures. They were caught by the tide, their hats blew off or one lost a shoe. John was vigorous and healthy and he thrived. My parents were more relaxed and had a lot going for them.

A brief sketch of my mother would always need some reference to her family background. She set store by her close contacts with her parents and brothers and sisters and saw them frequently. If visits were ruled out, then the telephone was in constant use. I learned a great deal about the relations from the numerous one-sided conversations I overheard. As they took place in the open hallway, they were impossible to miss. My mother seemed to come into her own as a member of this extended family and for a long time did not feel very much at home in the Forest with its different cultural overtones and lack of finesse as she saw it.

We went to her old home at the Vale quite often. I always looked forward to those visits. My Robin grandparents still lived at

Summerville, Longue Rue, in the family homestead which had been built for their marriage in 1890. Like many islanders who had inherited fields and built greenhouses, they had made their living from growing flowers for export, mainly gladiolus, narcissus, asparagus fern and sometimes the arum lily. A large packing shed, overhung by lilac, stood behind the house. Gran was quick and skilful at bunching, but everyone available lent a hand.

She and Grandpère had brought up six children, of whom my mother was the youngest. There were three boys and three girls, who had appeared in quick succession between 1891 and 1897: Amicie, Eugene, Helene, Arthur, Cecil and Miriam. Amicie and Helene had remained unmarried and Eugene was a Methodist minister on the mainland and married to another Helene. They had no children. He and Arthur (father to Ruth and Jean) had been in the Army in the First World War and there were still on display, as if in remembrance, some souvenir squares of embroidered silk which they had bought in France as presents. Cecil was married to Ada in 1934.

In the large garden at the back, Gran had her own small conservatory where she grew geraniums, begonias and exotic plants, which flourished in response to her loving attention. She cherished a magnificent herbaceous border with its splashes of red hot pokers, delphiniums, dahlias, lilies and a mass of daisies and chrysanthemums. Sweet-scented roses and hydrangeas grew in profusion and appeared round every corner of this delightful garden with its overhanging trees, thick bushes and unexpected turnings. We would dodge the trailing creepers to play tag and hide-and-seek and ball. Gran's pride and joy was her long row of sweetpeas with their delicate hues of blue and mauve, pink and scarlet. Loganberries and raspberries, blackberries and indoor grapes grew in abundance and there was always a plentiful supply of vegetables for the house. The burst of apple blossom in the orchard came as a spectacular spring miracle to be followed by the saddening drift of petals over the bluebells in the grass. A massive Virginia creeper turned the front of the house into a wall of autumnal crimson and birds perching on its tendrils came in for a feast of tiny spiders.

My grandfather, Frederick Pierre Robin, had come from Les Longs Camps, a farm just a few minutes' walk away from Summerville. His brother, John, still lived there in the homestead built by their grandfather. At least thirteen children were born to John, my great uncle, and nearly half of them had died when they were infants. He had become a Jurat in the States of Guernsey (the island government) and held an office that, in those days, combined political and juridical functions. When he was a young man, Grandpère wanted to be an écrivain, a right-hand man to a solicitor (called an 'advocate' in Guernsey), but his father had forbidden it and, since 1910, he had used his administrative abilities in the role of Treasurer and Secretary of an insurance company, L'Alliance Réciproque and so, in this way, complemented the practical work of the grower.

Rachel Mary, my grandmother, came from Baubigny and her forebears, named Blampied, had intertwined with Grandpère's branch of the Robins. When she married, she left the Anglican Church, where she had been confirmed, to become a Methodist like my grandfather.

When I was small, our visits to Summerville were frequently on a Saturday or a Sunday afternoon (after Sunday School). Brian and I would rush into the scullery area and give the pump handle a friendly jerk before we burst into the living room.

My grandparents were welcoming. When the initial kissing of a tickly moustache was done with, I found my grandfather nice. He was always in a grey cardigan on Saturday and a black suit on Sunday, and sat with one hand on each knee, making little comment till female chattering subsided. Gran was cheerful and outgoing and quickly had things organised. Her large deep-set eyes emphasised the prominent cheek bones and her wavy white hair was caught back in a bun. She wore glasses with mottled black and grey frames and laughed and found amusement in her grandchildren.

Aunty Am (Amicie), who lived at Summerville, hovered in the background in her familiar brown dress, dotted with tiny sprigs of flowers. She was never obtrusive and always available, treated, it seemed, more like a trusted servant than the eldest in the family. She was very short-sighted and peered weakly through small metal-framed glasses which had thick lenses tinged with blue. In her late teens, she had read an article on colour blindness. This was the first she knew of it and suddenly it explained her disadvantage. She had felt stupid and to blame for ineptitude. No one had guessed the cause of her disability. Her speech was slow and her manner gentle. She had a marked respect for her parents and a very generous spirit. Sunshine intensified her blinking and she spent most of her life indoors doing much of the cooking and housework. We always knew she would make a scrumptious apple pie for our tea. She played the piano well and took a keen interest in theology, had a thorough knowledge of the Bible and read whatever newspapers and magazines came her way. In a different time and place, she might have received a university education. She could easily be persuaded into a game of Ludo or Snakes and Ladders, while my father was replacing a broken pane in a greenhouse or removing leaves from a blocked gutter (not on a Sunday!).

Sometimes, she took us up to her attic bedroom, which she had once shared with my mother and Helene. On the opposite side of the landing was a matching attic room which had been used by the three boys, her brothers. Under the sloping rafters, it was suffocatingly hot in summer. There were many treasures to be found here and we often came away with an unusual coin or foreign stamp. Soon we were starting our own collections and were further prompted to hunt through the atlas and search the *Children's Encyclopaedia* to find more information on a striking stamp's country of origin.

On wet afternoons, while the grown-ups chatted, I sat with a tin of assorted buttons and lined up the decorative ones in sets, remembering their history. "These came from Aunty Am's coat, when she was a girl." "This buckle was attached to a belt Gran used to wear with her best dress." "These white buttons are kept for Grandpère's long underpants." Tired of all this, I threaded tiny blue and black beads into a long necklace or flicked through the family album.

On the windowsill was a pile of garden catalogues and Grandpère allowed us to take home the coloured picture of a flower which was inserted in each issue. The living room, where we sat, was shaded by a high clipped hedge and an island of bamboo and fig with much taller trees beyond. Screened away between this hedge and the windows, stood an upturned wooden box on which was kept an enamel basin and soap dish for Grandpère's use when he came in from hours of weeding in the fields and greenhouses. He wiped his hands on a frayed old towel and threw it over the twigs to dry. Then, removing the mud from his boots on the foot-scraper, he followed old Mac, the tabby, into the house for a meal.

At Christmas-time, there was always a large family get-together at Summerville. Tables were placed end to end and covered with the best cloths of white damask. A centre piece, embroidered by one of the daughters, set off a rich fruit cake, while the use of starched white tray cloths and doilies edged with hand-made crochet, marked this out as a special occasion. Bottled logan-berries and pies were plentiful. Everyone pulled crackers and induced their paper hats to settle properly for the games. As people seated themselves round the parlour for the favourite, they grasped a long circular string on which was threaded an elusive curtain ring. It passed deftly and secretly from one clenched fist to the next, while the person in the middle spun round to detect its whereabouts. "Le furet du bois joli," we chorused, "Il a passé par ici. . . . Il court, il court, le furet." It all started very solemnly. Suddenly the string jerked. Uncle Art had pounced on an imaginary ring. Sucking in his cheeks with ferret-like astuteness, he distracted everyone with his diversionary antics and witticisms.

Partway through the evening, the youngest of us were taken upstairs to sleep. We envied Ruth, who was allowed to stay up with the crowd, because she was older. We sank into the unfamiliar feather mattresses and as the dimmed gas lights flickered, we watched the leaping shadows dart across the roses on the wallpaper. On the dark journey home, I looked out for the glint of cat eyes, as, disembodied, they sped towards a hedge to avoid the approaching car.

In the summer, an extended-family picnic excursion to the beach was arranged at a time when Uncle Eug (Eugene) and Aunty Helene, his wife, were on holiday in Guernsey. He had the care of some Methodist churches in Shropshire and later, in Edgworth, near Bolton, in Lancashire. My father fixed benches to the back of his small black lorry and rounded up those who could not easily reach the chosen destination by bus. He was the only one in the family to have a car or lorry.

As children, we clambered over the rocks and bathed. The middle-aged adults suddenly found the annual energy to sprint after a disappearing ball. The elderly and inactive sat on the dunes, protected from the spiky weeds and insects by a dark brown rug. Cucumber and tomato sandwiches were made memorable by the sprinkled addition of salty water and sandy grit which clung to eager fingers. Guernsey biscuits, rather like unsweetened tea cakes, spread thickly with Guernsey butter, were removed from their wrapping of greaseproof paper, and bunches of Summerville grapes waited for their turn in a sturdy wicker basket.

My grandfather's two sisters lived near Summerville and they had married two brothers. Together with their extended families now spread across three households at Les Annevilles, they formed another network of relations whom we visited. So, within a few minutes' walk of each other were all these interrelated homes where, among the numerous cousins, my mother had grown up and made her girlhood friendships.

Her sister, my Aunty Helene, lived for a time at the Forest. She acted as housekeeper and companion to old Mr. Mauger at L'Epinel. Frequently, she dropped in at Rue des Landes for an afternoon chat with my mother. They liked making clothes and, while Lily cleaned the bedrooms, they sat sewing. Aunty wore the beautiful floral dresses she had made and when Ruth and I were bridesmaids at Uncle Ces' wedding, it was she who made us the frilled outfits of apricot georgette.

In the early spring, I would skip along the lanes with this Aunty in search of the first violets and primroses. Soon, the hedgerows were alive with many beautiful wild flowers and we picked them to our heart's content, arranging the lemon primroses and the celandines over a circlet of green leaves and scenting the rooms with honeysuckle. In summer, when the cliffs were ablaze with yellow gorse and heather, Aunty walked down the valley with us to Petit Bôt, which was the much-loved beach near home.

The two sisters chose a smooth rock to lean against and, spreading their towels side by side, they sat down on the sand for a good old Guernsey yarn. Some who did not know the family well mistook them for each other. They were of the same height and build, quite short and trim. Both had wavy brown hair, bobbed loosely and aunty's eyes were large and deep-set like my grandmother's. Second-best straw hats shaded their faces from the summer sunshine.

On the rare occasions when my father joined us on such beach outings, he rolled up his trouser legs and edged his way gingerly into the water. Nervously, he watched us jumping into the oncoming waves. "Be careful!" he shouted, frozen by the spectre of his uncle said to have drowned when wandering in a drunken stupor. We were warned not to go beyond thigh level. How could we ever learn to swim without flouting his authority? I grew wary of the sea and was plagued with cramp when its coldness gripped me.

My father wanted me to follow in his family's musical footsteps and arranged for me to have piano lessons with his cousin Hetty. I progressed through several grades, but was always drawn to the haunting melodies of the violin. He himself had played the instrument as a young man during the musical evenings at Milestone. Then came the First World War and towards the end, he was drafted to France and received a bullet injury to two fingers of the left hand. He could never enjoy his skill again.

The Forest Methodist Church at le Bourg played a significant role in our lives. My parents were members and as young children we sat in a semi-circle of small children in the Primary section of the Sunday School, being taught by 'the grey one' and 'the brown one'. I was identifying Doreen Heaume and Daisy Bougourd by the colour of their coats. They displayed large pictures of Bible stories on an easel, and after they had said their piece, we copied the scene and sang 'Praise Him!'

As we grew into Juniors, we crossed the road to the older building, which, in my grandfather's youth, had been the chapel, where he was organist. Once, far into the service, he realised he had forgotten a crucial piece of music, so, while the long prayer was in progress, he slipped down to his home on the adjoining property and was back at the organ before people had opened their eyes.

Our teachers were dedicated and caring and we learned as much from their example as from the content of the lessons. My father was for a long time a leading light in the Sunday School, sharing a major teaching role with Mr. Wilfred Heaume and Mr. Theo Allez. He was also a Local Preacher and took appointments in the chapels scattered over the western parishes. On a Sunday morning, he usually preached in French and in the evening it was in English. His preparation was always thorough and he could be overheard in our dining room eloquently addressing the table and chairs.

He liked to take me with him sometimes on his regular visits to the old and sick and housebound. I ran to keep up with this stocky striding figure, whose trilby was pulled down well over the eyes. As his walking stick struck the ground, he swung the top round in a circular rhythm and all could recognise his good-natured pride and confident bearing. He stopped only to greet a neighbour driving home with horse and cart stacked with milk churns. Hens scattered as he approached an open farmhouse door, and, knocking loudly, he would call, "Are you there, my friend? It's Bazil from Rue des Landes." He would draw a chair close to the deaf old man seated next to the fire, which was kept alight all year round to boil the kettle. As he passed on the local news, I would play with the cat, perched on the wooden frame of 'la jonquiere' or green-bed. This wide rectangular day-bed on four short wooden legs had survived from previous generations and was used by the elderly or the exhausted, who stretched out on it for a few minutes' break from the heavy work out of doors. Its hollowed middle was filled with dried fern or bracken rather than a mattress and was usually spruced up with a green baize cover. My father would then lift the large French family Bible from the dresser, open its golden clasps and read the selected Psalm or Gospel passage which he followed with a prayer of blessing and thanksgiving in French. We would invariably come away with fresh eggs for la dame Brehaut.

He knew all the families in the locality and often went into the cottages to take the measurements of a body for the coffin. Some homes were little better than hovels and sometimes he would carry out basic repairs without charge and do most of the work himself. If there were fleas, he changed out of his overalls and all his clothes in an outbuilding at Rue des Landes and did not let this deter him. Many of the families took heart from his impulsive kindness and my mother sometimes supplied a bundle of outgrown clothing. Children played barefoot round the lanes and some were bandy-legged with rickets. Wages were low and there was little provision on the island for those who had to meet crises.

On some Sunday evenings before John was born and while my mother was at church, Brian and I would roam through the fields with him far beyond the Milestone boundaries. We would give a friendly pat to the grazing cows as we sauntered by. Then, as the setting sun tinged the sky with a crimson glow, we would climb up the hedgerows to find our bearings by the spires of the churches at St. Saviour's and the Forest.

These rambling walks, although filled with childish chatter, left me with a lasting sense of the island's great silences, of the abiding value of the land as a means of livelihood, of the Christian faith perpetuated down the ages and of my father's pride in his little family.

Soon all this was to change dramatically. Bulldozers came to flatten the same hedges. Brian, in his Wellington boots, followed the novelty tractors as they levelled out the land. Seagulls swooped down to an unwonted daily feast. Then the newspapers announced the forthcoming opening of the airport. Our windmill was in the way and was demolished. It was May 1939. Regular air services would now run to the mainland. The small patch of dune land at the north of the island used by small private aircraft was now relegated to the category of the outmoded and outgrown. Mr. Cecil Noel's aerobatic exploits which had once seemed foolhardy, now looked tame.

My father as a member of the Forest Douzaine (the Parish Council of twelve) was one of the dignitaries at the opening ceremony. His property with all the greenhouses behind Milestone abutted on to the airport and he had arranged for wooden benches to be positioned on the boundary hedge for the onlookers. We had a grandstand view of all the planes as they landed and took off and hailed them with the wave of a balloon and streamers.

Opposite our house, where there had been pasture, a large hotel was erected with its name 'Happy Landings' displayed over the entrance. Loud music boomed out late into the evening and the volume of traffic past the house increased. Instead of being woken by the cocks crowing in the nearby farmyards, we were deafened by the planes flying far too low over our stable. Kite flying was forbidden.

In the meantime, my father was consolidating his business based at Milestone. He built bungalows and sold paint, nails and timber to neighbouring farmers and growers and put up new greenhouses for them as the tomato industry flourished. Sometimes I rushed to the packing shed after school and helped to grade his tomatoes, arranging them in 12 lb chip baskets of wood, lined with the colour of tissue paper that denoted their size and quality. They were sent away to Carmarthen, to Newport in Wales, London, Sheffield, Manchester and Scotland. There were usually six regular full-time employees, three for the greenhouses and outdoor work and three in the workshop. Others came when needed.

* * * * *

At school, the end of term hymn was guaranteed to produce a few tears, 'Lord dismiss us with Thy blessing . . .'. In the summer of 1939, it was my turn to feel the poignancy of the opening lines of the last verse:

> *Let Thy father-hand be shielding*
> *All who here shall meet no more;*
> *May their seed-time past be yielding*
> *Year by year a richer store;*
> *Those returning,*
> *Make more faithful than before.*

I was eleven and I was leaving the school, as I had passed the scholarship examination to the Ladies' College, an independent school which received backing from the island government, the States, and was rated rather more prestigious. It aimed, eventually, to provide a level of education similar to that available to boys at the historic Elizabeth College, which ranked as a Public School, albeit a minor one.

My father told all his customers of my success and Gran from Milestone gave me my first watch. It was gold with my initials engraved on the back. A dressing table was bought for my bedroom, to mark this further stage in my life. I began to think I must have done something quite important.

I started my new school in September 1939 just as war broke out. The navy blue uniform of the Girls' Intermediate School was replaced by the green tunic and brown velour brimmed hat of the Ladies' College. I did the work with ease and was greatly surprised to find myself top of the class for nearly everything. Marks rarely fell below 75%. I began to have more confidence in my abilities and some of the old childhood anxieties receded. There was a much greater formality in this school. Miss Ellershaw, the headmistress, had a cultured and restraining influence and conveyed an aura of English upper middle class values. School activities were well organised, although slightly hampered by the architectural shortcomings of the building where the school was accommodated. I thought life was rather bleak for the boarders.

# Chapter III

## *'Pack Up Your Troubles'*

Till May 1940, the war seemed remote from Guernsey, which felt like a quiet backwater, detached from all the battles which raged elsewhere. Many people still held to the conviction that, no matter what, Hitler's armies would never land on British soil. They would be held back and defeated. The islanders were proud of their allegiance to the British Crown and drew comfort from the victories of the First World War in which many Guernseymen had given their lives to defeat the Germans. Everyone remembered Cambrai and Ypres ('Wipers' to the English), the bloodstained poppy fields of Flanders and the sodden trenches of the Somme. The man that Aunty Helene hoped to marry did not come back. Was all such sacrifice to be in vain?

Abruptly now, the peaceful carry-over from the 1914 war was ended. The lull of the Phoney War in the west was shattered by the lightning advance of the German Panzer Divisions across Holland, Belgium and France. In response to an appeal, I hurried with my knitting of a blanket of coloured squares for Belgian refugees. The homeless from the Continent were arriving in the safe haven of the island.

By the end of May, large contingents of the British Expeditionary Force were being driven west towards the beaches of Dunkirk and many thousands of its fleeing troops were dumped unceremoniously on British shores by the rescuing armada of little ships. On June 14th, Paris fell. The speed of the ensuing German Blitzkrieg across the rest of France took everyone by surprise. Soon the advancing Nazi armies reached the coast of the Cherbourg Peninsula which could be seen clearly from the Guernsey beaches on a cloudless day. Across the thirty miles of sea, rumbles of gunfire were audible. The Channel Islands waited with a mounting sense of foreboding.

Would the Germans come? Surely the islands could be of no strategic importance . . . and yet . . . would Hitler want them as a stepping stone for the invasion of England? My twelfth birthday was hardly noticed as we tuned in to all the news bulletins on the wireless. What would happen next?

Rumours and warnings began to circulate. Some islanders, hearing about the torture of people in Poland, dreaded what might be in store. My parents were conscious of our house's nearness to the airport. It seemed more vulnerable than most. My father took the spare leaves of the extending table out of the corner cabinet in the dining room and carried them into the parlour. He used them to block its windows and set about making this a place of refuge in the house. He moved some heavy furniture towards the door, ready to barricade us in. Candles and matches were assembled in case the gas and electricity went off. My mother bought in extra sugar and tins of fruit to stock there. As we had always relied on our own home-bottled stores, this step in itself seemed ominous.

Would we be trapped in that one room with only this for food? As I peeped into the darkened fortress, I saw the shapes of our gas mask boxes piled in readiness.

What were my parents expecting? Was there going to be fighting outside the house? A siege? Bombs falling on the airport? Shattered glass from blast? A tangle of unanswered questions ensnared us all in a web of confusion. Already I could hear the scrunching of enemy feet on the gravel outside the parlour windows. Rifle butts broke the windows. I woke my parents with the nightmare. And nothing happened. School continued as usual and we ate our meals in a routine way.

On Wednesday, June 19th, the local newspaper, the *Star*, announced that the BEF had been withdrawn from France and the world awaited Hitler's terms. The words were tossed out with a mix of the grandiose and inconsequential. The French were seeking an armistice.

Then in the afternoon, a special edition of the *Star* was hastily distributed. When I came home from school, armed with an official letter, I found my parents in a state of consternation. The headlines ran:

ISLAND EVACUATION
ALL CHILDREN TO BE SENT TO THE MAINLAND TOMORROW
MOTHERS MAY ACCOMPANY THOSE UNDER SCHOOL AGE
REGISTRATION TONIGHT
WHOLE BAILIWICK TO BE DEMILITARISED

What?        Now?        We were stunned.

In making his momentous announcement concerning the demilitarisation of the island, Victor Carey, the Bailiff, was speaking on behalf of the States of Guernsey and relaying a decision of the British Government. The Royal Guernsey Militia and the Guernsey Defence Volunteers would be demobilised immediately and all firearms must be surrendered. Those of military age could leave for the mainland if they wished to serve in the British forces. There was no conscription on the island.

People tried to surmise the meaning of the announcement. Would the islands be seen as a tempting vacuum drawing in the German armies whenever they chose to land? There would be no resistance whatsoever. If they did come, would the British bomb them out again? Would such action be even more damaging? The *Star* said all air services to and from the island were being suspended. The only links would be by sea. Would food supplies last out if the islands were to be completely cut off from both France and England?

With such disquieting thoughts, my parents read about the practicalities of the evacuation plans. The British Government was making arrangements for school children and mothers with young children under school age to go to reception centres in the UK. They were to leave the following day. The former had to be in their schools with parents by 9 a.m. the next morning. Mothers with young children had to be registered by 8 p.m. that evening with the Vicar or Rector of their Parish and turn up at their Parish School by 10 a.m. All others who wished to leave must also register by 8 p.m. that evening, but with the Constable of their Parish. No reference was made to the time when they could go. It presumably would be later. The operation was taking on the hue of lifeboat drill.

Everywhere, hasty family consultations were being organised. Ours took place at Summerville. A succession of aunts and uncles came and went. We crowded into the living room shaded by the familiar leaves of the fig tree. Mac, sluggish in old age, rubbed himself against the visitors' legs in greeting and turned to his bowl of bread and milk flecked with Marmite. Aunty Am produced some cups of tea. Ruth, Jean, Brian and I were sent outside into the garden. We chased each other in perfunctory spurts, jumping over the wisps of 'Mind your own business' which were advancing fast across the pathways. We climbed onto the granite pig sty walls, now overgrown with brambles, and leapt across the gaps that had been gateways, just because we'd always done it. Now it seemed childish, pointless and devoid of challenge.

Frequently, we panted into the house and found the adults still deep in earnest conversation, but a pattern was emerging. Gran and Grandpère were evidently fixtures. They were too old for a

massive upheaval. They would face it out on the island, come
what may. Aunty Am would stay to keep house and look after
them. Likewise, Aunty Helene would stand by our old great-uncle
Tom, who, with only one arm, could not be left on his own to
fend for himself. By then, she had become his live-in housekeeper. Uncle Art and Aunty Adele would also stay and support
the old folk. Ruth and Jean would be evacuated with the States'
Intermediate School for Girls which they both attended. Uncle
Ces and Aunty Ada would stay behind with Marion, their four-
year old daughter, and the elderly relations. My parents decided
that Brian should go with his school, the Boys' Intermediate, and
that it would be best if I were to be evacuated with Ruth and Jean,
who were the closest I had to sisters. That way, we would be
together. They would ask Miss Roughton if I could be taken with
my old school and so be with them, instead of going with the
Ladies' College.

And John? He was then 3½ years old. Should my mother take
him away? Was his physical safety the prime consideration? But
was it really safe in England? The *Star* in the morning had
reported bombs being dropped on the Thames. Many thousands
of British children had been evacuated to the countryside to
avoid the raids on towns. Where would the islanders be taken and
would they be free from bombing?

The journey home from Summerville was sombre. This time,
there were no scented bunches of roses and sweetpeas to bundle
into the car, no clutching of tummies aching from too much
apple pie.

My parents considered their position. Should they wait till the
first waves of evacuating children had gone and then leave
together with John? Should they all three stay on the island or
should they split, so that my mother went ahead with John the
following day? If not trapped on the island in the meantime, my
father could join them later. There was the risk of an indefinite
separation, when my mother would have to earn a living on the
mainland. How?

They considered what was involved in walking out on
everything, without having the chance to make satisfactory
caretaker arrangements. They did not know which neighbours or
employees they might call on to supervise the business and the
premises. The house would be left empty. Would it be looted?
Milestone was cheek by jowl with the airport. What would happen
to Gran? Would she have to move elsewhere in case it was
bombed? Who would look after her?

My mother thought of all her possessions, the polished furniture and drawers of crochet and embroidered cloths painstakingly stitched at Summerville by the gas light of the Edwardian era. Would they be used to wipe the windscreens of German lorries? How much did possessions matter and could they turn their backs on all that had been their means of livelihood? Would all they had cherished be available later on, whatever happened? In short, could they up stumps so suddenly and be prepared to lose everything and see it go to pot?

With these teaming questions pounding in all our minds, we made our way to the Girls' Intermediate School and joined the throngs of people asking their own unanswerable questions. Teachers sat at trestle tables to register departures. There was a long wait to see Miss Roughton. Finally, my parents disappeared into the study for a snatched interview and she agreed to take me with this my previous school. The *Star* had announced a car curfew between 10.30 p.m. and 5 a.m. that night, so the crowds in school began to thin. Members of staff took it in turn to stay on duty all night to answer the telephone. It rang incessantly.

Miss Roughton had been given some advance warning of probable evacuation in a confidential meeting of head teachers on Tuesday, the day before the public announcement. Since then, she had been overloaded with the administrative task involved and had little time to deal with personal packing. As she hurriedly gathered up some essentials, she cast a lingering farewell glance at the beloved violin she had been given as a child. A few staff members could not leave because they had elderly dependants. It was made clear to the heads that all others were expected to go as escorts to the children. There was some fear that any people born in England and caught on the island might be deported to Germany. Many such anxieties arising from experiences during the First World War were surfacing. Rumours spread that all the old school records might be burned to destroy information. The danger remained unspecified.

In the meantime, our family rushed home again. Somehow, in the mêlée, my father had managed to dash to the bank in town and had bought a case. We had only one of a size suitable for children and that was allocated to Brian. We had never been away on holiday. The new case was brown with a little antler on it. My father said it was strong. It was for me.

Soon we were sorting out the clothes and consulting the check lists in the *Star*. We had to take our gas masks and ration books (the current one and the new). Children, it said, should wear a coat and take a mackintosh and a complete change of clothing. Suggestions were made as follows:

| GIRLS | BOYS |
| --- | --- |
| One vest or combinations | One vest |
| One pair of knickers | One shirt with collar |
| One bodice | One pair of pants |
| One petticoat | One pullover or jersey |
| Two pairs of stockings | One pair of knickers |
| Handkerchiefs | Handkerchiefs |
| Slip and blouse | Two pairs of socks or stockings |
| Cardigan | |

If there had been time, we would have sniggered at the antiquated language. The list must have been concocted by someone totally unfamiliar with children's clothing. No girl would have been seen dead in combinations and no boy would have referred to any article of his clothing as knickers (Ugh!).

Additional for all were the following items: night attire, comb, towel, soap, face cloth, toothbrush, and, if possible, boots, shoes and plimsolls.

No blankets would be allowed, but rations for the journey were necessary. Who had time and opportunity to match the absurd list given?

> *Sandwiches (egg and cheese), packets of nuts and seedless raisins, dry biscuits (with little packets of cheese), barley sugar (rather than chocolate), apple, orange.*

John was put to bed. My mother sat down in the living room and dipped into her wicker sewing basket as she had done so many times before. She stitched name tapes on our clothing and, as they were ready, we packed things in. There was room in my case for more than was listed, so extra items were pushed in quickly. They included some stationery and stamps and my small black Bible. I was enjoined to remember the teaching I had received and continue with my prayers. A family portrait was hurriedly found. I was told to cut off the mount, surely a scurrilous action.

As I look again at this tattered sepia photograph, I see my mother sitting with unusually upright posture. She stares forward with the suggestion of a smile. My father, in the prime of life, looks rather military. He stands foursquare in the centre of the group. I sit on a table, one leg awkwardly tucked under the other according to the photographer's instructions. My carefully arranged ringlets fall gently on to the dress my mother had made. I remember it was pale blue with pink smocking. Brian, with his fair curly hair, looks thoughtful in a neat home-made suit. He is clutching the lead of a stuffed studio dog. The picture was already seven years old. It did not include young John. A separate one of him was found taken two years earlier. There was no portrait of the five of us together.

When all was packed, I lifted up the case and walked the length of the house from the living room, past the office, and on to the far end of the kitchen. On this occasion, there were no chuckles at a receding fox tail and umbrella, no hint of a Queen Mary with majestic toque. The figure would soon be disappearing much further than the kitchen. The case was not too heavy, but I had all that I could comfortably carry. My mother slipped in a few words about menstruation that I had never heard about before, and my father counted out some change and gave us each some money. We were told to look after it well. I had 18 shillings (an amount equivalent to 86 postage stamps, then costing 2½ old pence for a letter). Although it was less than a pound and hardly a day's wage, it seemed a lot to have in one fell swoop.

At the unprecedented hour of 1 a.m., I crawled exhausted into bed.

My parents spent the remainder of the night wrestling with decisions about their own course of action. When we got up in the morning, my mother had a large suitcase partly packed for herself and John. She would go to the Parish School taking the push-chair which she would leave behind later on if it was not allowed on board.

In the meantime, Brian and I piled into the car with our cases. We had to be at school with a parent for 9 a.m. to get the latest instructions. My mother stood in the yard ready to wave us off. Fighting back the tears, she called in English, "Remember your brave mother smiling." It seemed so artificial and unreal. Abandoning the patois we'd been using all the time, she consigned herself and us to an extraneous world which wasn't hers and wasn't ours. It had another language.

As we approached the school gates, we found many parents unloading their children and saying goodbye. They were not allowed to remain on the school premises. Overcrowding and distressing scenes must be avoided. The staff were there in force. Some, like Miss Ella Mahy, teacher of French, had been up all night. Exhausted, she had gone home late the previous evening and started packing. In the early hours she said goodbye to her father and, strapping a holdall on to her bicycle and shouldering a rucksack, she set off to take her turn of duty on the school telephone around 5.30 a.m. She remembers how the trees, fields and houses stood out in sharp clarity. Riding down the Ville au Roi, she took note of the handsome old beech trees with their rough grey trunks so reminiscent of elephant hides. She wondered if she would ever see them again. "I realised that my throat was painfully dry and that strange groaning noises were quite unaccountably coming out of it. . . . After that, it was all a question of getting on with the job and no regrets. I suppose I had come to terms with the situation all unwittingly."

Miss Roughton had been dividing the registered children into thirteen groups, lettered from A–M. The heads of schools had been instructed that each group should be led by a teacher, partnered by another adult. A number of mothers volunteered, seizing this opportunity to accompany their daughters and travel with the school. A few other helpers were added and some groups had three to lead them. The numbers in their care fluctuated by the minute, as parents made alternative plans, withdrew their children or wanted them transferred to other groups to be with friends or relatives. Some anxious parents asked at the last minute if theirs could be added on.

Miss Roughton's master list named 223 pupils, including some of the younger girls and boys at the lower end of the school, aged only five or six. It seems that several more were actually taken so that the final figure may well have been 239 and 29 members of staff and helpers.

After we had waited at school all the morning, we were allowed a short break as long as we could return by 4 p.m. Miss Stewart rushed back to her home for a scrambled egg, but could not stop to wash the pan. All her belongings had to be left in their accustomed places. There was no time to arrange for storage. I returned to Rue des Landes, but was soon being whisked back to school by my father. The waiting seemed endless. By mid-evening, there was still no word of our departure. We were told to get blankets if we could, as a night passage was now envisaged. Miss Clayton fetched seven blankets of knitted squares made by the girls and intended for European refugees. She distributed them to those who would otherwise have had to do without. I telephoned home and my father said he'd come and bring a blanket and some sandwiches. Most of us had eaten what was intended for the journey. My mother had not left. She was at home with John. She had waited in vain at the pick-up point in the Forest near le Gouffre and returned to Rue des Landes when it was clear they would not go that day.

At 8.30 p.m. my father arrived with a familiar light brown blanket which had an edging of white stripes. It was the colour of the chocolate filling of a swiss roll and folded like one, to be carried as a roly poly back pack. He had tied it with looped string to go behind the neck, then forward and under the armpits. With my gas mask, sandwiches and case, I was now everyone's picture of an evacuee.

After a quick perfunctory kiss, he dashed off again in his usual brisk and business-like manner. It was his third last goodbye that day.

An hour later, we were heading for the harbour. I had a lift with others in someone's car. Buses were expected for the younger boys and girls. The seniors were told to walk if transport was not available.

# Chapter IV

## *'It Won't Be for Long'*

'Wish me luck as you wave me goodbye.' The words of the song had never seemed so apt as we gave vent to our feelings while waiting in the darkness of the harbour.

A gaunt cargo ship had moored along the quay. Little rowing boats were bobbing on the water to the rhythmic lapping of the waves on wood.

'Goodbye Sally, it won't be for long . . . Goodbye Sally, I'll be singing a song. . . .' The banalities of the current popular songs floated on the groundswell of a corporate identity. Separation had not yet cut into the flesh. Families would soon be reunited. In spite of the prohibition, many people had gathered at the harbour during the evening. Warnings that crowds might attract air raids had been given scant attention. By the same token, girls otherwise dressed in school uniform were not allowed to wear the regulation panama hats. They might attract the enemy! They had always been considered reactionary and girls who wanted to cock a snook at authority had pulled them out of shape or sat on them.

My own parents had stayed at home. Now the pupils of four schools, about 800 in all, filed into the Dutch SS *Batavier IV*. They were the Boys' and Girls' Intermediate Schools, the Elizabeth College and the Ladies' College. People waved vigorously and shouted encouragement, "Keep smiling!", "See you soon!", "Don't forget to write"! Someone threw an eiderdown on board for anyone to catch. There was a chilly night ahead. As we pulled out of the harbour round about 11.30 p.m., the singing of the waving crowds grew fainter. 'Cheerio! Here I go on my way . . .', 'Goodbye Sally, it won't be for long . . .'.

We were told to climb down a ladder into the hold. The acrid smell was indescribable. It was so overpowering that it was hard to breathe. We were told that this had been a cattle boat, afterwards used by troops. We lay on a dirty, bumpy floor, uncomfortable in our bulky life belts and huddled in our blankets if we had been lucky enough to get one in time. We slept fitfully. A girl was sick all over my case and I had great difficulty in wiping it clean again. Buckets were provided as the sea grew rough. One child went up to Miss Roughton and pleaded, "Can I be sick in your bucket, because ours is full?" A member of staff threw a blanket overboard into the sea. There was no opportunity to clean it of vomit. The owner was really dismayed as it was a brand new one.

At 5 a.m., we climbed up the ladder to the deck. All was bleak and grey. We threw our blankets over our shoulders and strolled along to see how others had fared. Jean had been sick, Ruth was managing and I felt merely queasy. In half an hour we sighted land. Some said we were approaching Weymouth. Progress was slow as the Dutch captain took a zig-zag course to avoid the mines. The hull of a sunken vessel protruded high out of the water. Crew members dished out tea from enamel pails. Only one of them spoke English. At last we docked at Weymouth and by 2.30 p.m. we had disembarked.

On English soil for the first time, I was filled with a spirit of adventure. The singing of the previous evening had lent the experience a sense of occasion. Never had I felt community solidarity so poignantly conveyed in spontaneous song. We would brave the future with verve and determination:

> *Glad hearts adventuring,*
> *The City of God dawns far;*
> *Brothers, take to the trail again,*
> *Sisters, follow the star!*

We soon found ourselves in a hall where we were medically examined. By then we had all acquired a luggage label to tie on to our coats. It was rubber-stamped with the words 'Borough of Weymouth and Melcombe Regis' and the letters N.A.D. What did they mean? Details of name and destination were never filled in and I have the label still.

In another building, we were given sandwiches and a cup of tea. A junior girl was spotted by a Weymouth helper who thought she was too young for tea. The cup was taken away from her and a glass of milk was promised. It was never brought and she had to move on feeling thirsty. Outside, crowds of Jersey people were waiting. I saw Brian in the distance standing near some deckchairs. Miss Brown, our group leader, warned us not to wander off, so I tried waving, but could not attract his attention. Some of us sat on our cases if they were strong enough. Mine was.

Finally some buses drew up. They had been conjured up to take us to the railway station when Miss Roughton explained that the younger ones in the party could not carry their cases all the way. We hadn't seen double-decker buses before and there was a rush for the stairs. Ruth, Jean and I had to content ourselves with the lower section.

At the railway station, we discovered that the Boys' Inter-mediate School, and Brian in their number, had gone ahead of

us. Miss Elsie Johnson with some of the younger children and
their teachers and supervisors were shunted into the empty
compartments of a waiting train. There was no room for the rest
of the school. It was with some difficulty that Miss Roughton
arranged for them to be bundled out again before the train
steamed out northwards into the unknown. She was at pains to
keep the school together as one whole unit.

Eventually around 6 p.m. our turn came. The journey is
described in the diary I started in my writing pad. As there was no
railway in Guernsey, the account is stuffed with the word 'first',
the first time we had been on a train, seen a station, gone
through a tunnel. It was also the first time I had seen a river, a
black and white cow and barrage balloons. They hung glistening
over Bristol, their cables intended to prevent enemy planes from
flying low over the city. We were tired and huddled up to each
other and dozed intermittently. In our compartment, my diary
reminds me, were Ruth and Jean, Mona Davey, Doreen Paul,
Agnes and Brenda le Page and Joyce le Tissier. Do they
remember?

Miss Roughton and others kept watch, patrolling the corridors
and curbing the exuberance of the younger ones who were
getting dirty from playing on the floor. One carriage had lost its
communicating door and any child might have leaned too far
and fallen on to the flashing tracks below. We still did not know
where we were going. Ruth had been reassured by her father that
if we were sent to Canada, she wasn't to worry. There would
always be some way of tracing us later on. Pat Hartland fingered
the locket on a gold chain that she was wearing. It was a family
heirloom left to her by her grandmother and marked this out as a
momentous journey.

We were told the train would stop in the darkest hours of the
night, so that no light could be visible from the air. We were to
settle down and sleep. One girl started wandering with her eyes
shut and her arms extended. There was much smirking and
poking. Was she really sleep walking? This had entertainment
value. At last we dozed, till woken up around 5 a.m. We were
approaching Rochdale. We shunted into the station about an hour
later and it was raining. There was a long wait till we were allowed
onto the platform. Bus drivers had expected us the night before
and had eventually given up waiting and gone home to bed.

A railway official came up to Miss Roughton. "Are you the lady
who was delivered of a baby on the train?" he asked. A search
went on to deal with this emergency. A bizarre rumour added

that the person concerned was locked in one of the lavatories and no one could find the key. We missed the denouement of this strange episode as the welcome buses arrived. We were divided into two large parties and herded in. Reception centres were at the ready. Close on 100 juniors, comprising the Kindergarten, Transition and Forms I, II and III were taken to Horse Carrs in Falinge Road with the Deputy Head, Miss Elsie Naftel, in charge. The seniors, starting with girls aged twelve and numbering about 140, went to the other end of the town and were deposited at the door of Roylelands along the Manchester Road on the way to Castleton. Sisters were allowed to stay together, so Jean, who was then eleven, came to Roylelands with Ruth who was fifteen, so she was thereby separated from her classmates who went with the juniors to Horse Carrs. But the three of us were still together.

All our cases and packages were stacked in the hallway at Roylelands, almost blocking a passage through. Members of the WVS (Women's Voluntary Service) welcomed us with sandwiches and hot tomato soup. It seemed odd to be drinking it from white chunky cups when normally it turned up in bowls.

We were told to go and sleep on the rows of camp beds provided. They were packed so close to each other that we could hardly walk between them. There was continuous noise and chatter and frequent trips to find a bathroom. Girls resisted this enforced inactivity before they could absorb their new surroundings. At last the extended period in limbo ended and we sat down to a plate of lamb, beans and potatoes, followed by bananas and custard.

Members of staff had used the much needed respite to nap and take stock of the situation. Schedules were quickly organised. We were allocated our sleeping quarters and allowed to roam the spacious grounds, so overgrown with rambling bushes and shrubbery, all coated with the black smoky film of the north. Twelve tall factory chimneys could be seen from the windows.

And so we eased into our new home. It had been hastily set up as an emergency centre, to be ready for bombed-out families or for Belgian refugees, who, in the event, never arrived. The house, although commodious, was overcrowded. Floors were bare. The large windows had no curtains or blinds, so could not be blacked out when it got dark. As daylight faded, everyone had to be in bed. We could not switch on the electric light at night in case of raids. Each camp bed, which had been supplied by the ARP (Air Raid Precautions), was covered with a blanket of tweedy material, a gift from the mills. Later, we were provided with a new, white, flannelette sheet, whose fluff wrought havoc with the navy blue uniforms in which the school was evacuated. We had no brushes to remove the clinging tentacles. As the beds were the only form of seating, there was no chance to escape the menace and we resigned ourselves to the speckled look. The staff did not. There were no pillows, so we made do with bundled coats and clothing.

Meals were eaten at trestle tables with forms, in separate sittings. A wan aspidistra stand was the only other piece of furniture.

Tea on the first day consisted of bread and margarine and jam and this was followed by a long-overdue wash. In the evening we had to hand in the food left over from the journey. I kept my apple and orange and ate one later. The other was stored carefully in the case. There were whisperings of another move. Now I had to look after myself and make my own provision for the future *in case* . . . . It carried all the things that I had brought from the familiar past and held them ready for the unknown future.

Some of the older girls had picked up head lice on the journey and late at night there was a frantic round of combing and shampooing to prevent its further spread. Most of us were free to find our own camp beds and have a good night's sleep.

The next day was Sunday. We were asked to sign a paper to indicate our church allegiance and then Miss Brittain, the Games mistress, headed a walk down the driveway lined with rhododendrons and along the neighbouring streets. The terraced houses of black-coated brick contrasted sharply with our Guernsey granite. The numerous mill chimneys formed a novel landscape and we compared each other's count when we returned. Sketchy memories of Geography lessons linked Lancashire with cotton. So this was what the text books meant.

My first letter to my parents was sent to Uncle Eug's address according to their last instructions. They expected to go to him soon after our departure. He was then living in Edgworth not far from Bolton and had promised them by telephone that he would try to put members of the family in touch with each other.

Most girls were Anglicans and in the evening a party was escorted to St. Aiden's in Sudden near Roylelands. A few of us walked to the Methodist Church in Castleton. We sat through the service rather dazed, but were glad to join in the familiar hymns.

I was just dressing after a medical examination the following day, when a wild call of excitement sent me running down the stairs. Uncle Eug was standing in the hall. Ruth and Jean had got there first. We had not realised he lived so near. He said that my mother had not arrived at his home yet, but if we telephoned him the following day at 4.30 p.m., we might be able to speak to her. He gave us sixpence each and went.

That night the strident crescendo wailing of the siren sent shock waves through the house. Was it a real air raid? Members of staff rallied us together in the dark. It was 1.10 a.m. and we were to take shelter in the cellars. I grabbed my Rochdale blanket and my own, located my coat and gas mask but failed to find my shoes. We were not allowed to switch on the light.

From the attic landing where I had been sleeping, I followed the line of girls groping their way down the three flights of stairs. We stood barefoot on the stone flags or squatted against the cold damp walls. Those who had come without a blanket or coat shivered in nightdress or pyjamas only, till they found a warmer friend who could offer cover. It seemed we had not escaped from danger. 'Woman in the churchyard sat . . . oo – oo – oo – oo . . . ah! ah! ah! . . .' As we chanted in the spooky darkness, all eyes turned to the gleam of a single flashing torch. We were curious to find out what our teachers were wearing in the middle of the night. Did they put their hair in curlers? An hour later, the all-clear sounded and I was soon asleep again in the attic.

Promptly at 4.30 p.m. the next afternoon (Tuesday 25th) Ruth, Jean and I jammed into a telephone kiosk down the road. We had been warned against leaving the house without a teacher on the pretext that we had no identity cards. Perhaps it was a ruse to keep us from straying too far. Miss Brown was with us and called the number. It was Aunty Helene who answered. She said my parents and John were still in Guernsey. They had moved to Les Fontaines and were staying with the parents of Ruth and Jean (Uncle Art and Aunty Adele), who had available space in their guest house. Brian was with his school in Oldham, she said, and I was given his address. Uncle had been to see him and had also located Olive and Peter Falla, our cousins from Les Annevilles. Peter was living near Brian, and Olive was with the Ladies' College, also based in Oldham.

I dashed back to Roylelands to write to my parents again, this time sending the letter to Guernsey. Had they decided to stay there after all? Perhaps something had happened to stop them leaving. I also wrote to Brian to give him all my news.

The following day (Wednesday 26th) when I had gone to bed, someone came up with a letter. I just managed to read it before it got too dark. It had been brought from Horse Carrs, which was the address passed round on the Guernsey grapevine. My mother had heard it on the Monday, two days before, and had written straightaway. The family was at Rue des Landes during the day but going to Les Fontaines to sleep. She had taken some of my clothes there as well as my stamp album, a few treasured possessions and our pet rabbits. The kittens, Sammy and Mickey, had been given away. The airport was quiet and there was no one at Happy Landings, the hotel opposite our house. My father was going to buy a bicycle as petrol for his car would be in short supply. There was a closing note from him explaining that he had sent money to Uncle Eug for our welfare, but he didn't state how much. We were to ask for shoes or any items of clothing we might need.

The next morning (Thursday 27th) a letter came from Brian describing his billet. He was with a Dr. and Mrs. Stewart and was allowed to use their son's books, toys and tools, while he was away at boarding school. There were two maids in the house, he said. On Saturday 29th, I wrote to him about the German bombing of St. Peter Port the previous day. Perhaps he knew already. There had been machine gunning of people in the harbour. Around thirty had been killed. As this was some way from our home and from Les Fontaines, I wasn't worried about our parents' safety, but I assumed that there would be a mass evacuation from Guernsey to follow. There might be a telegram to say our mother was on the way. I would write to Uncle Eug to see if she had telephoned.

By then, we had been at Roylelands for a week and were getting used to our new surroundings. We strolled through the nearby park and watched the growth of ten little ducklings. We played rounders and went on the swings. For country girls like me, unused to parks, it was a challenge to slide down a chute for the very first time. On walks along the canal, I collected tatty bits of fluffy cotton which were floating on the water. I sent a little tuft home as an explorer might send a specimen from a foreign land. We discovered the willowherb and many unfamiliar weeds so different from the dainty blue speedwell and the scarlet pimpernel which grew at Rue des Landes. Here, everything was black.

Meanwhile, domestic arrangements at Roylelands were taking shape and a routine was being established. Midday meals arrived by van in large canisters. We were all given tasks and mine was laying and clearing the tables. We knew little of the organisation behind the scenes, aware only that there were committees and bodies of helpers that were taking responsibility for our wellbeing. Soon we came to recognise the members of the WVS and the officers of the Public Assistance Board (a precursor of the DSS). In those first few days, matters relating to our ration books and our identity cards were settled and we were each given a number to be written with indelible ink on a tape for sewing on each item of clothing. Mine was 46. We did our washing in an outhouse.

Members of staff and helpers took on various areas of responsibility:

| | |
|---|---|
| *Bedrooms and housework* | Mrs. le Patourel |
| | Miss Brown |
| | Miss Mahy |
| *Washing up, washing clothes* | Miss McPhail |
| *Personal cleanliness and care of lavatory and bathroom* | Mrs. Underdown |
| *Hair supervision* | Miss Roughton |
| *Games and health, doses and walks* | Miss Brittain |
| | Miss Sayer |
| *Billeting lists and pocket money* | Miss Clayton |
| | Miss Mallett |
| *Mending* | Mrs. McPhail |

About thirty older girls were combed away from Roylelands and settled in Boothroyd, a house conveniently near. It was rented by Miss Roughton herself, mainly to relieve the congestion at Roylelands, where a room little larger than my parents' bedroom had twenty-one camp beds squeezed in.

Further news came from my father on Saturday 29th. His letter had been written before the German air raid on Guernsey of the previous day. There were about fifty cows brought from Alderney grazing on the airport. Two of his employees who worked in the greenhouses had been evacuated and the three who normally did carpentry work were picking and packing the tomatoes. On Monday 178 baskets had gone and 160 on Wednesday. The newly formed Food Control Committee was about to clear the stock from the small all-purpose shop on the Rue des Landes premises. The Minchintons who ran it had been evacuated and already burglars had stolen some cigarettes. The mail boats to the island had been reduced from six to two a week and he hoped that the one arriving the next day would bring them the first letter from me. (I did too.) He realised the cause of the delay as I had been told to write to them at Uncle's in Edgworth.

It seemed to me that the export of tomatoes must be running smoothly. Like others, my parents were carrying on their life on the island and it was business as usual. Weren't they coming? He made no reference to their future plans. I found that strange. If they had decided not to come, why didn't they tell us?

When some of us were walking back from church on Sunday evening, a car slowed down ahead of us and someone called, "Look, Lois! There's your brother!" Mrs. Stewart had brought him to Rochdale on a visit. Ruth, Jean and I jumped in and soon we were wandering round the grounds at Roylelands, exchanging news. Did the raid on Guernsey mean that our parents would be leaving? We didn't know what to think and could only wait in a state of muddled uncertainty.

With hindsight, it seems incredible that the telephone was hardly used. No girl at Roylelands, to my knowledge, had been urged by her parents to give them a ring on arrival. There was a sort of taboo on making long-distance calls. They were only for emergencies! (And for adults.)

On Monday, we went to school for the first time. Three classrooms had been allocated to us at Castleton Senior School, which was about a mile from Roylelands. The headmaster of this elementary school was Mr. Wilson and, from the start, he made us welcome. We could also have the use of the science laboratory and the hall when they were available. As we sat at the long desks with forms attached, we were given two new exercise books, a peach one for Maths and a blue one for everything else. In addition, we had a notebook, a pencil and a pen with a nib. At intervals along each desk, there were round holes for the enamel inkwells and these were to be refilled each week by members of the Castleton School. There were no lessons that morning, but the afternoon started with French and Divinity.

*Quelques idiomes avec avoir*
*Nous avons chaud*
*Nous avons froid*
*Nous avons faim*

It all seemed a bit unreal . . . as if the teachers were putting up a valiant front: "We're not quite on track yet, but we'll get there."

Every lunch time, we were told, we would walk back to Roylelands for a meal and return to school for the afternoon. To cope with the housework, there would be a rota of girls to stay behind. I was in the first shift and our working party made a start on Tuesday July 2nd, clearing the breakfast things, sweeping and dusting.

As the crowds surged in from school at the end of the morning, one girl, ahead of the rest, burst up the steps with a shout, "The Germans have landed! The Germans are in Guernsey!" Miss Roughton had told them all at Assembly. From the general hubbub, I gathered that there had been no fighting or bloodshed, but very few details were known. So it had happened. That was it. Some girls had obviously been crying. I decided I would let the news seep in slowly bit by bit. I felt a little cheated, because I had missed the main announcement. The news had been sprung on me second-hand in blurts.

I learned afterwards that Miss Roughton had started morning prayers with one of her favourite hymns, 'Praise, my soul, the King of Heaven' and it was in this context of faith and confidence that she had told the girls.

It was clear that the islands were now well and truly cut off and there would be no further contact. Would our parents be safe? Was there enough food to last? Many of the girls were subdued and tearful. One said Miss Mahy was good at cheering people up.

In the afternoon, some sports were hastily organised for all the Roylelands girls. I took part in several events, including a flat race, a skipping race and an obstacle race, and found myself competing with much bigger, older girls. I won some heats as I was quite athletic, but failed to win in the finals. My disappointment was absurdly out of proportion and seemed to channel the underlying mood of the day, which surfaced so unexpectedly in this particular fashion. I thought I must in loyalty remember my mother's words about being brave, when she was waving us goodbye and stop myself from crying. And so I did for several years.

The next day we went to school as usual and had French, Algebra, Divinity prep, History and English. Miss Stewart told us about the Industrial Revolution.

Thus began the five year period of evacuation.

# Chapter V

## *'For the Gang's All Here'*

At appointed times, Miss Clayton, the Needlework mistress, was to be found at Roylelands, with a cluster of girls pressing round her. She was the banker. Of enormous girth and dressed in her customary brown skirt, white short-sleeved satin blouse and tight brown cardigan, she sat with a handy notebook at the ready. We had been directed by Miss Roughton to hand over to her our vital little stores of shillings brought from Guernsey. She recorded the withdrawals for stamps, envelopes, shampoo and other small necessities and received the deposits of any sixpences that friends had given us. The system was working well and initial qualms were being replaced with greater trust and confidence. We had access to our money and, in her hands, it would not get lost or stolen. Most of us kept back a few pennies for local bus fares or unexpected needs. The security was short-lived. Miss Roughton got up to make an announcement. We had to make a contribution for our keep. The Rochdale authorities required this of us and it had to be done. Our savings, she said, would be reviewed and an appropriate amount deducted.

"No fear!" "I'm not letting anybody have my money!" A mixture of alarm, despondency or sullen acquiescence was registered on all our faces. How could we ever hope to pay our way? We badly needed the money to keep in touch with friends and relations and for small necessities. Who could we rely on when the last penny had gone? Some girls had no one.

Miss Roughton's task was difficult, since inevitably, some of us had brought a lot more money than others. A few had very little left. An equal contribution from everyone was out of the question. By what criteria would she determine the amount to be docked off?

We were aghast at the results. Six shillings had been syphoned away from my meagre deposit of fourteen shillings and sixpence. At the drop of a hat, nearly half my money had been swept away. It was gone for ever. How long could this go on? There was a general sense of outrage. It seemed that we had no control over our savings after all. Further fleecing would prevent us from buying stamps or stationery. We felt trapped, tricked and powerless. The thrifty had been penalised, some said. The more you had, the more was taken. Among ourselves, we compared the amount deducted. Why were there such wide discrepancies? What rule of thumb had been applied? Were those with relations on the mainland treated more stringently? Resentment fuelled angry mutterings of unfairness. Miss Roughton, surprised by the vehemence of feeling, assured us that no further inroads would be made. She sent £25.10.6 to the Public Assistance Department. A levelling process had taken place. There was a smaller margin between the rich and the poor and all were nearer penury and feeling more unsafe and at her mercy.

Close on the heels of this episode and two or three days after we heard about the German occupation of the islands, Miss Roughton called me for 'a little talk'. She said I must have my green Ladies' College tunic dyed navy blue, the school colour. I was taken aback and reluctant. Having just parted with my money, I did not want anyone to take control of my clothes and make decisions about them. This was something for parents to do. She was adamant. The tunic had to be dyed or I would have to have a new one and that would be far more expensive. How could I buy a new one? I resisted any more encroachments on my money.

I saw that I was to be an integral part of this navy blue school. My green uniform stood out and made me different. I was still feeling like a visitor included only on a provisional basis in a time of emergency. The girls who had previously been my classmates before the war now seemed rather distant. In the year since I had left, they had made new friends and alignments among themselves. Even the closest ones had grown away. I felt left out as though I did not belong to either school. In giving up my allegiance to the Ladies' College, I would have to forego the successes that my admission there had promised (or so it seemed). I glanced at my watch which Gran from Milestone had given me as a reward for passing the scholarship exam. All that it stood for mattered little to anyone here.

I handed over the tunic and it came back navy blue. What was to have been a short adventure across the sea had changed irrevocably. Its ending was lost to sight. The dye had fixed my stay in permanence. It was a shock. In this unwelcome way was the prospect of a long-term separation from my family really brought home to me. It meant that my future on the mainland was totally out of my parents' control and largely out of mine and coloured navy. Miss Roughton would have her way. She was in charge whether we liked her or not. She had taken the place of our parents as the decision-maker.

Authority had prevailed and I learned another lesson in compliance. Parents, home, money, clothes, friends, allegiances, all could vanish overnight. The buffeting affected all of us in different ways.

The routine life at Roylelands was taking shape. At 7.30 a.m.
Miss Brittain did the rounds and woke us up. After washing and
dressing, we queued downstairs to gargle at a designated sink.
This ritual over, we waited for the breakfast bell to ring and sat
down to cornflakes, bread and margarine. The chore allocated
for the day was tackled and then we made our beds and
assembled for the twenty minute walk to school which started at
10 a.m. We always went en bloc, escorted by a member of staff to
keep us all together and herd us on if there should be an air raid.
At noon, we trooped back to Roylelands for our midday meal. On
Fridays, it was fish cake, white sauce, beans and potatoes. The
second course might be sponge pudding or the glutinous sago
lumps so aptly christened 'frog spawn'.

Then the procession, as in the morning, skirted the canal
banks and made its way past the Dunlop plant and between the
mills marked Valley and Mars and Arrow and was timed to arrive
at school for 2 p.m.

Our trailing navy blue crocodile became a familiar sight to the
mill workers hurrying between shifts. To us, their clattering clogs
always seemed too hard and loose to fit. How could they keep
them on and find them comfortable? With black shawls over head
and shoulders, the women looked old and tired. We could hardly
understand the snatches of conversation we overheard. Their
broad Lancashire accent sounded foreign.

We were back 'home' for tea at 5 o'clock, when we regularly
had bread and margarine and jam. Cocoa was produced at 7.30,
to be followed by notices and prayers. The silence whistle was
blown at 9 p.m. when it got too dark to read or darn our socks.
All indoor lights were strictly forbidden, because we still had
nothing to cover up the windows. Air raid wardens made sure
that blackout regulations were strictly kept.

On Friday July 5th, Uncle turned up again at Roylelands. He
was given permission to take his three nieces to Edgworth for the
weekend. We scurried round in excitement. There was nowhere
to leave any of my belongings, no drawers or cupboards, so the
case with all its contents had to go with me. As there was no
packing to do, it was easy enough to set out straightaway and
catch the train.

Aunty gave us a warm welcome and our supper included a jolly
little tomato, which was in a batch sent by Gran from
Summerville just before the Germans landed only a few days
previously. It was like a rosy child arriving late and breathless,
after nearly being grabbed back by a kidnapper. A whole epoch

had gone by since the devastating news had reached us on Tuesday. For us, this was a little taste of normality in an unaccustomed world.

We shared the news in our letters and caught up with the events of the war. There was no access to newspapers and wireless at Roylelands. It was very comfortable to sleep on a proper mattress that night. The three of us shared a double bed and found it luxurious to have pillows and an eiderdown.

The next morning was spent in a much-needed cleaning operation: shoes and clothes and hair. My long, thick, swinging plaits seemed to attract all that was grimy in the Lancashire atmosphere. With Ruth's help, they were having their first wash since we had left our home a fortnight previously. The water turned embarrassingly dark.

Dressed in the best clothes we could muster, we set off in the afternoon with Aunty and Uncle to attend a garden party at the home of Miss Barlow, a wealthy local dignitary. After our first-ever game of croquet, we grouped around for a lovely tea of dainty sandwiches, strawberries and cakes. Our elderly hostess, an invalid, was wheeled through the grounds to escort her guests and we saw a Barlow building being transformed into a hospital: the family war effort, it was whispered. She employed a day nurse, a night nurse, a companion, a secretary, two maids, a chauffeur and four gardeners. One of her brothers had been Queen Victoria's doctor.

For my diary (started on the train from Weymouth) I was still using the writing pad and pencil brought from Rue des Landes. Now there were only one or two pages left. Uncle went out to buy me a red threepenny exercise book for the purpose and I said I would copy in the first two weeks' events and write up the diary regularly so that my parents would, one day, know what we had been doing. Ruth was also keeping a daily record.

Early on Sunday morning, Jean was sick and Ruth stayed in to keep her company while Aunty and I went to church. Uncle was preaching elsewhere. In the afternoon, we went to see the Wayo, a nearby reservoir. Uncle Art had previously been there when on a visit. We were treasuring memories of times that had gone for ever. Soon it was time to return to Rochdale. Jean had recovered. She and I had no money. We had left Roylelands so suddenly that there was no opportunity to go to Miss Clayton to withdraw some cash. Uncle gave us a shilling each and we were considered sensible enough to go to Bury on the bus, walk across to Knowsley Street railway station with the aid of a sketch map and catch the train, travelling three stops down the line to Rochdale. I felt my parents would have been very anxious had they known. It was the first time we had done such a journey unescorted.

At Roylelands, I headed for my camp bed, only to find it had been slept in by someone else. I was baffled. My niche had been taken. Where was I to go? I found one of the teachers who directed me to another room and here my case came into its own again, this time to mark my patch. I shoved it under an empty bed which denoted the rectangular area of my new home. I had discovered it could be changed without notice and in my absence and I could land up with anyone next to me without a say in the matter. I resented being so controlled by an outside authority. I had to wait till bedtime to find out whose feet would receive my goodnight whisperings. We slept in rows at right angles to the two longest parallel walls as in many hospital wards and with a pattern of alternating heads and tails to the wall, so as to avoid the transmission of germs, it was said.

Soon welcome gifts arrived to fill the evenings. Board games, cards, jig-saws and story books appeared and the Scouts sent cricket equipment. We chatted and wrote letters.

On Mondays and Tuesdays you could have wound your way in and out of great pyramids of washing. This was done in an outbuilding by those girls kept back from school for housework duties. They were assigned to a quota of vests or pants or blouses. Who wants to rub away at the shoe dye on mounds of other people's smelly socks?

The clothes were dried on lines in the yard and hung on racks in the kitchen. After a while, this highly uncongenial practice of communal washing was abandoned and we were each allowed to do our own.

\* \* \* \* \*

Horse Carrs, the house where the Juniors were based, was crammed. With its seventeen rooms, it had been large for the one family who had previously lived there, but now 155 people were jammed in. Miss Naftel, as our school's Deputy Head, had her allocation of teachers and helpers to look after the seventy-eight children under her wing. In addition, there were thirty or so children belonging to the Torteval Parish School from the west of the island with their supervising adults and a miscellaneous assortment of Guernsey and Jersey families, the largest of which consisted of a mother with her own seven children, aged from one to sixteen years. In all, there were 125 children, 5 men and 25 women.

Miss Hazell and Miss Johnson, who had taught the Kindergarten and Transition respectively, were fully stretched in looking after their charges. Together with Miss Stewart, Miss Ogier, Miss Simeson, Miss Hubert and various helpers and parents, they did what they could to comfort the younger ones, some of whom were thoroughly bewildered and miserable. They did not understand what had happened or why they couldn't go home. They were homesick and wanted their own parents. Most had never been away from them before. When one started crying in the night, others followed suit. Some were sick without warning and members of staff had to fumble their way towards them in complete darkness, since there was no blackout for the windows. All were exhausted from broken nights and unrelieved responsibility. There was no time off. Expectant mothers waited anxiously to see what might be in store for them.

The provision of toilets was totally inadequate and young boys, unable to find them or wait in a queue, urinated on the balcony. When the authorities brought in emergency portable toilets, this particular problem was eased, but there was the incessant hubbub of children on the go and fractious babies. Chickenpox broke out and most inmates were placed in quarantine. The sick ones went to hospital as there was no space to keep them isolated. Miss Hazell, who was used to controlling her young pupils by sending them into a corner of the room if they were too noisy, must have felt the strain. (I have acute memories of being banished to face the wall at her bidding in Guernsey.)

Miss Naftel, who was a Guernsey woman through and through and then in her mid-fifties, was shaken to the core when the occupation of the islands was announced. She said when she packed to leave her home at Les Fauconnaires in St. Andrew's, she had not fully realised the gravity of the situation. She expected to have some of her things sent on. Members of staff, like everyone else, had been restricted to one suitcase for the journey and were short of clothing. It was with a sense of jovial camaraderie that Miss Stewart shared her second vest with Miss Ogier. Miss Naftel rose to the occasion and applied her gifts of administration to encourage a sense of order and purposefulness. She was quick to offer the warmth of her personality where it was so desperately needed. She saw how much a friendly touch or hug could mean to young children who were shy or frightened and recognised how brave they were trying to be. Behind the husky voice and sometimes the flustery manner, there was a strong determination to make things work and they did. A household routine and rotas of supervisors were quickly organised.

Members of the WVS came every day and were responsible for breakfast and tea and the oversight of all meals, as at Roylelands. Here also, dinners arrived by van and so did not have to be prepared on the premises. Under Mrs. Stansfield, the WVS team members were vigilant and some said rigorous but kind. Children scuttled away from Mrs. S. with mutterings. They might have used the word 'martinet' if they had known it. The team opened doors to the local community, and Lancashire people were generous and good hearted in their response to the needs and sent games, amusements and clothes. But too many members of the public were popping in to catch sight of the young evacuees who were being helped and a tactful notice was placed in the local press to deter the spate of impromptu visitors.

Early on, one Jersey mother was admitted to the Marland Isolation Hospital with suspected diphtheria, but she was later found to be in the clear. Her husband had only twopence left and wanted to move to Burnley to see if he could find work as a motor mechanic. Financial aid was found and the couple with their little child moved on. Many people had left their homes in such a hurry that they could not draw on their savings. If they had tried, they would have found a £20 limit on withdrawals. Others had no bank accounts and were accustomed to rely heavily on their weekly wages. When they had spent the cash they had brought with them, they had nothing. (Later, those with deposits in the Guernsey branches of English banks were allowed to draw on them.)

Most of the island children had been inoculated against diphtheria earlier on, so the scare of an epidemic was kept well within bounds. Congestion was reduced when three of the adults left for Canada and the Torteval children with their supervisors were transferred to Alderley Edge in Cheshire. Numbers went down further as the Rochdale authorities found rooms and work for those family units which could be self-sufficient. The sixteen-year-old girl in the large Jersey family was given a job in the mills. When she got used to the overwhelming clatter of the machinery, she settled down.

Many Channel Island families, mostly Jersey people, had been given interim shelter at other Reception Centres in the town, also intended for bombed out families or European refugees. They were given lodging at the Cottage Homes in Wardle, at Westfield in Manchester Road and at Birch Hill Institution. When they moved into terraced houses, their neighbours often generously brought basic furniture, cutlery and blankets.

It was arranged that the Junior School of Greenbank near Horse Carrs, with Mr. Tweedale at its head, should allocate three of its classrooms to Guernsey children, who now had to forego their afternoon rambles on the moors and their newly acquired toys and buckle down to a timetable of lessons.

As the staff members were now teaching, there were few adults left in the house during the day. Most of the children were considered too young to do the housework, so it was decided to draft in some Roylelands girls to do the chores. They had to be selected from those who had already had chickenpox, so that they would not transmit the infection to Roylelands on their return. As I was on the list of the immune, I was sent on July 9th, with a partner, to sweep and dust, lay tables, serve at dinner and tea and wash up, the latter being a formidable undertaking when there were no dishwashing machines. The available tea towels always got sodden long before we reached the end of the first sitting's plates. In the afternoon, we hemmed aprons that were being made for 'the workers'. On subsequent Tuesdays, I returned to Horse Carrs with Kathleen Frampton or Margaret Palmer. We could be found wiping paintwork, washing grates, scrubbing floors, rinsing tea towels, cleaning cupboards and ironing. One of the supervising helpers watched me handling a broom, then clapped eyes on the heap of dust at my toes. "Always sweep away from you!" she admonished with asperity. I felt she was judging my home as well as my housework skills . . . a fundamental rule had not been properly implanted in me. As I had always done household tasks as a matter of course, I felt rather undervalued. Later, when I had a home of my own, I was always a little uncomfortable if, to avoid the furniture, I had to draw the brush towards me!

Another helper came round to examine the ironing. If she spotted a few creases, she wet the article again and the girls had to repeat their work. Some were reduced to tears. Piles were waiting. Perhaps it was only by maintaining her familiar disciplines that she could hold her world together. The distress caused by her incongruous demands was only partially offset by her generosity with sweets and second helpings from the leftovers at dinner-time.

The girls from Roylelands did much of the laundry at Horse Carrs, carrying buckets of hot water down to the cellar and rubbing away the Rochdale dirt by hand. Between their visits a parent/helper washed dozens of dresses and blouses.

Miss Roughton was now receiving mail from evacuated parents scattered over the UK. Some were anxious to claim their children. Friends or relations sent donations for immediate needs. Most letters were encouraging and supportive. A few correspondents, however, showed little grasp of the real conditions and struck an officious note. One man was enquiring after a Horse Carrs girl who appeared to have no close relations on the mainland. His letter went on:-

> '. . . *From the child's second letter received today it might appear she is not entirely free to receive and/or dispatch correspondence and also that there are somewhat severe restrictions in regard to pocket money; there is no direct complaint concerning these matters but merely the impression given by lack of reply to questions asked; there also appears to have been delay in the posting of each of her two letters.*
>
> *I should be very much obliged if you would kindly inform me what arrangements obtain regarding the conducting of correspondence by the children and to what extent pocket money is allowed. I sent her 2 shillings, but it appears doubtful if she has been allowed to have this. I fully appreciate, of course, that some restrictions may be desirable but perhaps you will be good enough to let me know what the position is. If she has not been allowed to have the money sent will you please say why this has not been returned to me or otherwise accounted for to me. A stamp for 2½d was also sent and has not been used.*'

We must hope that when Miss Roughton had crossed the town by two buses or cycled to Horse Carrs and shown the letter to Miss Naftel, that the girl in question was urged to use the stamp to thank her benefactor!

For some time following the German occupation of the islands, there were some girls who did not know whether or not their parents had been evacuated. On which side of the Channel were they and how could they find out? There was no official record to consult. One girl sent her first letters to both her parents in Guernsey, not realising that her mother and young brother had already left. She'd had no experience of writing to them before and didn't know how to finish. After calling them darlings she settled for

I remain,
Your loving daughter

Most girls had brought the addresses of friends, relations or family acquaintances on the mainland and wrote to them on their arrival in Rochdale. Margaret Palmer had left her widowed mother behind on the island. She had no relations on the mainland and wrote to friends in S. Wales to explain what had happened. She was astonished that it was her mother who replied. Mrs. Palmer had not yet tracked the school to Rochdale. She told Margaret how she had hurriedly left Guernsey on a coal boat. During a chat with the ship's engineer whom she knew, he had pressed her go to to S. Wales where his sisters and brothers lived and she had accepted this offer of a temporary base till she could find Margaret. She was hoping to get work near her daughter.

Monica Ball's father was in the Royal Navy and was serving on the *Esperance Bay*, an armed merchant cruiser, which had docked in Southampton. He was due for leave on June 29th and intended to go to Guernsey to see his family. In the meantime, Monica was evacuated with the school, and soon after she had gone, Mrs. Ball, waiting at home for news from her husband, received a telegram from him urging her to leave everything and come to the mainland herself. She hastily grabbed a few belongings and went down to the harbour, where she was admitted on to the *Duke of York*, which was packed mainly with mothers and young children. They arrived in Weymouth and soon Mrs. Ball was on a train to Southampton. Monica, by that time in Rochdale, wrote to her father's naval address and as soon as his leave started, both parents came up to Rochdale and stayed at a small hotel, while trying to find a room where Monica and her mother could live together when he had gone back to sea. After a short term with a Mrs. Smith, Mrs. Ball and Monica found a furnished room in a house belonging to the manager of the Regal Cinema.

Diana Falla was one of those who quickly made contact with her relations. She had an aunt and uncle in Swindon and a married sister in Reading. Although it was mid-summer, she was always complaining of cold feet and had medical attention for minor symptoms. It was still unusual to have a woman doctor. "Which one was she wearing today?" we would ask Diana. We had homed in on the stylish hat which seemed so mandatory for the professional woman. Lavish descriptions of her 'bird's nest' would follow. Another creation featured a long swathe of chiffon material that dripped from one ear and was flung across the throat and draped over the opposite shoulder. Then there was the purple plate trimmed with flowers that was tipped forward over the eyes and held in place by a band round the nape of the neck. Soon Diana was to leave us to stay with her aunt and uncle. Many others also went. We all knew that someone had been quick to trace Diana Wallis, since she sat on her camp bed in conspicuous splendour amid a bountiful display of sweets and ten whole bars of chocolate. She made the most of the kudos this gave her and bestowed pieces on all and sundry. Lesser mortals were obliged to share their smaller treats in thumb-nail portions.

We were sorry to say goodbye to our departing friends. There were no tangible mementos we could exchange, but they left behind a most acceptable gift – the space they had occupied. Gradually we were able to spread out a little and feel less squashed. In some rooms, we could stack the camp beds to one side during the day. Cotton sleeping bags arrived and those who had been Guides were distinguishable by the humps at one end of their beds. They had been favoured with pillows bought with funds from their opposite numbers.

It was now becoming apparent that many of the larger contingents of Channel Islanders were concentrated in the north, in Glasgow, in various Lancashire, Yorkshire and Cheshire towns as well as in Leicester, Bristol and other areas. Some individuals and mothers with young children had made their own plans and headed for the UK homes of their friends and relations, but many could not make preliminary arrangements before they left, often because those on one or other side of the Channel had no telephones, which were still something of a luxury. All were under great pressure and relied on assurances that there would be Government backing for them when they arrived on the mainland if they had nowhere to go and no means of support.

Sometime after the war, statistical details of the evacuation were released. Looking at Guernsey, it was shown that, from June 20th–23rd 1940, a total of 44 ships had carried away 20,202 passengers. In addition, other people had left on the regular mail steamer services. Almost half the population had gone.

Ministry of Health officials were concerned that evacuating schools should be placed in 'reception areas' rather than in 'neutral areas' which were considered less safe. Knowing that the Intermediate School bases at Oldham and Rochdale were in the latter classification, they had acted with commendable speed and even before the Germans had occupied the islands, they approached Mr. John Robert, a Guernsey civil servant, who had hurriedly left his island home and had a temporary base at the Victoria Hotel in Manchester. It was understood that he would become one of the three men to make links between the Guernsey States and the British Government in London, although, in the evacuation rush, it was unlikely that the three could have been given any verifiable authority. On June 28th, he had written to Miss Roughton outlining the Ministry of Health plans to send both schools to Thornton Hough in Cheshire. This move had the backing of Mr. W. Stringer, then an HMI, but previously Headmaster of the Boys' Intermediate School and so he knew it well. The current head, Mr. Fulford, and Miss Roughton were to let Mr. Robert know their reactions. The surroundings would be more congenial, it was argued, the residents were of a good type, and, on average, more well-to-do. He explained to Miss Roughton that Mr. Stringer saw further advantages:

> *'You and Mr. Fulford would share a modern school, a school which would be used by none but Guernsey children. The girls and teachers would be billeted with those people, so they would be living in homes at least equal to their own. Your helpers would have much lighter work, certainly no domestic work, not as far as I can understand. It would follow that their diet would be of a better standard than at present.'*

The two Heads visited the proposed host area in Cheshire and decided to resist going there. They did not make their reasons known.

* * * * *

A temperamental tank in the cookery building at Castleton school was enjoying its power to set the pipes a-gurgling. In mid-July, some of the senior girls had been poring over exam papers, trying to ignore the distracting accompaniment. They were bent on obtaining their School Certificate (the precursor of 'O' levels), for which they had been entered before the evacuation. Unavoidably, all their preparatory notes and textbooks had been left neatly stacked in their Guernsey desks, but as soon as their predicament was made known, Miss Keating, Head of the Rochdale Municipal High School for Girls, together with the staff of neighbouring schools, sent small batches of books. A vicar and a doctor living nearby offered the use of their studies as quiet

havens and a few girls dived into the basement at Boothroyd
where there was a billiard table and peace. When it was chilly
down there, they wrapped themselves in blankets and concentrated on cramming.

At that time, the Certificate was awarded only to those who
had, in one run, gained satisfactory grades in at least five subjects
taken from designated categories. A few core subjects such as
English Language, maths, and a branch of science were compulsory. Good results provided exemption from matriculation,
which was the basic requirement for university entrance,
although, generally speaking, much more than that was needed
in a competitive field.

Yvonne Robilliard had been entered for nine subjects. She and
the other examinees braced themselves for the challenge. They
were shut off at Castleton in a block separate from the rest and
we were warned with much gravity to keep away and be quiet.
When the normal trek to Roylelands for school dinner could not
be fitted into the examination timetable, the girls tucked into
threepenny pork pies.

Miss Roughton, realising how worried some of them might be,
assured them that a letter would be sent to the Oxford Local
Examination Board to explain the circumstances. Eventually, all
heard that they had got through very creditably, although, of
those who took Latin, Yvonne was the only one to pass.

Older girls now had to map out their careers. Some were
without parental guidance or financial support. Miss Roughton
wanted all to take advantage of any opportunities open to them
and set about identifying sources of help.

Anetta Crabtree, from Castleton School, who lived at Hartley
Farm nearby, was one of those who regularly brought her skipping
rope for break and lent it to the Guernsey girls. Together with her
friends, we practised the playground chants they used . . .

> *Jelly on a plate, jelly on a plate,*
> *Wibble, wobble, wibble, wobble,*
> *Jelly on a plate.*
>
> *Sausage in a pan, sausage in a pan,*
> *Turn them over, turn them over,*
> *Sausage in a pan.*

Suitable shaking and turning actions accompanied the sing-song
rhythms.

With many others, we mastered the skilful art of jumping over two clothes lines, each turned alternately in opposite directions by girl-pivots posted at either end. The trick for us was to time our entry into the rotating ropes so that our tunics were not whipped upwards over our backsides. Other Castleton children asked us to play marbles or hopscotch. They brought us comics and sweets and sometimes we could snatch a few minutes to go to their homes. In such ways I got to know Margaret Allpress and Agnes Gregory.

One Saturday afternoon, Agnes with two of her friends and her nine-year-old brother took me to the park where we played a ball game and ate sandwiches. "Come on! Let's go on the lake!" they shouted. It cost a penny for each of us. I remembered I couldn't swim and thought of my father's cautiousness about the water and jumped into the boat regardless. The motor started up and we were away. I felt I had left my father behind, powerless. He would not have allowed me to go. I had made a decision without his authorisation. This was a new departure.

There was little we could do to repay their hospitality, but I joined up with Marie Bisson who had been a great friend before the war and we invited two of the Castleton girls to Roylelands. They brought us a book and a coat hanger each and some comics to share. When they had seen the rows of camp beds, they had seen everything. The visit petered out in the overgrown garden. On one memorable occasion, our meagre tea was augmented by a lovely fresh fruit salad provided by the Castleton school. Perhaps some of the children thought we would miss the pineapples and bananas of a tropical climate. They had heard of the Guernsey sunshine, but had little idea where the island was. "What have you done with your grass skirts?" was their way of finding out.

After some weeks of playground activities shared with our hosts, we gradually seemed to fall apart into our separate school groupings, as if we were unable to bridge the gap of tradition, accent or lifestyle. We remained on friendly terms and had good reason to be very grateful for their personal interest and helpfulness. Their classroom conditions were far from ideal, since they had lost three rooms to us and were overcrowded in the remaining ones.

"Do you play the piano or the violin?" This question might have met with little response in Roylelands, except that a positive reply meant going to someone's house, ostensibly to practise. Mr. Fred Wilson, the Castleton Headmaster, had organised a committee to recruit local householders for this purpose. My hostess was Mrs. Livsey. I found her piano music very difficult to tackle on sight and floundered through the hour, grateful when she left the room, but aware that she could still hear my faltering efforts through the walls. I had been used to playing hymns in Sunday School, but this was more demanding. Tea and chocolate biscuits helped to make up for everything else and this visit proved to be the first of a long series. Some people lent violins to the school and Miss Roughton was able to renew her love of music, wondering at the same time whether she would ever see her own cherished instrument again. Pianos appeared at Horse Carrs and at Roylelands.

I slipped the penny I had been clutching into my pocket before opening my hymn book. The stewards at the Castleton Methodist Church often failed to notice our row when it was time for the collection. A group of us attended regularly and we were greeted warmly. Once, Ruth and I were each given a sheet with a hymn composed by the conductor of the choir, Mr. J. Hollows. I looked after mine with great veneration and laid it flat at the bottom of my case, so that it would not get crumpled.

The minister, Dr. Ralph Letch, came to Roylelands and invited a few of us to his home at Heywood on some Saturday afternoons. We strolled in a nearby park and learned to play Lexicon or Monopoly, till Mrs. Letch announced tea and plied us with cucumber sandwiches, trifle and home-made cake. Our host then saw us on to the bus and paid our 1½d fares. Later in the summer, he started a small group at Roylelands. It was to have a missionary theme and the first one was on work in Indian villages. Subsequently, Mrs. Letch brought a sari and allowed Pamela Tachon to be the model.

* * * * *

Although the congestion at Horse Carrs was greatly reduced during July when many children left to join parents or relations, there were still many problems which worried members of the Rochdale Public Assistance Committee. Following up the reports of its Emergency Sub-Committee, they decided to open another house nearby. On July 30th, Miss Johnson, together with some supervising adults, moved into Lyngarth, to take charge of a group of the youngest children, among whom were about fourteen boys, aged five to seven.

Rachel and
Frederick Robin

Rachel and Frederick Robin
the grandparents of
*(L ➤ R)* Ruth, Brian, Jean and me

The Robins *(L ➤ R)*

Amicie (aunt)
Rachel (grandmother)
Helene (wife of Eugene)
Miriam (mother)
Lois (me)
Helene (sister of Miriam)

Summerville, Longue Rue, Vale, home of the Robin family

Adele and Arthur Robin
of Les Fontaines
(parents of Ruth and Jean)

Eugene and Helene Robin (née Mahy)

Helene Robin (sister of Miriam)
and her uncle,
Thomas O. Mahy of
Courtil-a-Paix.

With my mother and John
shortly before the
evacuation.
(I am in Ladies' College
uniform.)

Rue des Landes, Forest, (childhood home), taken after
the war, but little changed over the years.

Mary Brehaut
(grandmother)
from
Milestone.

From John, goodbye!

Taken in the summer of 1940. The film was
in the camera, hidden inside a cushion,
till 1945. In retrospect, this provides a
poignant reminder of the parting at the
time of the evacuation.

The two family
portraits I took
to England in
1940

The Brehauts of Rue des Landes.
Miriam and Bazil (mother and father)
Brian (brother) and me.

John (younger brother)

One of these young boys, Peter Davis, remembers being fetched from Rochdale by his mother, who had been evacuated to S. Wales. Her husband, Peter's father, was away in the Forces. She had previously visited Peter while he was ill in a Rochdale hospital. He had been segregated from the other children to halt the spread of infection. Peter, then aged five or six, had been disgusted on two counts: it was an outrage to his pride to be placed in a 'baby' cot with sides that lifted up or down and he had not been allowed to take away from the hospital the toys that his mother had brought him on her visit. Sadly, Peter's grandfather, Mr. le Cheminant of the Arcade toyshop in St. Peter Port, was one of those killed in the German air raid on Guernsey, shortly before the Occupation started.

In the ensuing weeks, strenuous efforts were made to transfer the younger boys to the Boys' Intermediate School in Oldham and as soon as suitable billets were found there, they were escorted to their new homes and school, away from the teachers and adults they had come to know and trust. Once more they were pitchforked into the unknown.

The pruning down of the Juniors in various ways signalled an all-round shuffle across the school spectrum. Sisters were now separated from each other and placed with those in their own age group. Jean was sent to Horse Carrs, Ruth went to live at Boothroyd with the older girls, while I stayed on at Roylelands. The three of us were now parted. We all moved up one form and I found myself in Upper IV.

When this change took place, Ruth and I had just been to Edgworth again on another weekend visit. Jean was in quarantine for chickenpox and was not allowed to go. One of the highlights had been a tour of the Methodist National Children's Home and Orphanage as it was then known (now NCH), and we were intrigued with a black baby called James. Those of Afro-Caribbean origin were rarely seen in Guernsey. On Sunday morning, we had processed to the homes of the elderly before the morning service and sung hymns outside. This was a long established custom on the Sunday School Anniversary, still, in the north, termed Annual Sermons. One of the hymns was 'It came upon a summer's day', the tune of which was written by J.R. Barlow, a brother of Miss Barlow, whom we had met. We were beginning to recognise local interconnections.

In the manse at Edgworth, tea chests, trunks and boxes were all lined up. Aunty and Uncle were well advanced with their packing as they were due to move to a new appointment ready for

September 1st. Methodist ministers were used to an itinerant life, being based in one area, usually, for only three years. As all the furniture and fittings in the manse belonged to the local Methodist Circuit, they had to remove all their own possessions from cupboards, drawers and shelves and stuff them into whatever containers they could find and leave everything clean for the next minister's family. The houses belonged to the Church.

When they arrived at a new home, there was always a rapid tour of inspection. The household equipment was also Church property and left by the previous occupants for the newcomers. Its state depended much on its age and on past treatment. Had the sheets been patched and the blankets darned? Was the crockery of the thick white chunky kind? Were the enamel saucepans chipped? Was the cooker clean, were the pipes well lagged, the garden under control?

Aunty and Uncle were about to move to Summerseat, a village some two and a half miles north of Bury. Uncle was to have oversight of a few churches in that vicinity. Everything had been arranged long before the evacuation, but it so happened that he would be stationed only a few miles from Rochdale. Our visits could continue.

# Chapter VI

## 'We're Going to Hang Out the Washing on the Siegfried Line'

I woke up startled. The shrill rising crescendo of the Rochdale siren dwindled into a whine and was followed by a further strident shriek into the night. Rhythmically, it insisted we move fast. It was the beginning of August and soon the warnings in our area would become more frequent. Ready to hand were our coats, shoes and gas masks. A number of torches had been acquired since our first descent into the cellars, so now we could see where to spread our blankets on the cold stone floors. We tried to doze till the continuous even note of the all-clear sounded and we could warm up in our beds upstairs. In one black cavern, a bucket was positioned. Girls who could not wait to use the bathroom which was out of bounds until the raid was over, were forced into indignities.

Although the sound of the artillery barrage was rather muted through the thick walls of the cellars, we could tell that the warnings were for real. There was little sign of fear. Didn't everyone know that Rochdale was not worth bombing? But why was this myth being sustained? Was it to allay anxiety? Likely targets were Liverpool and the Merseyside docks, Manchester, Bolton, Bury, Oldham and perhaps occasionally the smaller towns, and always some place else. Yet, how vulnerable were we – really?

As we had no maps, we had only a hazy idea as to our own location, our distance from other towns and their geographical relationship to each other, but on various journeys by bus and train, we had noticed the ribbon development that linked the conglomerations of tall slim round factory chimneys, all belching out a pall of thick black smoke into which they tapered. It seemed that many towns ran into each other. Which ones were most likely to receive a pounding? Was Rochdale among them after all? The question was met with greater realism. We little knew what might be of importance to the Germans in the vicinity, but it was rumoured that the Turner asbestos works near Horse Carrs might well be singled out, although the buildings were heavily camouflaged to keep them secret from the air. Much went on underground we heard, but who among us really knew? For us, the human face was Lady Turner's. She was very prominent in WVS circles and had made herself known to Miss Roughton and offered her support.

The newspapers and wireless were not allowed to say which areas had been hit for fear of giving information to the enemy. 'Careless talk costs lives' was to become a familiar poster warning. It was only much later that we heard that many of the August raids were directed towards the Liverpool docks and Merseyside and the Lancashire cotton towns were in the flight line.

If you had been queuing outside a bathroom at Roylelands in the evenings, you might have overheard some angry protests. "Who's been using my shampoo? I'll wring her neck!" "You were first in the bath last time. It's my turn to have the clean water!" "Take your filthy socks away from my pile!" Sharing the same limited supplies of hot water by rota and constantly manoeuvring in a small space could be very irritating. When someone needed to use the lavatory in the bathroom, others got tired of the courtesy of 'not-looking'. Frayed tempers were checked if a supervising adult appeared, and vulgarities were provisionally curbed. There was little opportunity to be alone anywhere. Everything you did was seen or heard and subject to other people's scrutiny or comment. There was no privacy and nowhere to go to be on your own.

We were still living out of suitcases. Mine denoted the only space I could keep for myself and in it went the diary. I did not record my feelings freely. One day others might pounce on it and fling them back at me. I thought I would add explanations to my parents when they read the pages at a later stage.

Would we have to live in this fashion indefinitely? The prospect was daunting. Some girls were robust or aggressively assertive, others were painfully shy and reticent. All put a brave face on things. We had to carry on. Mostly, we had no one we knew well enough to confide in, although, gradually, as the mistresses came into frequent contact, a style of relationship developed which went far beyond that of teacher/pupil.

Miss Brown, who was neat and petite with dainty features and beautiful hands could be found bending over a camp bed, bringing pills to a girl racked with tummy ache. Miss Clayton took Ruth to town and bought her a pair of shoes and some wool. Was it with her money? Miss Mahy filled an old teapot with flowers from the garden. A merry bunch stood in greeting on the aspidistra stand. Miss Stewart produced quantities of cloth drawstring bags specially made by her mother for our hair brushes and combs.

There was a drive to keep the rooms clean and tidy. Every week they were inspected and the best one qualified its occupants for a privilege. Usually a special tea of cherries, plums and fancy cakes was chosen with perhaps a party game to follow. Once, a firm, whose equipment had broken down, bathed us in oceans of ice cream.

Girls were still involved in every household task. Miss Roughton had seen to it that there were more bowls, brushes and tea towels in all the houses. They were paid for, in part, by donations from well-wishers, varying from a few shillings to £10. There were schools who made collections for us.

Many years later, we learned that Miss Roughton was able to draw on the proceeds of an insurance policy which had matured shortly before. She was known to dip into her handbag for girls' fares or shoe repairs and did not always reimburse herself. Few records were kept of minor expenditure and the extent of her generosity remains undisclosed as she would have wished.

The WVS members were very supportive and, because they supervised the serving of meals, staff members at Roylelands could converge on the kitchen away from the hurly burly. It was with a great sense of shock that we learned of the sudden death of Mrs. Heap, who had led the team. She was well liked and had a real concern for the girls. If we had needed a reminder that life is tenuous, then this would have served. Death could come unexpectedly for reasons unrelated to the war and its catastrophes. She was to be replaced by Mrs. Casson, an able successor.

It wasn't till August 9th that a fortnight's holiday began. Our desultory lessons ground to a halt. Ruth and Jean went off to Cople near Bedford to stay with Mrs. Norris, who had been a regular visitor at their parents' guest house in Guernsey. Over the years she had become a firm family friend and was affectionately known as A.D. for Aunty Dorothy.

A number of girls had nowhere to go. Mistresses had to stagger their own holidays to supervise them and this could mean curtailing their well-deserved break to a week. Joyce le Tissier, facing a lonely time, confided, "When I lay in bed thinking that most of the girls would be going away, I might have been a little envious . . .", but she went on to describe the organised treks across the moors and her group's memorable trip to Hollingworth Lake, led by Miss Radford, who was on the Castleton staff. Well-built and firm in her handling of her pupils, she used a deliberate, loud and authoritative voice in school. Her commands reverberated down the corridors in a style so different from that of the Intermediate staff. Now girls were pleased to see her informally and to have a welcome home-cooked meal in her house. There were also outings to the baths and cinema, all designed to offset feelings of boredom and discouragement.

Administrative tasks fell heavily on Miss Roughton. Sometimes people wrote for permission to have the girls for weekends or holidays only a few days before the visit was due. They might omit to say whether they lived in reception areas, safe from bombing. They were vague about train times and fares. Details had to be checked by the exchange of telegrams. Postal orders received in the mail for fares had to be cashed. At the request of hostesses, hard-pressed staff members made special journeys to key railway stations to place girls in the care of the guard.

I didn't know till the day we broke up whether or not I was to go to Edgworth for the fortnight's holiday. Uncle had explained that Aunty was tired and he would let me know. In response to an urgent telegram of enquiry sent by Miss Roughton, an invitation arrived and I set off, for the very first time on my own.

The BBC news that evening was alarming. It featured RAF attacks on the Guernsey airport. Newspapers said that forty to fifty German fighters, twin-engined bombers and transport planes had been sighted on it. Heavy and incendiary bombs were dropped on the landing grounds. Gun posts round the airport had been machine gunned and fires started around the hangars.

Was Gran in her house at Milestone on the brink of all that when it happened? Was she alright? Were my parents inside Rue des Landes, only 500 yards from those hangars? Was this likely to be the first of a series of raids? Would the British Government try to retake the islands?

So my parents could be killed by bombing as well as by starvation. This was something else I had to absorb. More than ever, I had to be prepared to manage on my own without them. I might never see them again.

"Hello, Lois!" I heard. Aunty and I were strolling past a drapery stall in the Bolton market. I swung round in astonishment. Mrs. Heaume, a member of my church in Guernsey, was waving through a gap in the rolls of curtaining. When she had finished serving a customer, she told us she had been evacuated with her younger son, Eric. His older brother, Ernie, was in Cheshire with his school. Somehow it seemed quite the wrong setting for her. She was isolated and battling to survive. I thought of her husband who had taught us in Sunday

School. His intriguing squint had been such a puzzle when we were younger. When two of us stood in front of him, which one was he looking at? Now he was among the many married men on the island, who were separated from their evacuated families. The Heaumes lived in a lovely old granite farmhouse at La Villiaze, along another side of the airport. Was he safe? Mrs. Heaume, at the market stall, was now earning just enough for bare necessities. I imagined my mother in her position, obliged to stand all day and moving heavy bales of cloth. Would she have managed such a life alone? Clearly the answer had to be 'no'. I found out later that Uncle knew the Heaumes as he had been the one to marry them.

A day or two afterwards, I was lolling on top of Lil, the elephant, at Belle Vue Zoo in Manchester. The experience was funny and enjoyable. It was my first ever visit to a zoo, since we had none in Guernsey.

Between these trips, Uncle and Aunty finished their packing ready for the removal van and we were off to Southport to stay for a few days' break in a small boarding house. The vast stretches of grey sand with the sea receding out of sight contrasted starkly with Guernsey's small coves flanked by time-worn granite cliffs, strewn with dabs of brilliant yellow gorse across the sheets of ox-eye daisies. I collected some unfamiliar sea-shells and stuffed them in a Liquorice Allsorts box. I wanted to show them to my parents and say: "See what I found! This is what my life was like. Here's what you have missed. I'm trying to make up for all that." The shells are still in the same box, kept carefully in my suitcase.

My diary records, in merciless detail, the adventures in the escapist film *Typhoon*, well publicised for its new and glorious technicolor. With suitably grand sound effects, we were transported to the tropical island, there to follow the preoccupations of the girl with the man and the monkey, amply spliced with the brawlings of the drunken skipper and his crew. I had previously seen only four or five films, the most spectacular of which was *Snow White and the Seven Dwarfs*.

The boarding house proprietor gave me two shillings and sixpence and I bought a much-needed pair of scissors. I sat on park seats, knitting a navy blue pixie hood for the winter. It was clear that the war would be going on some time and I would need warmer clothes. In the gardens, Uncle started to teach me the Latin names of flowers. I glanced at Aunty, who happily referred to marigolds and lupins. If Uncle accepted the ordinary names from her, why should he want me to learn the obscure ones, I reasoned to myself. I made no effort to memorise them and eventually he dropped this fruitless display of erudition.

The Amusement Park seemed to beckon him and I followed his lead through Noah's Ark and along Jonah's Trail, where I watched him lose his balance, as segments of the floor impulsively rose and wobbled in unexpected places. Shrieks from other tourists provided an atmospheric sense of artificial danger. Was he putting himself through these capers to amuse me or was he enjoying himself for his own sake? I didn't know how to behave towards this middle-aged child. If only Jean had been with me! We would have cupped our hands over our mouths and had a good old giggle.

There were times that week when I felt like an onlooker. Here were two adults adrift, making do with a northern holiday. They were surely missing their annual visit to Guernsey and the warm welcome they always had from friends and relations. Aunty was accustomed to staying in the family home at Pulias and seeing everyone on a grand tour of the relations. This was the highlight of their year, and, locally, much was made of their visit.

Uncle was known to have wanted children, but there were none. My mother had said Aunty was too old for a family when she married (in 1926 when she was thirty-one). I knew that women of that age could have children, so what did my mother mean?

The two had been engaged for a very prolonged period. After Uncle's stint in the First World War, he had gone on to train for the Methodist ministry, which in those days took seven years. He spent them partly at Richmond College in London and also on probation, mainly in Jersey churches. He was not allowed to get married until after his ordination at the end of the training, in July 1926. For much of the interminable engagement, they were separated by the sea.

As we sat in the Southport parks, I tried to connect all I knew of the family story with these two people who were still strangers to me. Was I being a wartime burden, hindering them from doing what they might otherwise have chosen to do? I looked at Uncle. Was he seeing me as a replacement for the children he didn't have? Sometimes his manner suggested it. There were many overtones I did not have the maturity or social skills to cope with. I must stay clear and not be drawn into emotional seas too deep for me to fathom. The pain of my mother's stress some years before was still acute. I knew what it was like to be involved. With a sixth sense, I saw I must ward off Uncle's babying banter. It seemed so out of kilter. He wasn't speaking to me. He did not know who or what I was. I hid my insecurities. Perhaps all those worries would soon be a thing of the past and would recede along with the Latin names of fading flowers. Then things would be alright. I must hold my own and keep a sense of proportion, I told myself. I barely recognised the feelings in myself as anger and was ashamed to feel so negative.

When alone, Aunty and Uncle spoke to each other in patois. When I was with them, there was a free mix with English. I spoke to them only in English, although I was still thinking in Guernsey French and so had to translate continuously as I went along. Uncle, who had seemed so much of an Englishman in Guernsey, now seemed like a Guernseyman in England.

The choice of language was of more than passing significance. I was throwing over the old patois style of communicating and so of relating. These were cultural changes which, for me, coincided with receding childhood.

A Guernsey accent was painfully stigmatised as countrified and insular and definitely out of place on the mainland. I had to make my way in a new and changing world. To hasten the anglicising process, I worked on ridding myself of those remaining grammatical usages which were seen as 'errors'. These, typically, were made by Guernsey people translating literally from the patois: "She's to her Gran's", "He's going in town". These were things I was too ashamed to say, me. I set about modifying the vowel sounds and inflections which created the familiar Guernsey lilt. I had to make the point, "I'm not like that anymore."

There was a price to pay, a distancing from the past, almost estrangement. Every conversation was now conducted in the language of what had been, till then, the outside world, in English. The patois of the homely chat and daily inner life could not be used. These emotions, experienced in the Guernsey context, did not feel or sound the same expressed in English. The cultural value changed. Now, it was hard to find the words to correspond with what we'd known. We knew no English counterpart for the vocabulary of familiar ways, so many of us kept the memory of those strong relational ties and interplay in a protected place, where few had access. Somehow, we knew our rooted selves could not be recognised by new acquaintances of another genre.

In those days of upheaval, much of what we said was fairly
superficial. We dealt with food and clothes and the adjustments
needed when so overcrowded. At Roylelands, the adventurous
camping atmosphere had given way to a period when we needed
individual space and room for our belongings. The loss of
personalised interest in our welfare given by parents could not
be replaced by the care of tired teachers. We were a school and
we must help each other in the communal life we now shared.
Girls from the town areas of the island predominated and they
could not understand the patois. Every conversation was in
English. The patois was now so deeply hidden and obscured that
no one knew which girls could speak it. Ruth, Jean and I who
had rough-and-tumbled with it spoke to each other only in
English.

When the use of English was made compulsory in Welsh
schools, it was asserted by those struggling to sustain the cultural
heritage, 'Whoever controls the language, controls the soul of a
nation'. Without deliberate connivance from on high, the
Guernsey patois was dying out. No one ascribed any value to it or
prized its unique way of mulling over and transmitting past
experience. The new pressures were powerful enough to sweep
the patois to one side in the name of progress and self
development. There was no looking back.

Yet I was anxious to avoid seeming like an English foreigner to
my parents. The conflict between loyalty to them and the need to
adapt, remained, for a long time, centred on the use of language.
My parents' wishes came to mind in patois voices from their
Guernsey setting. I had to free myself from their tight hold and
see them with English eyes and on an English footing. I realised,
after a time, that I would not have to cut myself off from my
parents altogether or let them go, but could continue relating to
them in their absence from my new position.

I have tried here to unravel some of the conflicting feelings
that confused me in the early months of the evacuation. I
wouldn't have been able to explain them in these terms at the
time, but I was concerned by the mounting sense of having to
deal indefinitely and on my own with the relationships in my life.
The war might go on a long time and I would grow up and
change and see things in a new perspective, wherever I was and
whatever happened. Time could not stand still.

Much went through my mind as I sat in those Southport parks.
I think that in the course of that holiday week, Aunty, Uncle and I
took the measure of each other.

If one of the little sparrows, hopping at our feet along the pier, could have picked up vibes instead of crumbs, he would have had a merry time interpreting all that was going on among us.

In a few more months, I would have had a better all round picture of my aunt and uncle, although much of their lifestyle was already known. A thumb-nail sketch drawn at a later stage might have presented Uncle as taller than the average Guernseyman of a previous generation. He was lean and upstanding with faintly greying hair combed back without a parting. There were no traces of brilliantine, so overused by men. It was the wide-open eyes that drew attention as if they had a habit of being startled out of their state of preoccupation. A genial smile might supervene, till, in a mood of relaxation, the eyebrows rose.

Uncle cared about his work and gave it time and effort. He was sanguine, but lacked exuberance and energy. He often enjoyed the company of those in his churches and gave them encouragement and support. He relied on their good nature and responded well towards it. His sermons showed his easy optimism and a theology that might have been termed liberal. He was apt to hold up famous men as models and spoke highly of their achievements and their greatness. Such were David Livingstone and Albert Schweitzer. It was the uplifting versions of these controversial characters that he presented. He praised courage and devotion. We must be like them. He liked gardening and grew vegetables as well as flowers. He had learned a great deal about them in his youth at Summerville and supplemented his knowledge from books and magazines.

Aunty was rather taller than the women in our family and conscious of a growing middle-aged spread. Her short light brown hair waved loosely and was clipped at the sides over the ears. Her cheek bones and upper jaw were prominent and she had a tendency to bite her lip in a chewing fashion when she was anxious or in a thoughtful mood.

She had learned to play the piano and liked one hand to strike ahead of the other. This lack of synchronisation passed muster at small weeknight meetings in the local hall. She aimed to get the housework over quickly in the mornings and spent many afternoons with a book. She went to the library for biographies and the stories of travellers and had a complete set of the works of Dickens, whom she admired. She disliked mending and was not very good at it. She represented herself as not very strong, but was seldom ill. She was loath to take on long-term commitments.

She accepted with equanimity the shortcomings of all church manses where she lived, seeing her rather bare lifestyle as part and parcel of the fulfilment of Uncle's vocation, which she supported from her place behind the scenes. She was matter of fact in her manner, never spoke in public and participated little in activities outside the home, but when people came, she welcomed them warmly and enjoyed the conversation.

\* \* \* \* \*

Our school term started at the end of August. Summer days were ending. In the evenings and at weekends, some girls played netball at 'Kingsley' next door to Roylelands, where the owner had marked out a pitch in his garden for the girls. Some enjoyed their own variety of rounders and cricket. A few resorted to a hideaway where they judged who could spit the furthest.

'Confucius, he say' proclaimed Barbara Spiller's brightly coloured blouse, well before the days of the T-shirt and its captions. This had arrived in a batch from overseas. South Africa and the Canadian and American Red Cross were coming to the aid of the island evacuees. Red checked shirts of cowboy dimensions arrived and later bright salmon cotton stockings. Because they were so short, they put a severe strain on suspenders, which were attached to a liberty bodice and so pulled down on tender places. The long-legged among us endured unsightly gaps when bending forward.

Kathleen Cochrane knitted herself a warm navy blue jumper. Greatly daring, she deviated from the school plan to have a plain long-sleeved style and created short billowy puff sleeves to gather into the armholes. Then with a final flourish, she embroidered large mauve daisies round the neckline and waited for a wigging. Mrs. Livsey gave me some fine navy wool to knit myself some gloves, but they were to prove too thin to stop my fingers from getting numbed.

Second-hand clothing, stored in the Roylelands attic, was made available when the staff thought it was needed. Miss Roughton insisted that we all had dressing gowns. Most of us had worn our own coats to go down to the cellars. Now, those who couldn't get proper dressing gowns were handed old coats from the attic and Miss Roughton herself sewed some braid round the hem of one to make it look the part. Such gestures were variously interpreted as kindness or a waste of time. (Why wasn't she doing something more important?)

Members of staff were themselves short of warm clothes for the winter, since, like everyone else, they had brought only summer clothes from Guernsey. They were glad to have a few things from the attic. Shortly before the evacuation, Miss Stewart had collected from her colleagues in Guernsey some items of clothing suitable for the many European refugees expected in the UK. These had been sent to a friend in Scotland for distribution. Now this friend, unable to use the clothing as originally intended, returned to Miss Mahy the two suits she had donated. She was now the delighted recipient of her own discarded clothes and had one of them, a grey one, dyed moss green. She wore it so often that it is virtually impossible to visualise a wartime Miss Mahy in any other colour! Likewise, Miss Sayer is remembered with alternating red and yellow jumpers and a contrasting necklace of jet black beads.

To restock the attic, Miss Clayton made several excursions to Stockport, where the newly formed Channel Islands Refugees Committee, based in London, had arranged to have a second-hand clothing depot. This central committee with a Jerseyman, Lord Justice du Parcq as Chairman, and a Guernseyman, Mr. M.E. Weatherall as its Director General, raised thousands of pounds through public appeals on the BBC and in the newspapers. The funds were used to make clothing available and to relieve poverty and distress.

An estimated 30,000 Channel Islanders were adrift in Britain, the great majority having come from Guernsey. Mothers with young children were billeted as soon as possible, but it was the hostess who received the allowance for food and lodging and the mother got only a derisory one shilling and sixpence every week (the equivalent of seven postage stamps). It was impossible to buy clothes for the colder weather with only this meagre pocket money and to supplement the one caseful brought from the islands. If such mothers left their billets in any unauthorised way, they placed themselves outside the Government scheme and so had to take complete responsibility for their own housing and wellbeing. Jobs were obviously hard to find and keep if they had children. They were caught in a situation that could not easily be remedied.

In September, as the raids on the north intensified, better provision was made in the Roylelands cellars. The exodus of girls to friends and relations left more camp beds to spare. The ones that sagged badly from the heavyweights in our number and those whose bent frames registered the sorry results of bouncing and rough handling were humped downstairs. A few distorted specimens had protested in vain when, earlier on, a girl strode over their closed ranks to reach her corner.

In the cellars, we were told to sleep two to a bed, head to toe. We made a beeline for the better rejects, grabbing the least wriggly partner. If you had to have someone's toes protruding into your face, so much the better if you could choose whose they were! Miss Sayer and Miss Mahy came round with toffee and milk. We returned to our upstairs beds when the all-clear sounded and we were allowed extra time before the usual morning call. If the raids lasted a long time or were expected to recur, we stayed in the cellars all night.

At Boothroyd, girls slept under, on and around the billiard table in the cellar. Miss Clayton tried gently to coax a camp bed into taking her unprecedented weight. It collapsed unceremoniously beneath her. "You have my permission to laugh," she announced and everyone exploded.

Late one evening, before the siren sounded, I was caught with my roommates riveted to our upstairs window and applauding the entertainment in the sky. The display of sweeping searchlights was breathtaking. What was the large spark hovering in mid-air? Was it an exploding plane or a flare? As a penalty, we were banished to a ground floor room with a poorer view. This turned out to have many advantages. It was the only room to have some recently acquired blackout material to draw across the windows. This meant that the light could be switched on as the days grew shorter. What's more, high over the low profile of camp beds, rose two solid double beds which had come from we knew not where. By a self-imposed rota, we used them in roll-on fashion, perhaps taking our cue from Alice in Wonderland's table companions, who were always moving on to the next position.

A number of small brick rectangular shelters had mushroomed in the school playground, much like the ones dotted along the streets. We practised hurrying into them from various parts of the building. Mr. Fred Wilson, the headmaster, claimed in stentorian tones, that, once inside, we would be safe. His confident assertion carried the authority of the ARP, the RAF, the Government and the building trade all rolled into one. We allowed our own commonsense to be overruled. It was plain to see that such flimsy structures with their thin flat roofs could hardly deflect a scattering of shrapnel and shattered glass, let alone withstand the impact of direct bombs and blast. Far less reassuring was his advice to put cotton wool in our ears and keep our mouths open if the noise from screeching bombs became too deafening.

On September 3rd, exactly a year after the outbreak of war, the night was punctuated by two lots of air raid warnings between 11 p.m. and 3.50 a.m. The school day was likewise interrupted three times. We swung back and forth into the shelters like darting yo-yos. Then there were two more warnings in the night.

The school shelters had wooden seats attached to their longest walls, so that you sat facing others with your knees nearly touching. The faint flickering light of four candles was too dim for reading, so I tried knitting, but it wasn't till we emerged that I could check for any dropped stitches. Soon we were carried away into a far more exciting experience. From the unseen inhabitants of nearby shelters came the unmistakable strains of popular wartime songs. As we had no wireless at Roylelands, we had been slow to pick up the latest hits. Now we listened to our fellows from Castleton. We could join them or beat them!

As the Battle of Britain was fought over our heads and the war raged on into the following year, we drowned the noise of anti-aircraft gunfire with our own urgent imperatives . . .

> *Run, rabbit, run, rabbit, run, run, run,*
> *We'll have the Huns on the run, run, run.*

The tuneful whistle of the Seven Dwarfs as they marched to and from Snow White's spotless household attracted variations of the following:

> *Whistle while you work*
> *Hitler made a shirt*
> *Mussolini wore it*
> *Chamberlain tore it*
> *Whistle while you work*

Then visualising the ludicrously built-up headgear of Carmen Miranda with its voluptuous fruits spiralling ever upward into its gaudy plumage, we exaggerated her crooning stammer . . .

> *I, yi, yi, yi, yi, yi see the moon above*
> *Way, way, way, way, way up in the blue*
> *Then, then, then, then, then, then, then I fall in love*
> *And when I fall in love, I fall for you.*

The rhythm was exhilarating.

Abruptly the mood would change to one of grim determination, albeit out-dated in its stated aim:

> *We're gonna hang out the washing on the Siegfried Line,*
> *Is there any dirty washing, mother dear?*

In barely acknowledged ways, the songs enheartened and
unified the two schools and transformed the experience. We were
all in this together. We were allowed to yell and the sound we
made was good.

## Chapter VII

### 'Kiss Me Goodnight, Sergeant Major Tuck Me in My Little Wooden Bed'

Today, when I take from my old case the bracelet with its simulated pearl segments threaded on elastic, I remember the kind-hearted members of the Castleton Methodist Church, who sometimes invited us to tea and showed interest in our story. In one home, that bracelet was pressed on me with love. "Go on," they said, "take it. We want you to have it." Surely it must be questionable to accept anything so pretty and so cherished by the owner. I was embarrassed, but they were generous. I took it.

On another such visit, we were lent some books. One girl had *John Halifax Gentleman* and I had *Silas Marner*, but of more immediate appeal was Victor Hugo's *Toilers of the Sea* set in the environs of Guernsey, where the author had spent many years as a political exile from France. We all knew his statue in Candie Gardens, which commanded a magnificent view across to the islands of Herm, Jethou and Sark. With cape flying in the breeze, he strode perpetually towards the harbour. His eyes scanned the seas, which could be as wild and tumultuous as the haunting pathos of his stories.

Sprawling on my camp bed, I reached yet again for my handkerchief. I was feeling below par with a recurring temperature and heavy cold. I was painfully aware of my thinness and the knobbly look of knees and ankles. My responses had slowed down. I was considered sluggish and there were some who did not spare their taunts. I felt rejected with no power to surmount the sense of failing strength. When sores erupted on my face, the doctor was called in. Perhaps the buried grief was breaking surface. He said I was anaemic and prescribed a tonic and Cod Liver Oil. No one seemed to be thinking of delayed shock or mourning or even of the suddenness of the switch to communal living and the loss of the individual attention we had all received at home. If they were, they didn't say so and all we could do was to hang on to see what happened.

I realised that I had to look after myself and must plan ahead to have my clothes clean and mended and waiting in the case. I must not risk being caught unawares and unprepared as at the time of the evacuation. I must be ready for anything at any time; things seemed to have got rather out of hand. I was with older girls and feeling left behind. The 'train' of the dream must not go on without me. I would have to organise things well.

Marie Bisson, my friend of pre-war days, had just come out of hospital with chickenpox. She had swollen glands and likewise felt run down. We kept each other company but did not feel as close as we once did. We were allowed some days off school. It was a luxury to lie down since cotton sleeping bags and pillows had arrived.

One day an old black battered car turned up at Roylelands. Carefully, Miss Warren extricated herself from her load of books and packages. She had taught Art at the school in Guernsey some years before the war and was now on the staff of Stretford High School on the south-west outskirts of Manchester. Her girls had collected useful things for us and she brought a list of willing pen-friends. We were each allocated to a Stretford 'cousin'. Mine was Jean Adams. I was told that my name had been picked out of a hat and I would become a sort of adopted niece to Miss Warren. She said I could call her 'Aunty Lilian'. Soon she was to send me a lovely scarf she had woven herself in shades of green. She made me warm pyjamas and a lovely blue dress in a style that made me feel more grown up.

In the meantime, an administrative streamlining of procedures was taking place. Mr. John Wilson of the Public Assistance Board required weekly information about the number of residents in the four houses for the Ministry of Health. There were to be no admissions or departures without his written permission. Many arrangements could not now be made on an ad hoc basis. Relations could no longer claim a girl without going through the prescribed formalities, and the sanctioning of visits to relations was no longer so much in Miss Roughton's hands.

The members of the WVS were confirmed in various super-visory tasks out of school hours, so that it required a great deal of goodwill to adjust and keep a reasonably controlled balance between them and the school staff. The four houses were being run not as hostels, but as Reception Centres. The Public Assist-ance and Health authorities were still mainly responsible for the provision made.

For a while, there had been further talk of the school moving, this time to Wales. The Ministry of Health had found a place in Cardigan which was in a reception area. Miss Roughton went to see it for herself at the end of September and reported that the school would have to operate a shift system with the host school, since the building was not large enough for both at the same time. We might be a burden. She didn't feel welcomed. There were no shelters. She thought a military aerodrome some five miles away might attract enemy attention. There was a drought. The girls would be in billets.

She reacted as though the school were under threat and would be broken up, a prospect not envisaged by the Ministry. She was afraid that, if billeted, girls would leave and go off to other areas. The ties of community feeling among themselves would be broken and perhaps their sense of loyalty undermined. She may have foreseen a further weakening of her close control, which she judged essential to the school's continuance. It was as if her life depended on keeping the school together and taking it back to Guernsey whole. No, the sentence may be shortened without undue loss of truthfulness. Her life depended on it. It was an obligation and so a personal mission. She could not risk having her school divided and sections parcelled out to local schools, nor have the staff dispersed. (They would not leave, they said.)

Whatever her motivations, her strong reactions against the proposed move seemed a completely self-evident necessity to herself and to the staff, who gave her their loyal backing. Many girls did not want another upheaval and were a bit apprehensive about going into homes with people they did not know beforehand. The mood was in favour of staying put. Yet, there was a tremendous risk in staying on, hidden by the fact that many people had become blasé about the frequent air raid warnings. They supposed that planes flying overhead were always on their way to another area. In spite of the gunfire, the siren was sometimes treated as though it signalled another hoax, which must not be allowed to interrupt the daily round. Besides, hundreds of local children were staying on. Mass evacuation was not being advised for them. But what if some of our girls had been killed? How would she have explained herself to the parents then? They had sent their daughters away precisely because they wanted them to be safe. This was the time of the London blitz when thousands were being bombed and made homeless. Parts of Merseyside lay in ruins. Could it always be maintained that Britain had the upper hand in the air? Not in September. Further devastation was expected. Any place could be the next to receive a pounding.

Of great interest are the omissions in the argument. How much importance did Miss Roughton attach to the hardships of the communal life we were living, the stodgy diet, inadequate heating, our vulnerability to epidemics, and most of all the lack of personal homely attention which overtaxed staff members could not easily provide? Did she realise how much some girls were hurting? Billeting might have its risks and failures but there was a chance that affectionate relationships might grow. It is a matter for speculation whether she and the staff would have seen things differently if they had been married themselves with children of their own.

The Head of the Intermediate Boys' School was faced with a similar dilemma. He went to a village on the edge of Snowdonia in N. Wales, within reach of Caernarvon, to size up that area as a future home for the boys. He came away thinking there were not enough facilities to occupy them out of school hours and they would be bored out of their minds. Perhaps he felt the staff would be drawn into supervising and organising activities in the evenings. Although, as a reception area, this was safer, he decided to decline the Ministry's proposal to move there and to stay in Oldham, classified, like Rochdale, as a neutral area.

Miss Roughton wrote:

> *'We decided together to take the responsibility of asking to remain in an industrial area where there was admittedly a likelihood of air-raids and a certainty of bad weather and smoky air, but where the children were offered all the opportunities of a full municipal life.'*

What could a full municipal life mean to us when we were virtually 'confined to barracks' unless with our own relations and friends elsewhere?

After the war, in 1946, she must have felt the need to justify her decision to the Guernsey parents, as she quoted to them from a letter she had written to the Ministry of Health in 1940. Her plea to stay in Rochdale ran along these lines:

> *'Many have pitied us for being set down in an industrial town after an island with its pure air and wonderful coastline. But we have grown fond of this town. Here through the generous hearts of Lancashire, we have regained something approaching happiness. We have by this arrangement of living together in four big families kept a feeling of unity that we shall inevitably lose if you send us wandering. Our children feel secure with their teachers whom they now know not only as mistresses but as foster-mothers. Put them in billets in a strange locality after leaving them for three months to work out a new scheme of living, and we shall find them drifting off to friends and losing touch with that living bit of Guernsey which is their school. We are in a neutral area I grant, but we are very close indeed to Wardle and*

*Whitworth which are reception areas, and so far, though we are often hearing sirens, we have had no tragic happening.*

*Our town lies in a hollow and is often veiled in mist, which is no doubt a protection.*

*In three months our children have made many friends and would feel the parting: since they have, many of them, lost parents, homes and possessions, they set very great store by the friends they have made here. I wish I had the art to persuade you to hold your hand. A visit would perhaps help to convert you, but I am afraid it would be asking you too much to visit an obscure community from the Channel Islands . . .'*

Who was this person, whose determination so shaped our destinies and who wielded so much power over us? What was she like at this early stage of the evacuation?

Then in her early fifties, she had a face that was beginning to wrinkle. Her greying hair was cut short to a level just below the ear and the entire left side of her forehead was covered by a carefully positioned right-angled loop, which was held to the side by a slide and kept in shape by an attentive tweak of the wrist. It was usually pinioned down by a narrow black bandeau, circling low round the head. The style must have been fashionable when she was young, but was then rarely seen except in pictures of Red Indians. Early on, she had acquired an old sit-up-and-beg bicycle long past its heyday. The bandeau had some practical use when she was cycling, but was kept on indoors and became like the cigar to Churchill. No cartoonist would have omitted it from a caricature, which would also have depicted the triangular underside of an upturned chin. She had a habit of lifting it high with aristocratic mastery when she was addressing her girls.

She was tall and stood straight, keenly aware that deportment mattered and she was fond of exhorting girls to keep their tails in. Sometimes, a faint puckish smile might be detected, but it often created discomfiture, since the cause of the amusement was not always discernible. Was she laughing at us or at a situation or even at herself? She didn't allow us to know. There were times when she held herself apart, as if other concerns were claiming her attention; she seemed distant as though she occupied a mental world to which few had access. This trait no doubt arose from the need to maintain her status as headmistress in the uncongenial surroundings created by overcrowding and mutual encroachments. It was more likely to be related to her cultural background and sophistication which had little chance of expression in the first few months of the evacuation. More than this, she had the enviable gift of detaching herself and 'not-hearing' the raucous, crude and unrestrained remarks that the unfortunate might make within her orbit. ("Shut up, you idiots!") When she was forced to notice, she could flash with anger and mock the tone with exaggerated mimicry.

Girls automatically stopped a conversation when she came near. She had little small talk and was not given to chatting. Those girls who wished to relate to her did so on her terms. She was apt to size up disturbances as behavioural problems relating to the school – "She's not cooperative", "She talks too much", "She doesn't pay attention", and not "What's on her mind?" Sometimes she showed little overt interest in the feelings of the girls, although there were notable exceptions. She was greatly concerned that the most able should follow a path to a satisfying career and worked hard to find the wherewithal. There were others who attracted little direct support and encouragement. There were far too many to receive equal attention and help. Sometimes relations stepped in and took responsibility.

She made great use of her Oxford accent, which, in those days, still gave people an aura of social distinctiveness and authority. If she had been a man, the stamp of the officer class might well have been imprinted on her. She gave the impression that she was not entirely in her element, but was pitching in her all to make the best of the circumstances, which she would mould to her purposes. '*QUI VEULT PEULT*'. She made the school motto her own. 'Where there's a will, there's a way'. Sometimes she tackled things with prodigious energy, but could concentrate too long on minor matters. There were times when she was slow to delegate. She carried a great deal of information about people in her head or in notes scribbled into little books which she stuffed into old bags, easily slung on to bicycle handle bars.

Those who came to know her well and with whom she could relax were touched by her warm humanity and many personal kindnesses. She had a strong Christian faith which informed her daily living. She regularly took evening prayers at Roylelands and morning prayers in school if there was the space and opportunity. Many collects and prayers were used over and over again . . .

*'Teach us, good Lord, to serve thee as thou deservest;*
*to give and not to count the cost; to fight and not to*
*heed the wounds; to toil and not to seek for rest; to*
*labour and not to ask for any reward, save that of knowing*
*that we do Thy will.'*

She spoke the words with a clear, musical rhythm deeply rooted in her strong Anglican background. Her father had been a clergyman in Radwell-on-Sea, in Essex. She had a love of poetry and music which came through more ardently as the war progressed. The violin was her forte.

Many girls and members of staff were personally drawn towards her as if she provided a model for normative living. They aspired to her standards as if they were loftier than their own. She could inspire those around her to become more like her, to hold their heads high, drop their country accents, spell and behave better, without always consciously trying to do so. I can remember copying some of the shapes in her handwriting because I thought they were beautiful.

When she was in her eighties, I asked her what it was that had sustained her through all the pressures and packed hours preceding the evacuation. She recited parts of W.E. Henley's *Invictus* and William Blake's *Jerusalem*.

### Invictus

> Out of the night that covers me,
> Black as the pit from pole to pole,
> I thank whatever gods may be
> For my unconquerable soul.
>
> In the fell clutch of circumstance
> I have not winced nor cried aloud.
> Under the bludgeonings of chance
> My head is bloody, but unbow'd.
>
> Beyond this place of wrath and tears
> Looms but the Horror of the shade,
> And yet the menace of the years
> Finds, and shall find, me unafraid.
>
> It matters not how strait the gate,
> How charged with punishments the scroll,
> I am the master of my fate:
> I am the captain of my soul.
>
> *William Ernest Henley.*

### Jerusalem

> And did those feet in ancient time
> Walk upon England's mountains green?

*And was the holy Lamb of God*
*On England's pleasant pastures seen?*

*And did the Countenance Divine*
*Shine forth upon our clouded hills?*
*And was Jerusalem builded here*
*Among these dark Satanic Mills?*

*Bring me my bow of burning gold!*
*Bring me my arrows of desire!*
*Bring me my spear! O clouds, unfold!*
*Bring me my chariot of fire!*

*I will not cease from mental fight,*
*Nor shall my sword sleep in my hand,*
*Till we have built Jerusalem*
*In England's green and pleasant land.*

*William Blake.*

Miss Roughton said that one was humanist and the other religious. They were well in the forefront of her mind during the preparations for departure. She said she had felt humbled at the time and had asked, "What do we hold in our own right?" The responsibility had been laid upon her as a trust. A Day Book she kept has a list of the essential belongings that girls had to take on that journey into the unknown and beside it she had scribbled in pencil a verse of 'O God our help in ages past'.

Coat or mac
Gas Mask               *Beneath the shadow of Thy throne*
Ration book            *Thy saints have dwelt secure*
Case, labelled         *Sufficient is Thine arm alone*
Label round neck       *And our defence is sure.*
Food for journey

\* \* \* \* \*

Meeting someone from Guernsey that we knew was reassuring. Apart from the immediate warmth of the contact, it was good to know that the past was not cut off altogether and shoved away in some inaccessible recess. When I had met Mrs. Heaume, it was through her familiar voice and manner that I had sensed her personal concern and the weight of responsibility she carried.

Now I was to meet another Methodist from home, one who

knew my family, although he was not an islander himself. He was Rev. R.D. Moore, a minister who had lived at King's Road in St. Peter Port. Sometimes he had preached at our church.

Later, we learned that, at the end of June, he had been on the mainland on church-related matters, when he heard that the Germans had bombed the harbour at St. Peter Port (June 28th). His reaction was immediate: residents would fear further attacks, deducing that the Germans were ignoring the demilitarisation of the Channel Islands, and they would want to have a second chance to get away. (It transpired, after the war, that the British communication with Germany on demilitarisation had been bungled or made quite ineffective and the Germans genuinely did not know that the islands were undefended when the raid took place.)

Mr. Moore had hurried consultations in London in the hope that they would lead to ships being deployed to evacuate another wave of islanders. After the initial exodus (in which we were included), there had been a lull. Hesitant residents had been deterred from leaving by the eruption of a few challenging posters. The most effective warned DON'T BE YELLOW! So when the regular services to England were resumed, departing ships had not been filled to capacity. People were settling down again, to attend to their cattle and their greenhouses and were sending their tomatoes to mainland markets. At the same time, foreseeing that food might be in short supply if the Germans came, some island doctors were urging a further reduction of the population. More should leave.

It was during this period of urgent debate that the Germans did arrive. Mr. Moore was now stranded on the mainland and unable to go home to Guernsey as he intended. Immediately, he created a base at the Methodist headquarters in the Central Buildings at Westminster and set about registering the names of all scattered Channel Island Methodists, so that they could be put in touch with each other and receive help. Through the pages of the weekly *Methodist Recorder*, he issued lists of the evacuated islanders and appealed for clothes, money and offers of accommodation and employment. Before long, he had acquired a car and, with his wife, was delivering bundles to many parts of the country.

On October 3rd, when he came to Roylelands, he told us he had heard, through someone who had escaped from Guernsey, that there were 600 to 800 Germans on the island. They had confiscated food from empty houses, which, in some cases, were now occupied by troops. Clothes, including shoes, were rationed. Mr. Raymond Falla, a prominent Guernsey grower, had been allowed to go to France to get seeds for the spring crops. The greenhouses would be growing a wide range of vegetables rather than just the customary tomatoes and flowers. Fishing was allowed within a two mile radius. The teachers on the island had rallied together and the education of the children would continue.

The news was reassuring. There was every indication that life was proceeding in an orderly way. There were no reports of calamities or cruelties.

Although we exchanged only a few words after his talk, I felt that this had been another link with home and all that had once been familiar.

Now we had an epidemic of German measles at Roylelands and for a fortnight the sick were isolated, by day in an upstairs room and by night in a section of the cellar divided from the rest by sheets dipped in disinfectant and hung across on strings. Then someone at Boothroyd got head lice. This proved to be a most intractable problem, spreading throughout Roylelands. Like many others I had nits. Miss Roughton and Miss Mahy were exhausted with the repeated shampooing of everyone's hair and combing it through with a fine tooth comb. To prevent a recurrence, mistresses were allocated to various rooms to supervise hair brushing and to check that all was well.

I was moved to find among the wartime correspondence and notebooks left after Miss Roughton's death, the jagged remains of those same tooth combs.

The news came through in mid-October that we were not going to Wales. There was some sense of relief and yet great uncertainty as to what might lie in store. So if we weren't moving, what was the next development? We waited as though on hold, in hock till something happened. Any small explosions of excitement were welcome.

Brian was going to broadcast! We were thrilled. His school had recorded a contribution to a half-hour programme which was to be relayed on October 22nd, which happened to be the Golden Wedding of Gran and Grandpère from Summerville. Everyone hoped it would be heard in Guernsey. Brian had been asked to give a short message and Mrs. Stewart had helped him to compose it. It was then translated into patois by one of his masters. The English version was:

*'Here I am, Brian Brehaut. Hello Mum, Dad and John! I'm happy and comfortable and well and I'm growing and putting on weight. Lois and I send our love. Goodnight.'*

Unfortunately, the translation was into old stylised patois which approximated to 'good French' and did not at all correspond to what Brian would have said naturally. It sounded as remote as Elizabethan English seems to us today and ended, *'La Lois et me vous souhaitent bouen niet.'* This was like saying, 'Lois and I bid you goodnight.'

*'Souhaiter'* in the patois was an old fashioned word conveying a wish or greeting and was not used except by the formal or the elderly. The language had been skewed to seem more respectable than the vernacular and thereby lost its personal touch. He learned it off by heart and it was sandwiched among songs and other pieces.

On the crucial evening, we were down in the cellars at Roylelands, poring over Miss Brittain's wireless set. Promptly at 8.30 p.m. she turned it on, but no sound came. The batteries had gone flat. No one else had a set. It was very disappointing, but I consoled myself that it was intended for our parents and I hoped that they might hear it. In Brian's billet, Mrs. Stewart had difficulty in finding the right wavelength and he missed his own message also.

Air raid warnings were incessant, day and night. I recorded nine in my diary between October 26th and 30th. Marion Miles, Mary Chapman and others had left and now we could have a camp bed each in the Roylelands cellars and sleep more comfortably. After breakfast one morning, a girl told me I had spots on my face, so down I went to join 'the measleys' who had not yet surfaced from the cellars.

One by one, girls were disappearing into isolation and soon Miss Sayer and Miss Peggy Mallett fell victim. Miss Brown was away ill a few times and Miss Roughton was transported to hospital with quinsy. Girls contributed a halfpenny each to give her some brown eggs and roses. There were too few girls and teachers well enough to sustain lessons and school at Castleton was suspended. Numbers were still dwindling. Miss Roughton had been obliged to lose some of her staff members, since the ratio of teachers to pupils was too high after the depletions. Miss Simeson, who had taught Maths, left, Miss Hubert went and so did some of the other parent/helpers who had done some teaching from time to time.

Those members of staff who remained were required, from mid-October, to pay for their board and lodging at the Reception Centres. After an initial disruptive gap of two or three months, they were receiving their salaries again, but now as the employees of the borough. By that time, it was generally understood that all employing educational authorities on the mainland would be reimbursed by the Guernsey States when the war was over. In those days before equal pay for equal work, secondary school women teachers usually received £220 to £240 p.a. The charge of £1.1.0 a week could be considered fair, but there was no extra remuneration for the additional round-the-clock responsibilities which the staff were undertaking.

My recollection of having German measles is not so much of the itchiness and discomfort, but of the continuous grinding of teeth inflicted on us by one of our bedfellows in the cellars. There was no escape, but one or two treats came our way. Miss Roughton turned over to us, the 'measleys', a gift of oranges which she had been too ill to eat. We had half of one each. They had become very scarce. I was deputed by the girls to write her a note of thanks in my best handwriting. Brian sent crosswords he had made up and I read *Schoolgirl Honour*, a book sent by Jean Adams of Stretford High School.

Quarrelling was a real problem in those cooped up conditions. Then there came the day of the fight when two girls clashed beyond the limits of patience. After that, Miss Sayer and Miss Mallett, who were themselves recovering, came into our room more frequently to occupy us with Lexicon and jig-saws. Fortunately blackout material had arrived and many girls had previously spent hours, under Miss Clayton's supervision, stitching the hems of curtains. We could switch on the lights when it got dark. In good weather, there were regulated trips into the garden and, regressing to the juvenile, we played Cowboys and Indians in the shrubbery. The wild rambler roses climbing the arched trellises had withered, but there was still much of interest to be found in the tangle.

Miss Mahy and Miss Brittain were faithful ambassadors, bringing up loaded trays and coal for the fire. News came that the Red Cross had arranged for us to send ten-word messages to our homes. We had all to use the same words: '*Dear Family, All happy, well. Everything provided. Much love [name].*' I hoped they would reach their destination.

"We might be billeted!" The rumour spread quickly. We must find a partner, we were told, as we were likely to go in pairs. Notes flew backwards and forwards, ours via the ovens. Every piece of paper from our room had to be baked, to kill the germs it seemed. Who could I go with? Ruth? No, she would go with her sister, Jean, but as they attended schools in opposite ends of the town, this might not be allowed. If that were the case, then Ruth might pair off with me, but if we had to be with those in our own age group, we would each have to consider someone else. . . . So the protracted negotiations went on. There was not enough information to go on. It was with sighs of relief that we took our Izal baths, dipped our toothbrushes in the disinfectant and emerged from the 'Black Hole' as it was (unfairly) labelled. Vacated beds were immediately filled by others, among them Marie. Only six girls at Roylelands escaped incarceration.

There followed a few days with Aunty and Uncle at Summerseat to recuperate. School was still closed. I had already been to see them for two weekend visits, the second one being marred by my biliousness. This time, Ruth came for a few days, only to develop German measles herself and so she was unable to take full advantage of the break and had to stay behind while Aunty and I went on a shopping trip to Bury. We saw on display a battered Messerschmitt 109, which had been brought down locally. Aunty paid sixpence for the Spitfire Fund and I climbed into the cockpit. The local paper quoted a bystander's quip, 'Are t'stores selling them now?' After one or two such expeditions I went back to Roylelands with a dress, vests and warm stockings bought with the money my father had sent.

The manse at Summerseat stood on a corner near the top of a steep hill rising up from the station. It was large compared with many of the surrounding houses and had five bedrooms, one of which was used to store the trunks and tea chests ready for the move to the next appointment. The kitchen was damp and some of the carpets were threadbare, but the place was manageable. The house stood in its own garden ready for Uncle to develop.

Early in the mornings, I was woken by a series of sharp clacketty sounds in the roadway. They grew louder and more insistent as they neared the house. The first time I heard them, I leapt out of bed to watch the approaching horses, but all I could see were dozens of people intent on reaching the mill in the valley. The clatter of clog irons was disturbing evidence of the world of unremitting work, low wages and grim necessity.

In the distance rose the moors and, isolated from the rest, was the long shape of Holcombe Hill with Peel's Tower, the local landmark, standing sentinel on the skyline.

Brian had already been here for his delayed summer holiday in September, with Peter, our cousin from Les Annevilles, and John Mahy (Aunty's nephew), who were all billeted in Oldham. I had seen Brian on two or three of his brief visits to Rochdale, but now, free from quarantine and illness, I was allowed to go to his billet in Oldham. I saw the budgie whose discarded feathers he had sent me. I have them still stored in the case. He gave me some precious pieces of shrapnel he had collected from the nearby streets. For years, I kept them in a little yellow tin of Bisodol indigestion tablets. He was evidently very settled and comfortable and Dr. and Mrs. Stewart had made him welcome. He liked it there. As he showed me round the local museum, I thought it was very strange to be the guest of my own brother.

In the meantime, Miss Roughton had been to Carnforth at the invitation of the decision-makers, who were reviewing prospects for our future. Would billeting be best? Present were Mr. Allen, the Chief Billeting Officer for the Manchester area; Mr. Harris, a Board of Education Inspector; Mr. Royds, the Rochdale Director of Education, along with Councillor Crowder who was on the Rochdale Education Council and the Public Health Committee. Mr. John Wilson represented the Public Assistance Board and, watching over Guernsey interests on behalf of the States, was Mr. Harwood who related to the Ministry of Health.

It seems that there was little chance for Miss Roughton to make out her strongly felt case for the school to stay on in the four houses, since, right at the outset, it was made clear to her that both Roylelands and Horse Carrs were needed for their original purpose, to house bombed-out families in the area. Raids could create an emergency situation at any time. The girls would have to go elsewhere. There was some discussion about providing proper hostels (as distinct from Reception Centres), but these were not allowed for children under eleven. For the older girls, any alternative to Roylelands would have to be run under strict Local Authority control with stringent regulations and inspections. This would be more costly than maintaining the girls in billets. Mr. Harwood was mindful that the States in Guernsey would feel obliged to reimburse those UK authorities which supported Guernsey children. The mounting bill must be trimmed wherever possible. The war could go on for quite some time. It was left to Mr. Allen to stress the value of home comforts, warmth and the affectionate family atmosphere that a billet could provide. The consensus was clearly in favour of billeting.

Miss Roughton wrote afterwards 'I made the decision not to fight'. She felt it wasn't fair to ask the staff to settle into another house with new rulings and conditions. It was driving them too far, she said. Perhaps she was remembering too that the Roylelands girls now wanted billets. In reality, she had no choice.

She was partly consoled by the promise that a recommendation would be made to keep Boothroyd on as a small hostel for about sixteen senior girls. Billeting allowances would be paid for them. Soon after that, the Ministry of Health took the final decision to go ahead with billeting the majority.

A fancy dress party was hastily organised as our stay at Roylelands was ending. An Arab, a charwoman, a snowflake and a page-boy joined in procession and the music troupe swayed in with Miss Roughton playing her violin, Miss Brittain a piano accordion, Miss Brown a tambourine and Miss Sayer a mouth organ, while Miss Mahy and others, bringing up the rear, created sounds of interest from their combs and paper.

In next to no time, I was again in quarantine. As I wanted a comb to fit into a case I had made for Uncle's Christmas present, I called in at the Castleton shops on my way back from school. Ruth Robilliard was with me. She slept in the same room, across the aisle, with her feet pointed to my head. Abruptly, she was whisked off to hospital with scarlet fever. The doctor said that her roommates could not go to school and had to eat in isolation. We were barracked in at Roylelands. I worked on my presents: an embroidered needlecase for Miss Warren, a kettle holder for Aunty and similar small masterpieces for others.

Suddenly on Friday December 13th, it was announced that twelve of us would be billeted that weekend. (A few had already gone.) Marie was to go to Mr. and Mrs. Hindle in Heywood Road, and I would go to a house in Manchester Road a little further than the Castleton shops. I withdrew my credit balance of six shillings from the school bank, washed my clothes which froze on the line, and took my Izal bath which signalled my final emergence from quarantine. The case could no longer hold all my belongings, so I had to find a carton. For storage, many girls had by then been allocated an open wooden orange box with a division down the middle. Tipped on end, it looked rather like a hospital locker with a shelf half way down and housed shoes, books and oddments. These, now cleared, lost all trace of the user's personality. We were off. Subdued excitement kept us all awake till late.

At 10 a.m. the next morning, a taxi arrived. I bundled in my case and the rest of my possessions and, with Miss Roughton and Mrs. Casson, drove off to my new address. Soon we were knocking at the door of a small terraced house. A young girl, who had been sitting at the window peering through the net curtains, ran to open it. "Where is your Mummy?" Miss Roughton asked. "She's at work," came the timid reply. At that, Miss Roughton said I couldn't be left with someone who was out a lot of the time and I found myself back at Roylelands.

On December 15th, I remembered that little John was four years old. I wondered fondly what he was doing on his birthday and when I would see him again. There was no means of knowing.

The weather was wintry and the air raid shelters at school were sodden. We had no room for standing. We sang till we were hoarse.

During the chilly nights at Roylelands, we turned into a variegated landscape of colourful humps, with coats and any woollen clothing we could find flung over our spartan bedclothes. Jumpers and even pixie hoods and gloves were worn to encourage sleep.

Each day, a few more girls were billeted, till, gradually the thirty-five remaining at Horse Carrs and Lyngarth and the forty-five or so at Roylelands had all been quartered. School tailed off with a carol service and I still had nowhere to go. Roylelands was to close. Nearly everyone else was settled. Miss Roughton assured me that I could stay in a house which some of the mistresses would be using after the holidays. There would be room there on a temporary basis.

Shortly before I left for Summerseat, I was told of a prospective billeting hostess who went away for the school holidays. She could only accept a girl who had somewhere else to go out of term-time, so this billet was difficult to fill. Uncle and Aunty were asked if they would be prepared to dove-tail in and have me for the holidays on a regular basis and they agreed. It seemed as if I might go to that billet.

I said goodbye to Roylelands and later, when I wrote a jingle about our life together, I was surprised to discover there was such a note of fondness in the nostalgia.

A was for attic where old clothes were kept.
B was for Boothroyd where all seniors slept.
C was for cleaning; no small job for two.
D was for dinner; too often t'was stew.
E for excitement when asked out to tea.
F was for friends, whom we all liked to see.
G was for gargling by most girls avoided.
H was for Horse Carrs where juniors were boarded.
I was for ironing; we each did our share.
J was for jumble, all spread out to air.
K was for kitchen, a beehive of work.
L was for lessons, which we tried to shirk.
M was for mistresses, shocked at the noise.
N was for nightmares, great dormitory joys.
O was for orange, which we ate by quarters.
P was for postman quite laden with letters.
Q was for questions when we did not have any.
R was for rest when our camp beds were 'comfy'.
S was for sirens that woke us each night.
T was for tonic, the measles to fight.
U for umbrella, a dire necessity.
V was for vict'ry; we knew t'was a surety.
W the wishing for plum pies and tart.
X was for Xmas when we did depart.
Y was for yearnings for home bright and vivid.
Z was for zone which to us seemed the frigid.

That Christmas, Brian was at Summerseat along with John Mahy, the son of one of Aunty's brothers in Guernsey. They were brought from Oldham by car. Ruth and Jean went to Mrs. Norris' home near Bedford.

I needed an Emergency Ration card, so Aunty and I went to Ramsbottom Food Office. Wartime regulations made it necessary to buy rationed food only from the shop where the customer was registered. If you went away, your normal coupons were cancelled and you were issued with the Emergency card (for a week or half-a-week at a time) and then you could buy your rationed food elsewhere.

Air raid warnings were again frequent. We knew that whole sections of some towns had been devastated. They could not be named in the news, but Uncle heard from a visitor to our area that in November, it was Coventry which had been heavily blitzed. We expected similar treatment further north.

Sure enough, there was a very heavy attack on the night of December 22nd when the whole sky was lit up with a suffused glow. It was both eerie and beautiful. Manchester was on fire. Searchlights played across each other in an everchanging kaleidoscope of patterns. Parachute flares hung suspended and there were sudden bursts of light and unexpected flashes. The barrage of artillery fire was deafening. The whole house was a-shudder and my bed kept shaking in response. The din finally subsided around 4 a.m. and everything went quiet.

There was an awesome feeling about the experience. I felt I had been present during killings. There was power and a fascination in this wanton orgy of mass destruction. Manchester was only seven miles away. Had other places been hit? Next day, we tried to find out more about the devastation, but soon we were behaving as though nothing much had happened and we went on with our festive preparations. On Christmas Eve, I saw a lorry in Bury transporting the wings of a German bomber and wondered where it had come down.

During the evening, Brian, John and I assembled the presents we had brought for the others. They didn't amount to much or match up to our ideas of Christmas, so, grabbing an old pillow case for Uncle, we rummaged for his old gardening shoes and stuffed them in. Soon other packages, all individually wrapped in newspaper, were thrown on top: a carrot, a lump of coal and Aunty's dust cap. We hoped this diversion would make up for what was wanting.

The next morning, there was great excitement as we exchanged the presents. I received some paints and a nightdress case to embroider, a calendar and a sponge bag.

After the Church service, we had a very good Christmas dinner with chicken and we played Freddy the Fox, Monopoly, Beetle and Donkey.

And so ended my first Christmas away from home.

The Germans forgot to come.

## Chapter VIII

## *'I've Got Sixpence, Jolly Jolly Sixpence'*

It was near the end of the holiday and I still did not know where I was going to live. Nearly all the other girls had been settled before Christmas. Then a letter came for Uncle and Aunty from Miss Roughton. It confirmed that I was to go to the term-time-only billet and I learned that my hostess would be Miss Keating, the headmistress of the Rochdale Municipal High School for Girls.

Usually, the billets seemed to be dealt out like cards. Miss Roughton had announced that each girl would have a home that closely matched her own in Guernsey, but this policy proved to be far from practicable. We were not questioned about our accustomed lifestyles. In any case, the distribution of wealth, the ownership of property and the class structures of Guernsey had no parallel in the industrial north of England and could not be aligned or their significance compared. Billets were made available only as and when needed and none of us ever had a choice. It was a matter of 'take what's there' for everyone and it was the responsibility of the billeting officer to make the arrangements. Few of us were thinking about settling into a 'proper' home. It was temporary. We were game for anything – well, within reason.

By this time, I was assuming quite a fatalistic attitude to the future. My parents might die, the school might move, my billet might be uncongenial, others might show little interest in my concerns, so what? I would just have to get on with things the best way I could. At any time an air raid might end everything. I had somehow accepted that the worst could happen and had made my own adjustment to it, however inadequate and unsatisfactory. I had come through a good deal and could face more. I realised I was managing without my parents and could go on doing so. It was hardly the glowing response of someone who enjoyed having the wind blowing on her face, but I had come a long way in a short time.

Whatever lay in store, it wouldn't be permanent, so it was with some degree of detachment that I started collecting my things to put into my case, which, once again, would tide me over a period of transition. Nevertheless, the jibes about minding my p's and q's stirred up a mild anxiety. What would be expected of me in that billet? Was I up to it? I thought I was and yet I felt rather ashamed that in view of the far greater threats which I seemed to be negotiating or holding at bay, I was worrying over trivialities. What was I going to say when I saw Miss Keating?

As arranged, a car pulled up outside the manse in Summerseat. Rev. Quail, a Congregational minister, with whom John was billeted, had come with his wife to take him and Brian back to Oldham. They had said they would drop me off in Rochdale en route, so I was bundled in for the twenty minute journey (five to six miles as the crow flies). I was very surprised that you could get there so quickly by car, when our normal travel time took so much longer.

Soon I was being admitted to 34, William St. in Rochdale, an unpretentious terraced house where some of the mistresses were living since the closure of Roylelands, Horse Carrs and Lyngarth. Like Boothroyd, this house had been taken on a rental basis as a result of investigations by Miss Roughton's sister, Winifred, who was anxious to do all she could on her frequent visits to the town. It transpired later that a murder had been committed in that house and one of the inside doors had been taken away in evidence and was still missing. Perhaps other prospective tenants had heard of the crime and veered away. After a period of settling in, the new occupants noticed that there was livestock in the walls and one of them went to the library to identify the species. In the end, the whole place had to be fumigated.

Now, Miss Brittain was at hand to take me to my billet about fifteen minutes' walk away. We strode briskly along with my case and blanket, my gas mask and the other paraphernalia which had been transferred from Roylelands to William St. to be stored till I had been given a home.

A little breathless, we arrived at 22, Edmund St. A maid, dressed in black with white cap and apron, opened the door and ushered us into the drawing room. Miss Keating rose to welcome us. She was a slight and dainty figure with straight mid-brown hair combed back and twisted into a chignon held in place with tortoiseshell clasps. We were introduced to her ageing mother who was seated in an armchair by the fire. Her wrinkled face with high cheek bones and deep-set blue eyes was topped with wisps of thinning white hair swept upwards into a very fine hairnet. My ration book was handed over and then Miss Brittain was gone. Miss Keating spoke crisply but with kindness and in the manner of one used to assuming authority. A husky tendency in her voice took the edge off any sharpness. Practicalities were discussed. I was sent across the road to 13, Edmund St. Miss Sayer, Miss Stewart, Miss Naftel and a few other parent/helpers attached to our school were now living there in another small enclave. As bidden, I asked if I could go to school with the staff the following morning since I did not know the way. When I returned, Miss Keating said I had to be washed and in bed by 8 p.m. I was dismayed. It seemed so early, the lot meted out to an old-fashioned child of long ago. I felt shy, out of place and bewildered.

At 7.30 the maid brought in some cocoa and a biscuit, and I got up to prepare myself for bed. "I might be here a long time," I said to myself, and, on impulse, planted a kiss on each forehead and headed for the door. They looked surprised.

Upstairs, I tried some reassurance. "It's going to be alright. You'll settle soon." I would have to get used to things and learn to be acceptable.

I looked at the round brooch Miss Keating had given me, the one that has been with me all these years. It was like a disc covered with a pewter sheet beaten into a leaf pattern by one of the girls at her school. It felt like the token of a tacit contract. I would be housed and fed as long as I fitted in. If I wasn't suitable, I would have to leave. My part was to be compliant and adaptable. That I was conscientious, dependable and well-meaning was evidently not yet apparent, but would surely count, I hoped.

I got undressed and settled down for the night. My bedroom was the small one over the hall next to Miss Keating's and looked out over Edmund St. The middle bedroom in the house was Mrs. Keating's, and Vera, the maid, slept at the back next to the bathroom. I had unpacked my suitcase. My two dresses were draped from coat hangers hooked to a peg on the door. My underwear and other belongings were tucked into a small chest of drawers. In the corner was a quaint triangular piece of furniture with a bottom cupboard for shoes and on top of it stood two mirrors at right angles to each other. There was room for a brush and comb on the mat in front of them. The foot of the bed was just a chair's width from a sash window. Its top half was permanently jammed shut and Miss Keating emphasised that the bottom section must always be kept open a little to let in air. It was bitterly cold and the draught was level with my feet. It was hard over the next few weeks to get accustomed to this rule. Would I suffocate if I pushed the window down a little? I dared not risk such flagrant defiance. A hot water bottle was not allowed for children. In bed, I was to discover that if I moved my legs round and round as though cycling, my toes would slowly thaw or I would drop off to sleep exhausted. Later came welcome bedsocks.

Next morning, I was escorted to school as arranged. There was a ten minute walk into the Town Centre, then a bus ride to Castleton and a further short walk to the school which was now to start at 9.15 a.m. This allowed time for the Castleton children to use the hall for Assembly first and start their lessons. We had a two hour break for lunch, giving girls ample time to return to their billets even if they were quite a long way off. Afternoon school lasted from 2 to 4.10 p.m. Unlike most others, I was to have school dinners as it was not convenient to have me at 'home'.

Afternoon tea at Edmund St. was brought into the drawing room by Vera. Beautifully polished occasional tables were drawn up to the armchairs and covered with white cloths elaborately embroidered by Miss Keating or her mother. The silver teapot and hot water jug stood on a shining tray. Wafer thin slices of bread and butter with home-made jam were followed by cake which Mrs. Keating had made. She prided herself on keeping up high standards of domestic organisation and continued the practices of the household she had run when she was younger. A genteel, careful and thrifty aura enveloped the house.

The drawing room was formal, but comfortable. A prominent feature was the long fender stool upholstered with green patterned tapestry, the prodigious achievement of Mrs. Keating, who had also made floral tapestry seats for the dining room chairs. The three-piece suite had serviceable mid-brown covers, removable for dry cleaning, and there was an extra armchair much smaller than the rest, which was assigned to me.

At the front was a large bay window with heavy green curtains which were lined with additional lengths of blackout material. The net curtains quickly got grey in the Lancashire atmosphere and had to be washed frequently and dried in the yard on a sunny day. A piano stood against the wall opposite the tiled fireplace, but no one played it any more. A vase of bought flowers was reflected in a round mirror base, centrally positioned on a side table. A thick but well trodden neutral carpet gave the room an air of rather worn-down luxury, which it would not otherwise have possessed. The total effect was sombre, restrained and pleasing to its occupants, the end result of hard work, diligence and a disciplined lifestyle.

The house stood on a very windy corner where Emma St. crossed Edmund St. A tall privet hedge separated it from the road on two sides. Plants refused to grow in the forsaken flowerbeds at its roots. A tarmac pathway was laid between the walls of the house and the hedge, but only the cat used it.

Further up the street, the church of St. Edmund's rose imposingly to view, squarely based on its own island. Symbolically perhaps, the street had to divide to go round it and then reunite on the other side.

The Keatings were Methodists. Mr. Keating had been a minister and once a miner. He had died of cancer in 1934, before the move to Rochdale. The church they now attended was the one at Spotland about fifteen minutes' walk away. It was much larger and more formal in its mode of worship than our small country chapel at the Forest, but, from the first, people were friendly and warm-hearted and I was welcomed into the Sunday School which met at 1.45 in the afternoon.

On weekdays after school, I sometimes heard Children's Hour on the wireless, I did my homework, and if there was any time left over, I added a harebell or two to the nightdress case I'd had for Christmas. I was quiet and undemanding and disappeared early in the evening, well before a cooked supper was served at 8.30 p.m.

During the first few weeks, I learned to recognise the unwritten codes and conventions which governed the routine and relationships in this household. There were many things I was expected to know which were rarely made explicit. Most of them were concerned with deference, due respect and precedence.

At home, I was well used to reading my mother's face and trying to conform with her expectations. It was an art well learned and not difficult to apply here. I practised being alert to Miss Keating's expressions without directly looking at her face. Being accommodating was being 'good'. I was in no position to challenge. In my moments of such self assertion at home, I had been sent upstairs to my room in tears and labelled 'stubborn', my behaviour judged by the way it corresponded with my mother's views and needs. Here, if I deviated, I wouldn't be kept at all. The basis on which my security rested could shift and I was the one to keep it stable. I could almost hear the words not said, "It's up to you!"

The range of conversation seemed very limited when I was present and was confined, I imagined, to the things that would interest Mrs. Keating. I ruled out everything that I thought might cause irritation or annoyance. The stuff of our school conversations seemed totally out of place and irrelevant in this setting. I was no Anne of Green Gables, prattling cheerfully into the silence and it did not occur to me that lively chitchat might be welcome.

A visitor to the house in those early days asked Miss Keating how I was getting on. She replied that I was 'amenable'. When no one was about, I looked it up in the dictionary to see what my current rating might be. This must be progress. I thought it was the highest accolade I was likely to receive.

After a while, I took to calling on Vera in the kitchen on my way up to bed. She was preparing the Keatings' supper or sitting in a cane chair by the fire – deep in a novelette. If I stayed more than five minutes, a voice called from the drawing room and the chatting stopped abruptly. But it was a pleasant way to delay bedtime and a relief to hear Vera's complaints . . . how Mrs. K. kept popping into the kitchen to check that she was doing things 'properly'. So Vera and I had something in common. We were both being closely watched and Mrs. K. had a very sharp eye!

As an evacuee and a child, I had an ill-defined place in the household. I could not be aligned with the family or with the maid and I was not a guest. There was no precedent; I was neither fish nor fowl nor good red herring. But who cared any more? This was wartime.

As I was not tired when I went upstairs, it took me ages to go to sleep. I hated being bored, so I used mental games to fill the time. I would name all the towns or rivers beginning with A, then B, and travel through the alphabet, memorising the totals. Which letter would win? I progressed to complicated mathematical problems which I set myself and when I got more bold, I sat on the edge of my bed writing my diary, but the light was apt to attract attention and a voice would call me to turn it off.

One day, Vera divulged that Miss Keating had previously had a soldier billeted upstairs in the spacious attic bedroom. The authorities had required all the householders to declare the extent of the accommodation and officials had come round to note the empty bedrooms. When the soldier left, the Keatings were under pressure to have another or an evacuee instead. A child must have seemed a better proposition. I hope I was able to make it so, but, at the time, Vera's injudicious comments led me to feel that I had been foisted on the Keatings by force of circumstance. I was their war effort, an undertaking they were required to make. They would have preferred to be on their own, I thought. I didn't know how I was going to seem worth having. I could not take being in their home for granted as though they were my parents and so, for starters, I decided to concentrate on being helpful and on not-being-a-nuisance. I did not feel secure enough to try for anything more and was very grateful to have this as my home. By now I was getting used to the rules and conventions and they no longer seemed so restrictive. It was all in such marked contrast to the Castleton billet where I nearly landed up before Christmas. Another girl, I heard, had gone there and stuck it only for a few days. She was expected to mind the child, while the parents went to the pub in the evenings.

As there were no games in the Keating household and nothing much to do if I finished my homework and mending before bedtime, I always made sure I had a book on hand to read. That way I would not be a drain on the Keatings' time and so, I thought, would make my staying on more likely. It was up to me to make things work.

It sometimes took girls quite a while to settle in their billets, even though there was often a welcoming warmth and much goodwill. The billeting allowance received weekly was barely adequate. It was intended to cover food and run-of-the-mill expenses, but not our clothing. The amount was eight shillings and sixpence (8/6) for those under fourteen, and ten shillings and sixpence (10/6) for those older. Many homes provided clothes and little extras when they were needed and some were very generous in sharing what they had.

It's remarkable that so many people were ready to open their homes to children who were complete strangers. Some must have dreaded what might turn up. They were ready for a stern beginning, "Ee by gum, she'll 'ave to be'ave 'ere." The stereotyped picture of the evacuee, who wouldn't brush her teeth, died hard.

In households where space was limited and the income low, girls had to fit in quickly and learn the family ways. Adherence to the routine was the way to avoid friction. They all knew where they sat at table, when the wireless could be turned on and who filled the coal scuttles. The newcomer was not in a position to negotiate her role or upset the equilibrium.

It was comparatively easy for girls to get used to the Lancashire dialect, where 'starved' meant 'cold' and 'pots' referred to the crockery. Unfamiliar tripe, hotpot and parkin could be enjoyed. Sometimes, however, the expectations on both sides were unrealistic and needed reshaping and this took time.

One girl always thought she had been taken into her first billet mainly to be a companion to the girl of the house, who had difficult emotional problems. She herself was seen as the stable and reasonable one who would offset or foil the daughter's behaviour. Her own needs were apt to be overlooked in this rather inward-looking family.

Sometimes the images of us held by the adults in our world were harder to recognise and cope with. In my case, initially I was to be Uncle's kid sister's child and it was assumed I would enjoy his babying pattern of relating to young children. With the Keatings, I was to be the quiet, respectful, non-active child of a previous generation. It sometimes puzzled me that as a head-mistress, Miss Keating appeared to know so little about the home life of her pupils who seemed to live in a normal contemporary fashion. Or was it that she considered them inadequate role models and wanted me to fit into her lifestyle more comfortably?

The sets of expectations, hopes and fears which confronted Ruth and Jean in their respective billets were altogether different.

Ruth's billet was in Ashfield Rd., a street of terraced houses, and she was with Mr. and Mrs. Hebden, who were Christian Scientists. He was a grocer's roundsman and she stayed at home to look after their baby, Roger.

Right from the start, Ruth was treated more as a companion and a responsible older girl. Her hostess took her to a shop and invited her to choose the colour of a new eiderdown for her bed. It was a vote of confidence and counteracted the effect of another episode, which Ruth found both amusing and disappointing. The grandpa of the household took her on one side and explained that she had come to a good home and warned her with some acerbity that there was to be no swearing or loud-mouthed behaviour under that roof. No one was further removed from a supposedly typical brash EastEnder than Ruth, who was always courteous and thoughtful in all things and a responsible and protective sister towards Jean, four years her junior.

No dread of the lout was evident in Jean's billet. She remembers being delivered to her new home by Mrs. Stansfield of the WVS. "Be a good girl and do the washing up!" she was urged as her escort left. There was a warm welcome from members of the family who lived in a spacious house almost the size of Horse Carrs.

Quickly they produced a photograph. "Who is that?" they asked Jean. "That's me!" she exclaimed in surprise, but could not remember when or where the picture could have been taken. It was, in fact, a portrait of the daughter of the house, who had died not long before. She was Jean's age and the resemblance was uncanny. Jean soon found that she was treated as a replacement and given many of the daughter's books, games and clothes which had been kept.

One day, when Jean was playing outside with a ball and wearing the daughter's coat and scarf, she became aware of the parents' gaunt faces pressed to the sitting room window. It was their haunting look of shocked 'recognition' which made such an impression on Jean. In that moment, she realised just how she must appear to them – as their own loved child returned. At the same time, there was an element of horror which registered in their drawn features.

While she was benefiting from the generous provision made, Jean was increasingly aware of the drawbacks. "You'll never want to go back to Guernsey, now," they assured her. "We'll adopt you." She was hurt that they should suppose her own home meant less to her than theirs, but she felt she could not explain or protest and it was best to wait in patience. As time wore on, she knew she could not stay trapped in unrealities and remain so closely identified with a dead person. She would feel swamped. She had to be herself.

The parents' possessiveness and their son's conflicting feelings became more apparent after Jean had an unexpected phone call from Ruth. The sisters had not seen each other for a long time and they chatted away in Guernsey French, not realising that the boy was listening in on an extension. He was furious that his intention to eavesdrop had been thwarted by the use of the patois. Jean was a 'foreigner' he couldn't reach but wanted to bait, no doubt because he resented her being taken into the bosom of the family as though she belonged there. Jean had unwittingly fuelled his anger and, following his explosion, she was not allowed to receive any more calls from Ruth.

The confusion of identity persisted and there was no one Jean could confide in, since she rarely saw Ruth at the other side of the town and there were no others at hand to take a personal interest in her worries. To all intents and purposes, she was in a good home and she was well fed and clothed.

As the tensions within the family mounted, Jean's concentration on her school work diminished and she found herself at a disadvantage. In some desperation, she wrote a note to Ruth and asked one of her teachers at Greenbank to deliver it when she went to the senior end of the school at Castleton. With relief she watched the paper being tucked into a safe place – inside the leg elastic of her teacher's knickers, the normal home for her handkerchief.

Two weeks went by and there was no response from Ruth. The note had not been delivered. It was grubby and misspelt she was told.

Jean grew more nervous and apprehensive as her attempts to hint at the boy's intimidating tactics were dismissed by his parents. They could not accept that Jean, their 'daughter' could be seeing their son in such a poor light. It took further disturbances to remove the parents' blinkers.

In many billets, the adjustments were made quickly on both sides and warm relationships proved rewarding and lasted long after the war. Three sisters, Betty, Peggy and Pat le Gallez were given a home by the Laws who had a daughter of their own. The sleeping accommodation over their grocer's shop was rather cramped, but the girls were well liked and warmly integrated into the household. We sometimes imagined that while we were on strict rations, they were eating all the bacon bits flicked away by the slicer, supplemented by the eggs which were accidentally cracked.

For one girl, the first months in a billet were marred by a chronic cough and failing health. She grew very thin and frail and the standards and expectations in this home differed widely from those of her school. Small things could loom large at the time and she remembers with a smile that when given a sticky bun, she was sent outside to eat it. Miss Roughton had implanted a stern taboo on all chewing and eating out of doors and on buses and was apt to ridicule those who flouted her rules of ladylike decorum.

During her stay in this first billet, she had nightmares. Her billeting hostess decided to go away on holiday, taking her daughter. The father, who was a bus driver, worked all through the night. The neighbour was told that the girl would be in the house and if there were screams, it was only the nightmares and there was no cause for concern. The girl was given the responsiblity of making up a good fire in the evening, so that when her billeting 'uncle' returned, cold, at 5.30 a.m., the place would be warm. The grate was very near the foot of the stairs which rose directly from the kitchen to the bedrooms above. She was completely inexperienced in dealing with fires and this one had no guard. She was frightened that a hot coal might fall out while she was in bed and the house would catch on fire. If she screamed then no one would hear or, if they did, they would take no notice. She therefore sat up in the kitchen all night to keep check and only crept up to bed at 5.15 a.m., shortly before the 'uncle' was due back.

\* \* \* \* \*

I blew on my numbed fingers. The first winter in Rochdale was a cold one even by northern standards. Snow often lay two to four inches deep. I wasn't used to making snowballs. In Guernsey, the sporadic flakes soon melted away and some winters went by without any snow at all. I was perpetually chilled. I assumed that the bitter cold was something everyone had to endure and that I had to learn to be better at it. I must become more hardened.

The school playground was crisscrossed with tracks of ice, where Castleton children had taken a long run-up sprint and hurled themselves into a polished slide. They urged us to join in but most of us just fell.

Unexpectedly, I was offered some woollen vests. Miss Keating's sister, Mary, was up from London. She was the Headmistress of Hornsey High School and lived in Muswell Hill. On her visits, she livened up the household and is best remembered as an unusually short figure with greying hair and twinkling eyes which peered over her black rimmed spectacles as she chortled in amusement. When she realised how few winter clothes we had, she gave me the ribbed vests she had been knitting for the Red Cross. I have heard similar tubes dubbed 'bum-starvers'. At school, I was given navy knickers, and, in a mood of concession, a blue jumper to wear under my tunic, instead of the customary white blouse. We were always cold in poorly heated classrooms.

Air raid warnings persisted. If we did not take a wad of newspapers to school to line the wooden shelter seats, soaked through with icy drips from the ceilings, we'd invite the well-known quips: "So you've wet yourself again, I see?" "Time you grew up!" There was no room to stand, as the facing seats were so close together. In that dark, dank and sometimes smelly atmosphere, there was nothing else to do when we were tired of singing. Then jugs of cocoa were brought in and Miss Keating supplied me with an enamel mug so that I could have some.

If the siren went while I was in my billet, we all carried on regardless. Miss Keating took no precautionary measures, but there was a cellar where we could go if bombs dropped very near. I don't think I was ever really frightened. Most of us were inured to the fact that we could die or that our parents might. Raids were inevitable and to be ignored as much as possible. By then, I was so used to the siren at night, that I often dropped off to sleep soon after it had sounded and only woke up again to the shrill of the all clear. I could sleep through gunfire as though it had been thunder.

Early on in the New Year (1941), some houses in Sudden were demolished or badly damaged and there were casualties. I passed that way every day on the bus and noticed that the wreckage was only four minutes' walk from Boothroyd and six minutes from Roylelands. What would have happened if there had been a

second's difference in the Germans' timing when they released
the bombs? The girls at Boothroyd might have died. The *Rochdale
Observer* published photographs, but all it could announce in the
headline was 'Air raid damage in the North West'. The enemy
must not be told where it was. By then, street names and
signposts had been removed to avoid giving clues to stray
parachutists and spies, who could be lurking anywhere!

Later in January, we were shocked to hear that Stretford High
School had been flattened by a land mine. Fortunately no one was
there, since it happened in the night. Miss Warren thought the
building was mistaken for a factory from the air. She was thankful
no girls were killed, but saddened to lose her cherished Art room.
Houses roundabout had been damaged and her own home had
windows broken in the blast. Many of the girls were immediately
evacuated to Blackpool and everything was disrupted. Those who
had done so much to help us were now themselves at risk.

Jean Adams, my Stretford 'cousin' was one who stayed at home.
Her Christmas present to me had been a black leather case for
my gas mask. It looked very superior with a zip at the top and a
strap to go over my shoulder and I quickly replaced the tattered
box and string I had brought from Guernsey. We all had to carry
our gas masks everywhere we went.

Miss Keating told me I would have sixpence a week pocket
money. A penny would be allocated to the church collection, a
penny to the Sunday School, 2½ pence for a stamp and the
remaining 1½ pence was for other things. To keep up with my letter-
writing, I realised I would have to draw on my small store of 6
shillings, but I was delighted at the prospect of a regular income.
My parents had never supplied us with pocket money and when old
Uncle Tom had slipped us each a generous half-crown (two shillings
and sixpence), the coins went straight into our metal money boxes
shaped like a squat version of the Eiffel tower. I looked back to the
excitement of one Christmas when Brian and I had been allowed to
spend the accumulated contents on alarm clocks.

My parents with their frugal habits had always urged us to save
all we could. "Don't waste anything!" My mother was a hoarder
and nothing that could be used again was ever thrown away. One
of the dresses I had brought with me was made of navy blue serge
from a cast-off suit of my father's. She had tried this way and that
to cut the required shapes out of the unpicked pieces, but ended
up by adding a small triangle at the lower end of the skirt to fill a
gap. I was absurdly conscious of this join (hardly visible) as though

it shouted aloud of my mother's skimping and parsimonious life-style. I knew the family could well afford some new material, but she was used to the strictures of her own childhood when there were six small children to maintain and she found it difficult to adjust to the greater freedom as my father's business prospered. What's more, this dress had its neck-piece trimmed with outmoded zig-zag braiding of separate green and blue and orange strands. It added to the homely appearance and I was thankful to outgrow it. I was also wearing a misshapen orange jumper passed on when autumn turned to winter. The worst item by far was a dark blue coat inflicted on me by school. Miss Roughton was still insisting that we should all wear navy uniform and, with my Ladies' College coat, I was clearly not complying, till this specimen was dragged out of its hiding in a cardboard box. It had obviously been worn by a thin and humped old lady and was tight across the chest. Attached to it was a narrow fur collar, which looked as though a predator's orgy of chewing had been interrupted, so as to leave irregular patches of bare skin. "Lois, I hope I'm never seen out with you, while you're wearing that coat!" Miss Keating remarked, and although the tone was light-hearted, my discomfiture grew. I knew she meant it. On my way back from school, I always passed a shop that had a mirror in its window and I was confronted daily by this fleeting image of a mangy fur-necked waif. Attempts to improve the coat made little difference.

Later in the spring, Aunty and Uncle passed on to Miss Keating the sum of two pounds and ten shillings from my father's contribution to our welfare. The Bury shops were poorly stocked with children's clothing, they said, and they hoped Miss Keating would be able to find me a coat and hat for out-of-school use. There was little choice in my size and we came away with a blue coat whose belt at the back was too high for my low-waisted figure and I felt childish. The humiliating addition was a panama hat of the school uniform variety, the kind so bitterly scorned and left behind in Guernsey. A juvenile elastic was sewn on to fit under the chin, so that it could not blow away. It struck me that Mrs. Keating did not know I was too old for it. I did my utmost to tuck it into the crown out of sight in order to avoid the imagined jeers, "Can't you hold on to your hat, yet?", "Still a baby?" I wished that I could be the same as my contemporaries at Sunday School and have a plaited straw model trimmed with pretty artificial flowers . . . but perhaps they cost too much. In those days no one went bareheaded. I felt marked out as 'the evacuee'.

# Chapter IX

## *'I Know We'll Meet Again Some Sunny Day'*

After the severe disruptions of our first six months in England, there were only about 100 girls left, less than half the number evacuated. The authorities had continued to whittle down the allocation of teachers to correspond with the diminishing remainder. A realignment of staff was needed to cover the essential subjects and hold them in balance. It was a matter of closing ranks.

Under the new regime, Miss Roughton was to take French and English grammar. Her London B.A. Hons. degree (Royal Holloway College) was in German and, on that account, had proved of little practical use. The First World War had made the language too unpopular to teach in school and so she had switched to French. But this was the subject already being taught by Miss Mahy, who, as a graduate of Bedford College, London, had been appointed to the school in the mid-thirties. Now seeing the pressing need for Maths, she generously offered to take this on instead. With her usual determination and sense of responsibility, she brushed up by a correspondence course and was soon ready to take Arithmetic, Algebra and Geometry to School Certificate level. In her development of the syllabus, she was thoughtful and considerate, taking account of the girls' varying abilities and attainments, which had become so ill-matched by the upheavals. She gave lucid explanations and marked the homework promptly. Her care, commitment and cheerful manner elicited a good response. We all made progress and she convinced us all that there was value in logical thinking and precision. Some of us carry in our mind's eye the picture of a diminutive figure with short brown wavy hair. In her brogue shoes, she stands on tip-toe to reach the top of the blackboard where she is writing up the problems for our homework, since there were no text books. She steps back, adjusts her glasses and checks through the neatly written lines before we copy them.

Although she was then in her late twenties or early thirties, she had the sterling qualities which gave her the aura of someone older and, because she was a Guernsey person herself, she understood our family situations better than most and was well liked and respected. Every now and again, she would set aside the routine work for a spell of mental arithmetic. 'Begin with 8, add 22, divide by 5 . . .'. I have always valued her tips in judging whether a long string of figures could divide by 4 and how to add up quickly in nines. I found, however, that when I was tired, I resorted to the automaton's use of the dice-like dots learned in the Guernsey Transition class when Miss Johnson taught us. Now she was teaching the Juniors at Greenbank and I rarely saw her.

To Miss Sayer's main subject of Art was added set reading and English composition. We had finished an abridged version of *David Copperfield* while at Roylelands and now came Robert Louis Stevenson's *Travels with a Donkey*. Reluctantly we trailed the animal on its tedious journey over the Cevennes in the south of France. How I wished the poor weary creature would drop dead! I flicked the pages of some school's discarded textbook and counted the number we would have to plod through in its company.

When we finally progressed to Jane Austen's *Pride and Prejudice*, the staid characters hardly seemed more lively. They spoke to each other in stilted sentences, whose coded messages we found it hard to recognise. "What do you think of Mrs. Bennet's character?" Miss Sayer enquired. How could we say, "Plain silly"? We had to formulate a proper comment.

Some time later, when the film appeared in the local cinema with Greer Garson playing Elizabeth, I was astonished to find her animated. The restraint I had felt in the book was replaced by a pleasurable, sunny atmosphere and good humour. Flowers bloomed and nobody seemed too thwarted by the book's disasters, which injured no one. The bubbly characters behaved as though safeguarded in the haven of their own society and carried on their family chattering to their hearts' content. Miss Sayer held us firmly to the reading matter and encouraged us to consider the stories with a critical appraisal. With me, at least, she met with some success.

She was skilled in holding an Art class together while individuals were scattered over the room, painting at their own speed. We rarely took advantage of the opportunity for trouble, even when we had to go to the cloakroom to fill our jam jars with clean water. The least talented could rely on her friendly advice on shading or applying a wash.

In class, she sat prettily sedate. Her dark eyes were alert to every movement. She had thick black hair with tightly waving curls which were bushed to the sides of the head in a style then current. We were immensely saddened when we heard in March that her father had been killed in an air raid on the east coast. Miss Mahy's mother died in hospital and Miss Clayton fell ill with bronchitis. Miss Brown, who had been under strain was away sporadically and we missed her enjoyable lessons in biology. In the single exercise book we were still using at the time, there are sketches of cotyledons and corms interspersed with French verbs and notes on the prophet Samuel. Due to ill health, she finally left altogether and Miss Brittain, who taught P.E. and Games took over her work. During all these absences, our classes merged to make them viable.

The timetables at Castleton and Greenbank were made to dovetail, so that members of staff could teach at both ends of the town. Miss Sayer and Miss Mahy were often spotted cycling to and fro and Miss Naftel came from Greenbank twice a week to teach Geography.

Miss Roughton's bicycle grew in decrepitude. The web of string across the back attracted comments. Was it there to hold the mudguard down, to stop her coat from catching in the spokes or just to reduce the rattling? Once, after she had taught evening class in town, the bicycle was missing. She searched for it in vain. A tidy-minded citizen had thrown it on a nearby dump. As soon as she could retrieve it, she pressed it into further service.

No bicycle was ever built to suit Miss Clayton's bulging frame. She relied heavily on the buses. Her subjects were Needlework and Divinity and she presented Saul and David and other Old Testament figures with affection. She spoke simply of the ways God used them with all their imperfections. She encouraged us to explore our Bibles with imagination and in her carefully constructed lessons, she sketched in the history and topography behind the stories to place them in their context. The homework was well within our range, but challenging, since she expected personal interpretation and involvement – "What lessons did David learn as an outlaw and soldier that helped him to rule over his people?"

In the Needlework lessons before Christmas, she had shown girls how to use oddments of material to cover wooden coat hangers for presents or to practise neat darning or make alterations to their clothes. In the late spring, four rolls of floral material were delivered, each with a preponderance of a single colour: green, red, blue or yellow. These denoted the Houses we had been placed in when we joined the school in Guernsey. They were named after famous women: Elizabeth Garrett Anderson (green), Margaret MacMillan (red), Elizabeth Fry (blue) and Edith Cavell (yellow). Only their surnames were used. The numbers in each House were now lop-sided and there was some disgruntlement when transfers were effected. ("I don't want to be in Fry! So and so's in it.") I was green. Attempts to revive the

House system flagged as there were seldom opportunities for meetings or competitions. Under some duress, I finished my dress just days before the summer holidays!

Meanwhile, I was wearing a pretty frock from Guernsey. This one was special for my mother had bought some new material instead of making do with old. It looked rather like today's polyester and had clusters of pink and blue flowers on a white background and she had added matching trimmings. All the skills she had learned as a young woman were applied to make this a neat and well fitting dress. I was deeply upset when I eventually grew too big to wear it and was made to fling it in the school's old cartons. I watched the girls each morning till, later, I saw it resurrected on a younger figure. As she knew my family, I told her who had made it.

Miss Clayton continued her visits to the Channel Islands Refugees Committee's second-hand clothing store in Stockport and replenished the supplies to pass on to the needy in our number.

She, later, reawakened interest among the older girls who had been Rangers and, as a Captain, she made links with local companies and fostered joint activities.

Why were the front ends of her short grey hair tinged a fading yellow? If we had any doubts, we had only to look down at her plump fingers which were lightly stained with nicotine. The Boothroyd contingent confirmed that she liked to smoke. At breakfast-time, she could be found in their kitchen, stirring a saucepan of porridge. Fascinated onlookers glanced furtively at the progress of ash up the cigarette, which drooped limply from a corner of her mouth. Would flecks be camouflaged within their portion?

Some of the girls who had no parents on the mainland were glad to have her as their confidante. She dealt with problems helpfully and with discretion. "Is there anything you would like to ask?" she would enquire and sometimes a pastoral session followed.

Inevitably there were areas of contention. One senior girl refused to wash the Boothroyd doorstep when she insisted, and stormed off abruptly to find her mother in another town.

Miss Stewart was the History specialist and now she added Latin, which she had taught in Guernsey. We went back to beginnings. As I had a very good short-term memory, learning the vocabulary and an assortment of historical data posed no problems. Miss Stewart had linked our new surroundings with an outline of the Industrial Revolution, but now we had to turn to the stodgy textbooks which some school had sent. They dealt with the constitutional history of the Stuarts. Her attempts to coach us in the Constitutions of Clarendon were met with flat resistance, but we appreciated her efforts to build up a thriving library with the books sent in by well-wishers. Soon we were immersed in *Kidnapped* and *Ivanhoe*, *Lorna Doone* and *Great Expectations* without our realising how much they contributed to our understanding of the historical period they covered.

Miss Stewart addressed us earnestly in a softly spoken Scottish accent. Propped against a table-top and pressing her hands to its edge, she would lean forward to make a point. Her light brown hair, which she parted in the middle, was caught in a small tight roll behind. She wore fawn cardigans over quiet print blouses which hung in straight and unrevealing lines. Combined with sturdy skirts of tweed, they gave her a rather mannish appearance, only partly relieved by a plain necklace of wooden beads.

Striking a more flamboyant note was Miss Roughton's sister, Winifred, who now joined the staff on a voluntary basis. She had resigned from her post as music mistress at Cheltenham Girls' High School in order to join her sister's staff in Guernsey that January of 1941, but the evacuation intervened before all the formalities were completed and she was now caught between the two appointments and unemployed. To supplement her private income, she gave piano lessons in the lunch break, but only to those girls whose billets would pay the fees. She embarked with some gusto on a concentrated programme of classroom singing and soon she judged us good enough to perform in public concerts. She chose scenes from Shakespeare for experiments in drama and watched with satisfaction as the girls began to grow in confidence. Soloists blossomed under her tuition.

Did she or did she not wear a wig? The controversy still rages. Her dark wavy hair was secured tightly by a black band much like her sister's except that it stayed above the hairline which was low. "It's a bit skewwhiff today," we would whisper to each other, hoping for a thorough sideways slip. The curling pieces at the back were pinned haphazardly into a knot, a styling which did nothing to relieve the mystery.

Like her sister, she had a rather high-pitched voice, but could modulate it and make it versatile. She wore dark clothes, invariably black for special occasions. From a selection of beads, chains and brooches, she chose the one to enhance the outfit for the day. Unlike other mistresses, she had all her pre-war wardrobe to draw on. Her face was lined, but kept well powdered and, with lipstick, she accentuated the thinness of her lips. If some have described her as 'a bit Bohemian', they have been referring to her looks and not her morals. She had abstracted moments, when she sat with knees apart, one elbow on the table and hand cupped to tilting head. Through thick dark-framed glasses, she gazed into the distance, enwrapped in sounds beyond our human ken. A suggestion of the fey hung over her.

She seemed the only one to recognise a flatness in our singing and her hand would cut ever-rising steps into the air. We worked hard to relieve her of excruciation. 'There was a lover and his lass, With a hey! and a ho! and a hey, nonny no!' 'Nymphs and shepherds come away, come away. . . .' After the shrieking of the latest hits in the shelters, the dichotomy could not have been more absolute.

Champness Hall was a focal point for many civic activities in the borough and, for us, it was to have many memorable associations. The first time I went inside was for the Christmas party given by the WVS in January. But why did we have to wear school uniform? I had never seen Punch and Judy or a Charlie Chaplin film before. We played games and had a magnificent tea. Finally, the Mayor, as Santa Claus, pressed a shilling into each hand as we filed by.

We were soon back in the Hall for a concert of our very own, to express the school's thanks to those who had helped us and particularly to the WVS, prominently represented by Lady Turner, who made a speech.

At the close, we swung into 'Sarnia Cherie' which was a guaranteed tear-jerker. 'Sarnia' we had been told, was an old name for Guernsey, although of uncertain origin. Few of us knew the song before the evacuation, but it was to take on the dimensions of a National Anthem or theme song and we used it everywhere. There were few dry eyes in the audience by the time we reached its end.

> *Sarnia, dear homeland,*
> *Gem of the sea,*
> *Island of beauty, my heart longs for thee,*
> *Thy voice calls me ever, in waking, or sleep,*
> *Till my soul cries with anguish, my eyes ache to weep.*
> *In fancy I see thee, again as of yore,*
> *Thy verdure clad hills and thy wave beaten shore*
> *Thy rock sheltered bays, Ah; of all thou art best;*
> *I'm returning to greet thee, dear island of rest.*

*Chorus*
*Sarnia Cherie*
*Gem of the sea,*
*Home of my childhood, my heart longs for thee,*
*Thy voice calls me ever, forget thee I'll never*
*Island of beauty,*
*Sarnia Cherie.*

The second verse was ignored, since it would have had us in far-flung parts of the earth in search of diamonds, like disillusioned old roués who longed for solace in dear Sarnia.

Champness Hall became the venue for orchestral concerts, as the famous travelled around the country to entertain and keep up everyone's morale. In February, I was taken there with Miss Keating's school to hear the London Symphony Orchestra conducted by Keith Douglas. It was the first time I had been to such a concert and I found myself sitting so close to the cymbals that I was deafened. There was some commotion as one of the girls was sick and had to be escorted out by Miss Wilson. Behind the scenes, the renowned pianist, Myra Hess, offered the girl some Eau de Cologne and asked for Miss Wilson's help in packing her dress. In acknowledgement, she scribbled a hasty note in the teacher's diary. Such was my (very indirect) contact with the great.

* * * * *

'SAVE TO DEFEND THE RIGHT TO BE FREE.'
'THE MORE YOU LEND, THE SOONER IT WILL END.'

Such slogans heralded Rochdale's War Weapons' Week in early March. It aimed to attract investments in National Savings Certificates to help cover the war expenditure of £10,000,000 a day.

'Make it a million', the Rochdale posters urged. I responded by topping up the Savings stamps I already had to the required fifteen shillings in order to get my first certificate. I had put aside the regular sixpences from the Livseys, whom I had started to visit again, this time in the Wednesday lunch breaks.

Most schools, offices and factories had started their own National Savings groups and encouraged a friendly rivalry among their employees. At the end of the week, Vera and I walked down to the Town Centre to read the outsize barometer, whose

indicator had been rising daily. It pointed to an astonishing
£1,590,721 and this at a time when the borough population was
under 100,000, and white collar workers earned only £4 a week.

I was helping to win the war, not only by applying my money,
but by knitting for the Services. I had finished a navy scarf and
two Balaclava helmets in Air Force blue. For Empire Day, I
surrendered one penny and, in acknowledgement, received a
standard green certificate decorated with flags, which I duly stuck
in my diary. It averred that I had 'helped to provide comfort and
contentment to the sailors, soldiers and airmen of the British
Commonwealth, who have rallied to the cause of safeguarding
freedom, justice and security'. A verse from Tennyson was
appended:

> *We sailed wherever ships could sail,*
> *We founded many a mighty State.*
> *Pray God our greatness may not fail*
> *Through craven fears of being great.*

Such rhetoric masked the realities of the war situation. The lull
in the air raids during February had ended with renewed attacks
in the spring. By the end of May, the Germans and the British
had lost so many aircraft that an uncanny period of silence
followed. While the Government was maintaining that it had
proved its superiority in the air, ordinary people waited intently
for the German invasion to start. Which part of the coastline
would they choose? 'Dad's Army' was at the ready.

The Americans grew increasingly alarmed as they watched
from afar the Nazi invasion of Yugoslavia and Greece and the
serious isolation of the British on the outskirts of occupied
Europe. US supplies to Britain were under constant threat of
attack by German U-boats which were quietly proliferating. The
enemy blockage of the Atlantic was biting. We all knew of the
dangers in spite of the restrictions on newspaper coverage. Our
battleships were being chased and convoys broken up. Emotions
had run high when in September 1940, a ship carrying British
children evacuating to Canada and the US was torpedoed and
seventy-three of them were drowned.

It was a welcome signal of support when the American Lend-
Lease policy came into effect and Britain did not have to rely on
schoolgirl pennies. I asked Miss Keating what I could do. She said,
"Work hard at school and be well prepared for the future when the
war is over." Through all the vicissitudes, there was an innate

assurance that the conflicts would be resolved in Britain's interests. As a people, we could not be liquidated and taken over (in spite of the plain fact that the Channel Islands, like most of anti-fascist Europe, had. So why should the UK have such a favoured fate?)

My view of my Guernsey home was now beginning to change. I was seeing it from the opposite side of the Channel, more as someone outside it would. As I settled into my billet, school and neighbourhood, I felt the island rather distanced from me and cut off. To survive, I had been forced to separate myself from my parents. They were not available or of any practical use. Already, I was thinking and acting with less emotional reference to them. They were 'other', in a world of their own beyond my reach. In fending for myself, I had found that I could. I now liked my billet more. The initial uncertainty and misreadings had given way to more comfortable feelings. I had proved that I would not be disruptive and I knew the Keatings well enough to appreciate their worth. I centred myself on my billet which had become something of a home. It was more than a place to stay. Summerseat was for school holidays and peripheral.

Strangely, a factor which contributed to this sense of detachment, the viewing of the island as if it were a thing apart, was a lecture by Professor Fleure, himself a Channel Islander. He came to the library in Rochdale and many of us went to see his slides of Guernsey landmarks and views. I was very pleased to recognise Petit Bôt Bay and the Forest Church and to see the two ancient grandmères, the granite menhirs of gatepost size, whose carved faces and female forms had by repute been associated with rites to bring fertility to the fields. One was positioned outside the Câtel Church, very near the home of Ruth and Jean at Les Fontaines and I had seen it. There were pictures of old granite houses much like Rue des Landes and some had an older wing attached. When the grandfather of the family died, the ageing widow went to live in it, leaving the main homestead to the eldest son, who took on the responsibility for the farm or greenhouses. The details came too thick and fast to register and some girls yawned.

I was impressed. I was hearing a presentation of the island's history for the first time and was amazed that an eminent academic thought it worth his while to choose this for his subject. The island story had been given credence and could be respected. It was somehow redeemed from the downgrading emotional attitude which consigned the patois and the Guernsey ethos I had known to a position of inferiority. Guernsey was alright. The lecture gave an objectified view of it. It could be thrown on a screen to be seen from a detached position. We could see it as the place which we had come from and to which we had once belonged. Now we were positioned outside it, the feeling tone had changed. Many exiles have felt the same as they put down roots in a cultural setting which they would have to make their own.

In the meantime, Miss Roughton was making further efforts to perpetuate the school life that had been practised in Guernsey. There was her notable insistence on uniform, even though, at times, the only aspect of it that could be copied was the colour. Then the House system had been given an airing (though with negligible gain) and there was the re-introduction of Latin to mark the school out as academic in its aims and to indicate its status. A good education involved learning Latin, regardless of its usefulness or interest to the learner. It was important mainly for those who might need it for University entrance, an unlikely prospect in our circumstances.

Then, at the end of the Spring term, came Final Prayers. In Guernsey, this had been a grand finale. Songs had been practised to perfection. On the last morning, we had cleared our desks and flapped their lids to the mandatory chant:

> *No more Latin*
> *No more French*
> *No more sitting*
> *   on the hard old bench.*

Then we had filed into the hall to sit cross-legged on the floor while parents poured in to occupy the forms set obliquely to the longest walls. Dignitaries graced the platform with Miss Roughton holding the central position. This was her school. The girls' achievements were acknowledged and speeches were delivered. Before the sad notes of 'Lord dismiss us with Thy blessing' faded into an emotional silence, we had sung the famous Bunyan hymn:

> *Who would true valour see*
> *Let him come hither . . .*

and the rousing strains of

> *Glad hearts adventuring*
> *The way is wide*
> *Valour and faith*
> *Shall shield the pilgrim's side.*

Yes, valour . . .

Miss Roughton stood for valour. She was that valour. It was a noble setting.

Now, in Rochdale, before the Easter holiday began, efforts were made to recreate the atmosphere of the pre-war Final Prayers. The Juniors from Greenbank crossed the town to join the Upper School at Castleton. It was one of the rare occasions when the two parts came together. Those parents who lived in the Rochdale area (though few), were invited, as well as all the billeting hostesses. We waited expectantly for them to come and only Mrs. Spiller (Barbara's mother), and Mrs. Ball arrived. We sang as to a multitude.

My report as usual had been stuffed with A's but as I looked at the line headed 'Conduct', I read, 'Good, but lacks initiative'. Here was the spur to go to the dictionary again. I was put out. For survival and acceptance, I had geared my behaviour to fit in with others. I was undemanding and not-a-nuisance. At Roylelands, at school, in Summerseat and in my billet, I had turned 'accommo-dating-myself-to-others' into a virtue. It was a trait well learned at home. Now it was judged inadequate and even faulty by the very people I had tried to please. My attempts to accept the parameters of each environment and use the opportunities they presented seemed to have gone unnoticed. It wasn't fair. But had I been restrained and too amenable? Unwilling or unable to take a lead?

So I lacked initiative, did I? I decided I would get some.

The Easter holiday in mid-April (1941) was spent in Summerseat. The five of us were there: John, Ruth and Jean, Brian and I. We sped through jig-saws and Monopoly. To get some respite from the unaccustomed noise, Aunty dispatched us all for walks. She said we needed the fresh air.

High on the bleak and elongated ridge of Holcombe Moor, we circled round Peel's Tower. Viewed from afar, its dark grey stone pierced like an obelisk into the skyline. By its prominence, Sir Robert Peel was stamped in solid state against the fleeting clouds of memory. The tower upheld the worth of the industrial north and stood in tribute to the manufacturing zeal of his own forebears, whose wealth derived from cotton.

The monument acclaimed his work in Parliament. Today he is remembered for the Metropolitan police force he set up to cut the crime rate. Recruits were dubbed with his own names and known as Peelers or as Bobbies. He relieved the severe conditions of his day by promoting the repeal of the Corn Laws which had restricted the import of corn and thereby increased the bitter poverty caused by the potato famine of 1848–9.

Standing at the tower's base, we read the warning on the door: KEEP OUT! Was there inside a dangerous staircase leading nowhere? This had the haunting eeriness of *Kidnapped*. But the cold effect of those forbidding walls was to exclude.

We turned our backs on them and on the past. Alive, we sprinted headlong over the toughened turf and scraggy vegetation, which the onslaught of the winds had flattened. Caught in the gusts, we swooped with outstretched arms and let ourselves be flown. Our shrieks to fellow birds were tiny voices lost before they reached their destination. But no one minded. For each of us, this was a lone experience, atop the highest level of our world. Below us were spread-eagled little towns and hamlets and further off, in pockets, the pencil chimneys of the mills emitting smoke which masked the workers' homes and screened off tedium.

The valley of the Ross was little changed across the century.

Before we all returned to school, Uncle brought out his camera to use up the remnants of a film on our small gang of five. This was the last he could obtain in wartime. The shops no longer stocked them.

On April 20th, I noted in my diary that it was Hitler's fifty-second birthday and that I did *not* wish him 'Many happy returns'.

\* \* \* \* \*

"Lucky blighter!" "What did yours say?" The news buzzed round the school that messages from Guernsey were trickling through. They were sent under the auspices of the Red Cross and came via Geneva.

Each message was limited to twenty-five words and written on a telegram-like form. They conveyed little information but the tenor reassured. The Germans seemed to be respecting the islanders, and making few encroachments. There was no mention of shortage or starvation, but perhaps the censors were at work.

Each morning, we waited tensely in the classroom in case there was some news for us. As Miss Roughton walked in, we looked to see what she was carrying and scrutinised her face. Who would be next?

When the phone rang in the Keating household on May 15th, I was surprised it was for me. Uncle and Aunty had received a message! The families were well, they were living in the same houses, John was growing and they had had two messages from us in England.

I felt so light-hearted that when I was sent to the kitchen to fetch something, I skipped all the way back. Surely it was the first time in many years that those floor-boards had creaked to the tripping of excited feet.

As I reflected on the message contents, I wondered if my parents were still living at Les Fontaines, the home of Ruth and Jean. What had happened to Rue des Landes? Were the Germans in it or did my parents consider it too dangerous to live there after the British bombing of the airport in the summer? Such raids could be repeated any time.

I tried to picture little John, now almost old enough for school. Did he remember his brother and sister? I missed the cuddles and the rough and tumble of his toddler days. They were intense and I'd been almost like a mother.

The message Uncle had received was a reply to a ten-word one he had sent at the end of December and was written on the back of the same sheet and signed in Guernsey on February 22nd. The round trip had taken four and a half months, but it was news at last.

A week later, Uncle and Aunty had another message. Our families were well-fed and clothed and my parents were attending Ebenezer. This was a church in town and I wondered why they were going there. They had written on March 4th (1941) in reply to a message sent by Uncle in early November (1940). The double journey had taken over half a year.

When I had the very first message of my own, it was much later, eleven months after the evacuation, and I was back at Summerseat for Whitsun. The tantalising envelope stood waiting on the mantelpiece. It was from my father and I read:

> *Mum, Dad, John, Grans, Grandpa quite well.*
> *Living Manse, King's Rd. Often visit Summerville.*
> *Dad carpentering. Glad you visit Uncle Eugene.*
> *Loving greetings Brian, yourself.*

The manse, on the northern outskirts of St. Peter Port, was the house owned by the Methodist Church, where Rev. R.D. Moore had lived before the German Occupation. I deduced that the local church authorities had allowed my parents to use the house which had been left empty when Mr. Moore was stranded on the mainland in July.

Which of the possible reasons prevented them from living at Rue des Landes? I knew they would never choose to live in town. I could picture the road, but not the house. It was strange to imagine them in that setting. I hoped there was no German sleeping in my bed.

On the reverse side of this welcome reply, I read my original outgoing message with its mandatory wording, sent from the measles room at Roylelands in November:

> *All happy, well. Everything provided.*
> *Much love, Lois.*

Knowing our parents were safe gave us some sense of personal security, but made little difference to the practical running of our lives. We could not consult them or ask for their advice. I felt mine inaccessible. They existed for me in a kind of postponed way. It was as though I was still living out of the case, which I couldn't properly unpack because I knew I wasn't settling. How long would our stay in England last? It had its limits and would end, but when? Always, we had to be ready to go back, so making everything provisional. Emotionally I was staying partly packed ***in case***. . . . Much of myself remained on hold; I was keeping things stored up; not using everything; still treading water, pending our return. I had to preserve an element in me intact to meet my former parents who would re-emerge into my life in unfamiliar guise, altered by their own experiences. I could not afford to change too much myself or we would not know each other. It was too great a risk.

As with many anxieties, mine had their own illogicalities. My life was intended for my parents. If I lived it out too fully and shared it with a lot of people, it would be used up or gone from them to someone else and I would be cheating them of their due. I must somehow save it up and capture its outline in my diary.

Yet we had to manage living in the present and adapt.

The Red Cross messages were so sketchy and took so long to exchange that they could hardly be used for developing relationships, but they were markers to the passage of time. My parents whom I had addressed as Mummy and Daddy in my first-ever letter to them sent from Roylelands, now referred to themselves as Mum and Dad. This made them seem even more distanced and remote as though they had outgrown their previous roles and had given themselves new names to match their changed identity. They lived in a home I hadn't seen, and had an unfamiliar life style under an alien regime whose nature was unknown.

My commonsense told me that I was too old to call my parents Mummy and Daddy any more, but there was a sort of hurt as though I ought to have been party to the new arrangement.

\* \* \* \* \*

In spite of the anguish which sometimes registered in her face, Miss Winifred Roughton must have been pleased with our singing, because she approached the BBC for an opportunity to go on the air.

Her choir in Cheltenham had broadcast a number of times and she knew the ropes. Our March exams had been suddenly interrupted by a summons to Manchester for an audition. We saw for ourselves the rubble at Victoria Exchange railway station and the dereliction along the streets, which seemed to have been hit at random in the senselessness of air attacks. What were the targets? Soon we were queuing up the steps to the side of a bank, before being admitted to the studios which were in hiding over it. The enemy must not know where they were. We were warned not to tell a soul.

Having passed muster, we prepared for the great day. On May 27th a group of forty-five of us, aged twelve to seventeen, returned to the studios and ranged ourselves in neat rows. We were mesmerised by the assortment of tilting booms and microphones being jostled into position. Miss Winifred sat at the piano during the warm-up and her hand cut the air in ever-rising steps.

As the red light came on, the well-known Children's Hour presenter, Nan Macdonald, opened brightly with her customary 'Hello children . . .'. It was the signal for us to sweep into 'Sarnia Cherie'. Two girls introduced the old patois songs, 'Jean, gros Jean' and 'Le jour du lavage' (wash-day) and Frances Hemming in her strong, deep voice gave substance to her solo part in 'The Fisherman's Evening Song'. Marian le Tissier and Maureen le Page harmonised in the duet 'Santa Lucia' and we all trilled our way through 'The Polish National Dance' and 'Morning in Tyrol'. Two songs, 'Verduron' and 'Petronille' were in French.

Miss Winifred was disappointed that 'The Old Folks at Home' was not included. She had composed two lovely cascading descants for it and hoped that the song would carry special meaning to the families in Guernsey if, by chance, they were allowed to hear the programme.

At a press interview, camera lights flashed. Jeanne Guille and Molly Duquemin, the Head Girl, were questioned. It was with amusement and chagrin that we read the heading of a newspaper column a few days later:

LITTLE EXILES SING THEIR THANKS.

# Chapter X

## *'There'll Always Be An England'*

If you had just gulped your tea and you were an adult standing in a school playground watching an ARP warden with a bucket at his feet operating a stirrup pump, you would be receiving your training as a fire watcher. This was a duty which all able-bodied citizens were required to take on. The course would be completed when you had located the handy piles of sand-bags and the First Aid kit, for this knowledge would equip you to deal with sticks of incendiary bombs if they fell on your patch.

The Castleton school premises had to be guarded from enemy action at night when threatened, and there were times when Miss Roughton and a staff member slept on camp beds in the small staff room, their tin hats and gas masks at the ready. Boys were apt to thump on the outside door, when they realised there was someone there they could disturb and escape from. On other shifts, Mr. Wilson stayed in his room at the other end of the building. Once, Yvonne Robilliard, as a senior girl took the place of a teacher when she was ill. By then, older teenagers were required to join those who patrolled the streets at appointed times if the warning sounded. They had to report any damage, but were not allowed to tackle the trouble themselves. It was a good opportunity for two or three senior Boothroyd girls to parade in a tin hat.

Miss Mahy ruefully remembers basic fire and rescue drill with local enthusiasts. They were practising the quick evacuation of a building where people had been 'injured'. As she was lighter than most, she was picked to be the victim of the mock air raid and soon, at the hands of the blunderers, she found herself bumping backwards down the stairs, each painful bruise indicating the need for more expertise.

Miss Keating was exempt from firewatching during the night because of her mother's age and palpitations, but she might occasionally have to be at the High School for 7 a.m. or do her share of weekend duty. Then she would sit in her room and get on with her school work. If she was there on a Saturday afternoon, Mrs. Keating and I would pack tea for three in a basket and walk up the hill to her school. After the indoor picnic, I would stroll along to the kitchen, spick and span in its newness, to do the washing up and chat with the caretaker or any cleaner or teacher who might be on fire watching duty that day.

In an expansive moment of pride, Mrs. Keating had explained to me that the building of the new kitchen had been a triumph for her daughter, who had cajoled the local authorities into providing these facilities, when she found the School Meals Service to be so awful. In her view, it failed to deliver dinners that were sufficiently appetising and nutritious, and this before food rationing seriously affected the menus. Now the school was reaping the benefits and the meals were hot, wholesome and well served.

Like hundreds of other children in the town, I was having those same rejected dinners and they were getting steadily worse. I had developed a technique of swallowing the hated sago and other unpalatable food without really tasting it. Every day, when I returned to my billet, Mrs. Keating always found it difficult to make a bridge between her day and mine. "And what did you have for dinner today?" was her invariable solution to the problem. I treated this as a quiz or minor exam. It never occurred to me that she might want to know. For a long time, I floundered in my descriptions. How was I to say which animal had provided the meat we were given? It bore no resemblance to anything I had eaten at home or in my billet. I was vulnerable, supposing my lack of knowledge to be a sign of social shortcoming, till I hit upon a face-saving idea. I would christen what we had every Monday as 'lamb' and every Thursday as 'beef'. The scrawny, gristly bits floating in watery fluid on Tuesdays and Wednesdays would be soup one day and stew the next. On Fridays, we always had fish for the sake of the Catholics, but as it was drowned in a nondescript white sauce, it was both easy and true to say that I could not recognise the species. Coming from an island where mackerel, whiting and shellfish were plentiful, I knew that it wasn't anything like those.

I avoided describing to Mrs. Keating the stale smell of the so-called Cookery room where we ate. She would have been genuinely shocked and upset if she had experienced the conditions for herself.

When the noise grew too loud, a dinner lady would bang a ladle on one of the large drum-like canisters which contained overcooked cabbage dyed a bright green, and, to the metallic crescendo of triple raps, she would bawl, "Quiet!", "Sit down!", "Shut up!", all to no effect. When she had given up, the boys would line up their ammunition. Soon strings of unwanted gristle would suddenly find themselves propelled overhead to a targeted trestle table and the catapulting fork would prod round for

COMITÉ INTERNATIONAL DE LA CROIX-ROUGE
Palais du Conseil Général

*B.R.C.*
*Mess: Bur: 201* GENÈVE (Suisse) **CML** 5829
4

**DEMANDEUR — ANFRAGESTELLER — ENQUIRER**

Nom - *Name* Breheut 1407

Prénom - *Christian name* - *Vorname* Lois (21)

Rue - *Street* - *Strasse*

Localité - *Locality* - *Ortschaft*

Département - *County* - *Provinz*

Pays - *Country* - *Land*

**Message à transmettre — Mitteilung — Message**
(25 mots au maximum, nouvelles de caractère strictement personnel et familial) —
*(nicht über 25 Worte, nur persönliche Familiennachrichten)* - (not over 25 words,
family news of strictly personal character).

All happy well. Everything
provided. much love
Lois

Date - *Datum* 23 Janv 1941

**DESTINATAIRE — EMPFÄNGER — ADDRESSEE**

Nom - *Name* Breheut

Prénom - *Christian name* - *Vorname*

Rue - *Street* - *Strasse* c/o Mr Robin

Localité - *Locality* - *Ortschaft* Les Fontaines

Province - *County* - *Provinz* Castel

Pays - *Country* - *Land* Guernsey C.I.

| ANTWORT UMSEITIG | RÉPONSE AU VERSO | REPLY OVERLEAF |
|---|---|---|
| Bitte sehr deutlich schreiben | Prière d'écrire très lisiblement | Please write very clearly |

The Red Cross
message with its
mandatory wording,
sent from
'the measles room',
Roylelands. Nov. 1940.

Jean Robin

With Ruth Robin (left) and Miss Holmes.

With Brian at Summerseat, 1941.

The States' Intermediate School for Girls in Rochdale. Summer, 1944.

Part of the second row from the front in the group above.

Margaret Palmer    Kathleen Cochrane    Lois Brehaut      Miss E. Johnson      Miss E. Mahy

Miss E. Naftel      Miss N. H. Roughton      Miss B. W. G. Clayton      Miss F. E. Sayer      Miss E. R. Stewart

Monica Ball      Jeanne Guille      Marie Bisson      Hazel Maplesden

Bazil and
Miriam
Brehaut
with John
taken in 1943
and sent to me in
England in 1945.

Marion
Robin

With Brian and John,
grouped behind Helene
and Eugene Robin, and
Miriam (mother)
in the middle.

All that remained of Milestone, 1945.

In the field where their mother once somersaulted
at Rue des Landes: Margaret, David and Paul (front) 1967.

At the age of seventeen
and later to be the mother
of the three on the left.

another tit-bit to follow. Bawdy jokes delivered in a broad Lancashire dialect whizzed round at equal speed.

In the first year of billeting, I was often the only Guernsey girl staying at school in the dinner hour and felt quite isolated. Over the subsequent months, many efforts were made to reduce the noise level and humanise the pushy atmosphere. Finally, both Guernsey and Castleton staff members were press-ganged into taking supervisory roles and things improved.

Everyone seemed to be involved in dealing with the exigencies of war. Miss Keating responded to the Dig for Victory Campaign by growing potatoes and parsnips in the flower beds at school. Others were urged to do the same. On some Saturday afternoons the headmistress, her maid and the evacuee could be found hard at work on the patch. Here was a new situation, where the old social distinctions were both blurred and blended in the cooperative energy required to deal with the war. Spirits flagged when all the parsnips were stolen!

On many a Saturday, I had to make a bee-line for the bathroom wash-basin when I came back to my billet at lunch-time. My hands were stained a bad yellow as though I had been chain-smoking or working with tomatoes in the Guernsey greenhouses. They had to be scrubbed hard with Vim. The colour came from hessian, poorly dyed into a motley range of greens and browns. A group of staff members and girls regularly joined other volunteers for 'camouflaging' in a small disused warehouse near the Town Centre. We wove strips in and out, up and across large tracts of netting, which were stretched vertically on upright supports. Spread underneath each unworked net was a completed model and all we had to do was to copy on to the top net the design of the strips already woven into the underlying back drop. The finished nets were then stacked ready for their protective work of wartime camouflage.

One cold winter's morning, Doreen Nicholson arrived with her usual enthusiasm, but when Miss Mahy noticed the painful chilblains on her fingers, she sent her home in case they became infected from the dye. Once we arrived with lank hair and dripping chins and noses. We'd been caught in a heavy shower. No one owned an umbrella and our rainwear was not waterproof. Only one person had had the presence of mind to bring a towel. Risking splinters from the floor-boards in bare feet was better than spending the morning in sodden socks and shoes.

\* \* \* \* \*

The Livseys were a very incongruous pair, he and she, and it was a mystery to me why they had married. It seemed that Mrs. L. was Mr. L's third wife and she had been a widow. Snippets of information came from one of our girls who was billeted nearby. Both the Livseys made my weekly visits a welcome interlude in the unappetising run of school dinners.

Her yellowed silken hair was turning white and, in bygone fashion, it was looped into large plaited coils over each ear. Dressed always in black with lace about the throat, she was staid and upright in her bearing with narrow shoulders, low bosom and broad hips. A passé photograph of earlier days showed her to have been enormous. Now, reduced to half her previous size, she still relied on corsets. Rather stiffly, she bent to reach the poker from the grate and aimed it at the coal with dainty prods. By her demeanour and even by the fact that she had him for a husband, she signalled how deprived of affluence she felt. The rooms of the small terraced house were stuffed with cumbrous furniture, a solid legacy from her past. It would have felt more at home in the space we had at Rue des Landes. Like her, it seemed to have outlived its grandeur. Both had seen 'better days'.

Mr. Livsey spoke in a broad Lancashire accent, using northern words I found hard to understand. But somehow his bulbous nose and genial smile were reassuring. He was often plagued with coughing and, as a concession to his health, had been relegated to a minor supervisory role in his mill, prior to his retirement. This undemanding work was clearly underpaid and given to tide him over.

During meals, there was much chuntering between them. She was fond of denouncing Hitler and all his works, so showing solidarity with me, the one she saw as victim. To stop her going too far, he chided mildly, "Nay, Beth! Nay, Beth!" "Dinna fash yourseln" (or so it sounded). I sat back and held my counsel. Perhaps it was on that account the visits were continued.

I was worried about eating their rations. They said they wouldn't ask me if they didn't want me to come. It was a pleasure. I praised a bread and butter pudding sprinkled with dried fruit. It gained the status of 'Lois' favourite' and turned up often. Any food they gave me was much more wholesome than the overcooked off-putting dinners I escaped from. I was very glad to have such tasty meals, a world away from the stale and rowdy Cookery room at school, where we were hoarded.

He always accompanied me to the bus-stop, shuffling diagonally behind. In the cold weather, hunched inside his overcoat with turned-up collar and scarf, he peered down from a great height, smiling on my beret. The peak of his cloth cap masked his bushy eyebrows, and his kind voice emanated hoarsely through the untidy tufts of much moustache. As I was about to climb into the bus, he would take his gloved hand from his pocket and slip me a silver sixpence. "Here! Here!" he would urge, as though to stop me getting on the bus before it was too late. Perhaps SHE must not know the secret.

Once I was given two dresses, unwanted by Mr. Livsey's daughter, engaged in some far-off unnamed hush-hush work for the Ministry of Information. The pink one proved short-lived as the deteriorating fabric tore. The other blazed exotically in flames and yellows on the sky-blue of the tropics. No wonder it seemed out of place in school and church and billet. It was pocked with moth holes and lay abandoned like the forsaken feathers of a bird that's flown.

Miss Keating, looking to my future, thought I could do well in School Certificate, but that I might not reach the required standard unless more consistent provision were made at our school. We didn't have all the necessary books and the timetable was continually being disrupted. She was careful to say that no one was to blame. She asked me if I would like to be transferred to her school. The Rochdale Education Committee was likely to give its consent and she would still be paid the billeting allowance. She consulted Aunty and Uncle who held out no objection and saw it could be helpful. I was happy to go, but there was a small reservation. It meant another change of school, the third in two years and then back to the Ladies' College when we returned to Guernsey. Would that be in 1942 or 3 or 4? No one knew. I thought things over and decided to take the opportunity offered.

Miss Roughton refused to let me go. She said that just before the evacuation, when she had seen my parents, she had given them a solemn undertaking that she would keep a watchful eye on me. I wondered why that promise seemed more special than that given to other parents, but could imagine my father in his anxiety shaking her by the hand and pressing hard, "You will look after our little girl, won't you?" The resulting "I will" would go on ringing in her ears. On that traumatic day in June 1940, most parents had only to stand at a trestle table to register their children and that was that. It was only because her permission was needed for my readmission to the school, that my parents had had to see her in person.

I couldn't see why she was so adamant in her attitude towards me, especially as she had, seemingly, been almost casual about others leaving. In many cases, she could have little long-term guarantee of their security or even of their proper care. But then, this was wartime and in its heady atmosphere everyone was taking risks. Decisions had to be made quickly without thorough safeguards and reflection. And who determined which decisions were hers to make?

My situation was one which pointed up the unresolved dilemmas of our predicament. Where did authority really lie and who had the kind of responsibility which parents exercised?

Since our own parents (in the main) had not conferred authority on anyone except by default, the effect was predictably muddled. Authority was assumed by this person or that body on a rather pragmatic ad hoc basis. Could an uncle, for instance, just announce that a niece would be withdrawn from the school and taken elsewhere? By what right? We didn't know at the time how such decisions were reached.

In practical terms, written permission from the Billeting Officer was now necessary for all the comings and goings, whether at holiday times or when girls were joining or leaving school. And we all had an underlying sense of security. We would not go destitute. The Local Authority was obliged to provide maintenance till we were fourteen (or longer if we extended our education) and they would place us in suitable accommodation and see that we went to school. We knew that if the crunch came, we were not in the hands of our headmistress or billeting hostess or any relation and that something would be done to tide us over till we were old enough to earn money for ourselves. Miss Roughton herself, we felt sure, had a keen sense of personal responsibility for the welfare of the girls while they attended school, regardless of any official authority which might be vested in her. Her caring often went far beyond the call of duty.

Her supervision of the girls ended when they left school and girls had to learn quite suddenly to be responsible for themselves. Ruth remembers this moment. She was returning to Rochdale very late one evening as her train had been delayed. When she let herself into the Hebdens' house, where she was still living after starting work, she crept quietly upstairs and went to bed. It was then that she realised that no one would have known or made enquiries if she had been stranded altogether. She was on her own and would have to become self-reliant.

Those few girls who had no close relations or friends on the mainland to offer some support often felt very isolated when they left school and billet. They had to be enterprising and a few found live-in jobs as a general help or nanny and so created a new base for themselves, tenuous though it might be.

I was never quite sure whether I was tied to Miss Roughton herself or to the school. In either case, the responsibility must relate to my education and not to matters of domestic life, since I was in a billet. I sometimes wondered why my schooling could not have been delegated to a respected figure, one that she knew who lived in the same town. She could easily keep in touch with me if I stayed where I was. But she was keeping her word, she said. It was a matter of honour. This, I reasoned, must be evidence of the valour and faith of the song that had come to epitomise her aims. Such a lofty explanation did not stop me from feeling trapped.

In keeping, Miss Roughton also refused to let me take up my scholarship at the Ladies' College, by then well settled in N. Wales, in Denbigh, near the castle. Since I had been a pupil at the school it was obvious that my parents approved of it. It so happened that Miss Keating had long known its headmistress, Miss Ellershaw, as they had once been on the staff of the same school in Bolton. I gathered that various letters between them had led nowhere. I judged it best not to share all these discussions with the girls at school.

Brian met with no such impediments. Along with others, he had passed the scholarship exam to the Elizabeth College and joined the school in Derbyshire in June 1941. He was sorry to leave his billet, where he had received such excellent care and supervision, but wanted the greater opportunities he thought the College could provide.

Both the Ladies' College and the Elizabeth College had survived the early upheavals. After a short period in Oldham, they had moved in July 1940 to Gt. Hucklow, a small village on the moors in the Derbyshire Peak District. The boys slept in the hangar of the local Gliding Club and in wooden holiday huts which the Unitarians had built for the deprived children of surrounding industrial towns. The girls were in two stone-built houses which had also been holiday homes owned by the Unitarians. These were referred to as Barleycrofts and Nightingale. With the prospect of a bleak and windy winter ahead, arrangements were made to transfer the girls to Denbigh in N. Wales, where Howell's school (a girls' public school) had offered separate classroom accommodation, and the joint use of their facilities. In September 1940, the girls had moved on to Denbigh and were billeted.

Back in Gt. Hucklow, the junior boys of the Elizabeth College occupied the two houses which had been vacated by the girls, and the senior boys were relocated to Whitehall, a large house three miles from Buxton. The school was thus split between two sites some miles apart. Brian joined the Juniors at Barleycrofts in Gt. Hucklow.

Later, it was with some sense of disappointment and frustration that I noted how easy it was for two eligible Intermediate girls, who were offered scholarships to the Ladies' College, to be transferred. No obstacle was put in their way. Yet, in wanting to take up my scholarship, I had a gnawing sense of disloyalty to the Rochdale staff and was made to feel that I was somehow rejecting their hard work and commitment. I was now an Intermediate girl. I decided I would make the best of the opportunities given. Miss Keating had proved my champion and held the torch for me. I sensed a growing confidence in my relationship with her. I had a home.

* * * * *

Rochdale had been singing along with Gracie Fields ever since she had become a leading attraction in music hall and cinemas. Never did the townspeople forget that she had been born over a fish and chip shop in Molesworth Street. She was theirs and in 1937 they had given her the freedom of the borough. Soon she was being labelled the highest paid star in the world. For her mother, a dream had come true, for while she was charring and taking in washing for a local theatrical company, she had said to her daughter, "One day, tha'll lick t'lot, luv". Gracie had.

Now we heard that Gracie was to visit Rochdale. The town was agog. People fondly overlooked the opprobrium she had attracted in 1940, when she had gone to America in the company of her prospective second husband who was Italian and so likely to be interned as an alien in Britain. Public opinion had veered strongly against Italy since the fascist Mussolini had joined forces with Hitler and declared war on Britain and France in June 1940, shortly before our evacuation from Guernsey. Gracie was married in the protective climate of a neutral country across the Atlantic. She was not going to let a little thing like her man's nationality get in the way and she broke through the cool public aftermath with her heartfelt rendering of the patriotic song, 'There'll always be an England' and went on to raise 1½ million dollars for war charities.

One of the highlights of her visit to Rochdale was to be a concert at Turner's, the asbestos works, and she would be broadcasting. As I was strolling through the playground in the lunch break, I was astonished to hear music drifting through the open window of the staff room. Someone must have brought a set to school. I grabbed Delma Torode who happened to have stayed to dinner that day and together we crouched on the hot tarmac directly underneath the window. Safely flattened against the wall we avoided detection and the threat of being sent away. And that's how we got to know what was meant by 'Our Gracie'. We can now be told that, in the States, she received enough approbation to warrant having all her teeth extracted.

My stay at Summerseat for the August holidays was to be interrupted. Miss Warren urged me to join her in the Lake District. Her mother and her niece, Marian, who had become my pen-friend, would be there, in Kendal, where they were lodging on a temporary basis to get away from the bombing in the south. Miss Warren had been offered the use of a hut where the four of us could stay for a few days. By arrangement I met her in Bolton. Her little black Austin 7 was loaded with groundsheets, ropes and a miscellany of camping equipment. She had been with a party from her school, pea-picking on a farm not far from Liverpool. School children were being employed by Hartleys for their canning industry as so many men were caught up in the war. Those who went to such camps thought in terms of war-effort-with-fun till they got there. The pea-fields stretched to the horizon with their endless demands.

I threw my case and blanket into the back of the car and we headed north.

By that time I was getting to know Miss Warren better and felt more at home with her. I remembered my expeditions to Manchester when she had taken me to see the pantomime Cinderella or we had sauntered round the shops. I had admired her sketches of Guernsey beauty spots and recognised at once the old cottages at Le Variouf in the Forest near my home. She had sent me the *Girls' Own Paper*, winter gloves, a jumper and a summer dress.

Marian turned out to be a very unsophisticated girl of fifteen and Mrs. Warren a homely, dumpy woman with grey hair. I could see no resemblance to her daughter, Miss Warren, who was taller and had very straight brown hair which seemed to have been cut off abruptly by quick scissors in orphan style, and never coaxed into the fashionable page-boy styling. Her plain, dull, baggy

clothes and old walking shoes seemed a world away from my
mental picture of an artist, whose appearance, I thought, would
show an appreciation of line and colour and visual effect.

The wooden hut, where we stayed, was called Langdale View, a
name appropriate when there was no cloud hugging the towering
peaks above us. Its corrugated iron roof reacted loudly to the
deluges of rain it suffered. The only bed was assigned to Mrs.
Warren. Marian and I had a camp bed each and Miss Warren
unrolled her blankets on the floor. She plugged a hole in the
flimsy structure when my bedding got a soaking.

In the mornings, we fetched our water from a stream and that
is where Marian and I washed and brushed our teeth. Where
were we supposed to spit? It was a light-hearted moment when I
realised there was nobody there to tell us!

The farm nearby supplied us with fresh milk and eggs. They
had hardly heard of rationing. In the old kitchen, a toddler came
to inspect my plaits. So if he pulled them hard enough, they
would come away in his hands, would they? He reminded me so
much of John.

Miss Warren had been able to save some of her ration of petrol
for this holiday. She had enough to take us to Windermere,
Esthwaite and Grasmere. I saw Wordsworth's grave, but it was not
till later that I came to value his poetry. Hosts of golden daffodils
dancing in the breeze was the image he kept immortalised for
schoolgirls. It was too late for us to see them. But we were
immersed in the majestic grandeur of the mountain scenery and
watched the play of sunshine on the conifers and the broken
reflection of fleeting clouds on ruffled water. I found joy in the
harebells and the heather. We picked wild raspberries which we
threw into Marian's rain hat and ate with our sandwiches in
sheltered hollows. The smooth, barren slopes carved out by
glaciers and the impenetrable blackness of Blea Tarn inspired me
with their elusive beauty and depth.

The mountains seemed so far removed from the grey streets of
Rochdale and the Guernsey beaches. Their immanence reduced
me to a little dot bobbing down-river to an unimportant war, too
distant to be relevant. For eons, they had breathed down on the
valleys, through lurking mists and rainbows. They had knowledge;
they transmuted their dour contours to the sinister in moments.
Then, impulsively, they changed expression to the wildness of
their brooding mauves.

Our final expedition took us to Grange-over-Sands, where the
sea was grey and distant and we saw how poles were embedded in

the beach to stop the German planes from landing. Between the trips, we played word games and I knitted khaki gloves for the army. We even heard the piercing sound of Gracie distorted on the battered wireless. Then it was time to go. I packed inside my case Miss Warren's gift of a small print of Crummock Water, cupped in a welter of undulating mauves.

I had hardly paid attention to Miss Warren's daily trips to the farmhouse telephone to find out if her home was standing.

* * * * *

My disintegrating diary for that summer of 1941 bulges with a folded newspaper page. Over maps of the Russo-Polish frontier are splayed black arrows pointing eastwards. By the middle of August 1941, the German armies were only 150 miles from Leningrad, the key city guarding Russian trading opportunities in the north.

For a time, it looked as if a German victory in the USSR was assured and that Hitler's armies would be released to head west and concentrate on the invasion of Britain. How would the Channel Islands fare then? Would they be used as a German springboard for attacks on the south coast, thus turning them overnight into prime targets for British retaliatory measures? This could not be ruled out. After all, the RAF had already strafed the Guernsey airport in August 1940 and that for reasons which seemed quite flimsy. Suddenly the islands could become pawns in giant hands, an eventuality feared at the time of our evacuation.

In British pubs, local pundits guessed that Hitler might be confident enough to split his forces and deploy large contingents across the Channel ready for invasion. So where would the landings be? They laid bets on Hastings or Dover, Cromer or the Tees estuary, as long as they were far enough away from their own locality. Nearby beaches were dismissed as highly unsuitable: 'Too easily spotted', 'Too far from anywhere', 'Too near the airport'. The speculators had become instant tacticians, but 'Too near us!' was the unspoken dread in everyone's mind.

Yet, somehow, there was a feeling of camaraderie, of all being in it together, with Churchill at the helm. It was said in later years, that his reputation as a leader lay in his ability to give voice to people's dreams and strengthen their resolve. From his first days at Downing Street, he had harnessed the spirit of honour and determination, distilling it into memorable phrases.

*'One bond unites us all, to wage war until victory is won and never to surrender ourselves to servitude and shame, whatever the cost and the agony may be. . . . Upon all . . . the long night of barbarism will descend unbroken, even by a star of hope, unless we conquer, as conquer we must, as conquer we shall.'*

*'I have nothing to offer but blood, toil, tears and sweat.'*

It didn't seem to matter that he never travelled by bus or tube and rarely spoke to the ordinary worker or that subsequent speeches lacked lustre. The tenor of his earlier perorations had been requoted into everyone's psyche. He had become the bulldog of the cartoons, ponderous and good humoured, one whose casual lighting of a cigar showed he could blow smoke into the face of the enemy. Behind this public frontispiece, the feelings of regional independence stayed screened. As far as the war was concerned, Channel Islanders identified with the UK, although they were always proud not to be part of it.

When Churchill's vibrant tones boomed into the drawing room at 22, Edmund St. at the end of August 1941, the note was one of reassurance. The Atlantic Charter had been signed. Roosevelt, representing the vast reserves of the USA, was supportive without actually entering the war. The American Lend-Lease policy would continue and food would be sent to us across the ocean. We need not feel quite so vulnerable. Everything would be alright. This was the mandatory mind-set required of us all. Perhaps we chose to be lulled by those lionised Churchillian speeches, which we latched on to for their chuckling references to Hitler, just as if he could be laughed off, provided there was enough determination to humiliate him.

Clearly everything was not alright. How could it be when such horrific slaughter was decimating thousands of people on both sides in Russia and when bombing had already demolished the core of many British cities? We knew this, even though we were not told publicly which they were or how extensive the damage, and we knew that many European cities had also suffered from destructive attacks by the British.

Nothing seemed to matter till more of this frenzy had been expended, leaving one or other side impotent. All the appalling killings inflicted by both sides were supposed to stop the opponent. Claims to rightness and honour seemed now to be obscured by the obsessive need to get the upper hand. And for what? To secure again each country's pre-war boundaries?

Re-establish the status quo? Was that so sacrosanct and right that
it justified the slaughter? It was clear that nothing would ever be
the same again and we would never revert to Square One. I
thought a lot about the dilemmas and was mystified. I looked at
Uncle as one who had been personally involved in the First World
War. He'd been promoted to the rank of sergeant. He must have
given orders to others. How could he? He didn't seem a
bloodthirsty type, nor, as far as I could tell, did he feel guilty.
People seemed to think that war was inevitable, but that their side
would win. Clearly this had not been the case for Guernsey or for
France, so why should it be any different for England and the rest
of the British Isles?

And were the Germans that barbaric? They were often
ridiculed for their Prussian militarism, the goose step and the
swastika. But I thought of all the Red Cross messages I had seen
from friends at school and from our own relations. The Germans
seemed to be relating to the islanders in a civil manner. There
was little hint of interference in people's lives, except to take over
empty houses and regulate food and fuel supplies, an
understandable necessity. As far as we knew, the islanders still had
their wireless sets, they were not being made to speak German
and they were going about their everyday lives much as before
and unmolested. We had stopped being afraid of atrocities on the
island.

But the game of war, once started, must be played out, it
seemed, whatever the cost. We did what was expected of us and
carried on with the usual routine. There seemed to be little
alternative.

September 1st was rumoured to be the day selected by Hitler
for his triumph . . . THE INVASION OF BRITAIN. We were back at
school already, since we had only a month's holiday. We glanced
up from our desks and gave each other knowing looks. 'Not yet!'
they said.

While our evaluation of German intentions, their methods and
ultimate aims swung round rudderless, so a down-turn came
when news reached us that an Intermediate boy was nearly killed
in an Oldham raid. A bomb hit his billet before the siren
sounded. The son of the house and the mother were killed, while
he and the father and daughter survived. Did this devastating
experience prompt some self-questioning by the Heads of the two
Intermediate schools? Had they been wise to stay in such
industrialized towns when they had offers of safer reception

areas? What if a Guernsey child was killed? How would they explain their policy to the parents?

Vera was now anxiously watching for the postman. It was twenty weeks since she had heard from her husband. He was in the Forces far away in some undisclosed part of the world. She had jokingly dismissed him as gormless, someone who happened to be around at a convenient time. (They had worked in the same establishment, he in the garden and she in the house.) News came that his friend in the same regiment had been killed. Now she was angry. "If they go and put lead through my ole man, I'll go and make lead to put through them!" And she went to work in the munitions factory in Chorley, so enormous, Miss Keating said, that it took several minutes to pass it on the train.

It was now October (1941) and the household was without live-in help. Soon, Mrs. Neaven was found, but she could come only from 8 to 11 a.m. So Miss Keating had to rush home for lunch to check that all was well. In the afternoon Mrs. Keating managed on her own, snoozing, reading a library book from Boots and making little tapestry purses to be sold for Red Cross funds. The cat kept her company and often slept in black and white oblivion on her knee.

This was no ordinary cat. It behaved like a dog. Miss Keating would stand in the centre of the drawing room and throw a thimble, sometimes with such force that it would ricochet back from the skirting board. The cat pounced and brought it back in its mouth, dropping it at her feet. On January 10th 1942, puss deigned to sit in my lap. The occasions were so rare that I noted them in my diary. There was a well understood rule that whoever was nursing the cat should not have to move. Someone else would put coal on the fire or fetch wool. On no account must the cat be disturbed.

I shared with Miss Keating the task of guarding it at those times when tom-prowlers were likely to be lurking in the privet hedge. Although once or twice it escaped, there were never any kittens. Its name 'Kitty' was seldom used and it was simply addressed as 'cat' or 'puss'. Much was made of my tendency to drag out the vowel to 'Poossy' and this aberration was ascribed to my Guernsey background (or backwardness?).

I noticed that Puss sometimes received greater attention to its creature comforts than I did. It amused me. Indulgently, I told myself it didn't matter. It was only a cat. When Mr. Oliver Keating was due to visit his mother it had to be taken in a basket to a cat

shelter. The fur set off his asthma. I rarely saw him as he taught in
Derbyshire and came to Rochdale in the school holidays, when I
had gone.

"Don't linger!" Mrs. Keating warned. On my way home,
between school and home, there lay a zone of danger. It was the
Town Centre, where crowds of boys poured out from the High
School and queued for buses or shouted raucously across the
streets. Did she seriously think I would be attracted to those pock-
faced louts, who were always swinging their satchels at each other
and dropping litter? Or perhaps she thought I would wander
through Woolworth's and fritter away my meagre pocket money
on gaudy trivia? As I was never tempted to either hazard, I could
not see the point of continuing the warnings. Did she fear I
would go off the rails or was it her daughter's reputation which
concerned her? But perhaps it was just a matter of being back in
time for tea. In my own mind, I unkindly dismissed her anxiety as
the pointless preoccupation of an old lady out of touch with
school behaviour.

In the evenings, the drawing room was a hive of industry. I was
doing my homework and the others were mending or knitting for
the Forces. Miss Keating might be sewing a fresh white collar on a
dress to liven it up for school next day. Clothes rationing had
been introduced in June 1941 and each adult had an allocation
of sixty-six coupons for the ensuing twelve months. The
newspapers had sprung the scheme on retailers and customers
alike and the unused margarine coupons in our ration books
were reassigned, thus making it possible to start the scheme
overnight.

The newspapers had been fulsome in their explanations:

> *There is enough for all if we share and share alike.*
> *Rationing is a way to get fair shares.*
> *Fair shares  –   when workers are producing bombs and
>                         aeroplanes and guns instead of frocks, suits and
>                         shoes.*
> *Fair shares  –   when ships must run the gauntlet with munitions
>                         and food rather than with wool and cotton.*
> *Fair shares  –   when movements of population outrun local
>                         supplies.*
> *Rationing is not the same as shortage. Rationing or fair shares is
> the way to prevent a shortage without interfering with full war
> production.*

Examples were given of the number of coupons needed:

| | Men | Boys | | Women | Girls |
|---|---|---|---|---|---|
| Overcoat | 16 | 11 | Coat | 14 | 11 |
| Jacket or blazer | 13 | 8 | Woollen dress | 11 | 8 |
| Pullover or jersey | 5 | 3 | Blouse or jumper | 5 | 3 |
| Trousers | 8 | 6 | Skirt | 7 | 5 |
| Shirt or woollen combinations | 8 | 6 | Overalls or dungarees | 6 | 4 |
| Pants or vest | 4 | 2 | Petticoat or combinations | 4 | 3 |
| Pair of boots or shoes | 7 | 3 | Pair of boots or shoes | 5 | 3 |

Miss Keating who liked to wear a different outfit to school every day, soon began to feel the pinch. She blew sixteen coupons on a new suit and by that time had very few left, relying on her mother's promise to pass on spare ones. Mrs. Keating's own stock of underwear and home-made winter dresses of thick woollen material lasted a long time and would not need such quick replacement.

Miss Mary Keating occasionally came for a few days. The two sisters enjoyed shopping trips to locate pretty unrationed yarn and soon they were knitting open-work stockings and jumpers to ring the changes. When the waist stretched in an unflattering way, they sewed narrow unrationed elastic behind the welt line to keep the look of trimness which they loved.

By that time, Miss Mary Keating was based, in part, on Gt. Gransden, then in Bedfordshire, where some of her school had been evacuated to escape the London bombing. The girls were billeted in local homes and the mistresses who had gone with them were adapting to the task of teaching their second subjects when needed. She herself was revising her Latin and keeping two or three lessons ahead of a class. She must have learned the language once since it was a subject required for her first degree in English and for her second in Law. In her day, those who aspired to the headship of a London grammar school needed an extra degree to prove their worth and, before her appointment, she had worked at Law in the evenings, while she was teaching full-time during the day.

Once or twice, when her health permitted, Mrs. Keating went to stay with her in the village.

In holiday time, the Keating sisters, who had no car, often went away together to walk over the moors and get away from the demands of school and home and war. Sometimes, they were joined by Miss Knight, the Games mistress at Hornsey High School and a great friend of Mary's. They would base themselves in Whaley Bridge or Goathland on the Yorkshire moors and when freed from the usual constraints, who knows what they talked about or thought?

In this quiet period of adaptation, anxiety was reduced. We were all acclimatised to the war and making things workable within the restrictions. I, for one, was more emotionally attuned to those around me and perhaps they to me. I felt more settled and firmly based. I recognised the demands on me more readily and could respond with greater spontaneity. I was freer in the use of English and less guarded. I did not have to ask myself, 'Is it alright to say this?' I knew. There was less of the automaton as the sense of shock wore off and I didn't have to keep myself so deeply hidden.

My case was shoved into an attic cupboard and only brought down for the holidays in Summerseat.

# Chapter XI

## *'Keep the Home Fires Burning'*

The Red Cross messages now started arriving a little more frequently. By the end of 1941, after eighteen months' separation, I had received four short messages from my parents, all written on the back of my outgoing ones. (At that stage, they were not allowed to write except in reply.) Our network of relations on the island had evidently been reassured about our welfare and, knowing we were settled, they were now ready to concentrate on detail and even ask a few questions.

For my part, I had, early on, twice sent a closely written page of news under the auspices of Thomas Cook, the travel agents, who, through many connections in Europe, had negotiated a means of conveying mail to the islands for a short period after the Occupation. We thought they used facilities in Lisbon, since Portugal was a neutral country, but we had no means of knowing whether those very early letters had reached their destination.

Soon it was the Red Cross that was monitoring communications and through Geneva. There were strict limits to the number of messages we could send and the usual wartime censorship rules applied with their ban on place-names and references to events which could interest the enemy.

From Roylelands I had sent two such messages (at that stage restricted to ten words), then later, I had written three of twenty words, taking advantage of the increase allowed.

At the end of November (1941), I was delighted to have a reply to the message I had sent on June 8th. My outgoing one read:

*Living headmistress, High School. Methodist. Very kind. Celebrated Gran's birthday. Both keeping diaries. Happy school. Growing. Five feet two. Lois.*

Their reply, written on the back said:

*June message delightful. Continue diaries, education. What about music, hair? Everyone well. John lively, strong. Longing for reunion. Taking care of your treasures. Love, kisses.*

It had been signed on September 1st, so had taken only three months to come. That was quick! Things were looking up!

I thought of little John and pictured him chortling as he trundled a wobbling toy up the stony yard at Rue des Landes.

Then I came to. That image of a waddling toddler was already out of date when I left home. He must be learning English words, writing his name, getting ready for school. But were there any kindergartens on the island now?

And which of my belongings were being classified as treasures? I thought of the scrawny blue rabbit I had hugged to baldness and the stamps I had collected since Aunty Am had sparked my interest. A small black notebook recording the important events of my life had been left safely tucked into a canvas pochette, which I had covered with gaudy mauve and yellow stitches. Were the small brown ostrich feathers still wrapped inside a plea from my pen-friend in the Gold Coast to send a camera in return? I hoped the sachet for my handkerchiefs was safe. Of the palest blue satin, its lovely sheen was embroidered with a posy of red flowers framed in a white ribbon tied in dainty bows. This had been a present for my ninth birthday from Aunty Helene (my mother's sister) and it was stitched with the greeting 'Loving Christmas Wishes'. She knew I'd like it. Another of her gifts was a little mirror with a beautiful handle of patterned green glass. Were all those things retrieved? No doubt the furniture itself was still at Rue des Landes. So was there really a German in my bed? I still didn't have the answer.

What difference could any of these conjectures make to my life now? I pushed my memories back. What did a few items I had once cherished amount to anyway? If I ever had them back, I would probably stow them away in a drawer, unused and half-forgotten. I thought of my mother's implied exhortation to be brave. It must mean being willing to turn away from all you couldn't have. Everyone was sacrificing something in this war. I had become very pragmatic and dismissive of the things I'd prized (or so I thought). They belonged to a world I could no longer own. It had gone irrevocably. We were settled into a new life, leaving the other in a shadowland behind the present. Kicking the cat could alter nothing. We'd been forced to come to terms with being cut off and if we couldn't accept our new life styles, it was embarrassing to say so, tantamount to an admission of failure: we lacked courage; could not adapt or relate to people; we were socially inept or emotional miseries. Being unhappy seemed to be equated with being inadequate and this was inexcusable.

In my two single-page letters sent through Thomas Cook in the early days, such 'reasoning' lay behind my absurd zeal to assure my parents I was happy. Since I had never had to consider for myself how to create conditions that gave rise to happiness, I resorted to making use of the impressions thrown up by those around me: if you had food and relations on the mainland you were OK. Happiness consisted in having immediate needs met and a fall-back or guarantee of long-term security if all else failed (provided, of course, you could be free of bombs, invasion and illness). Anything extra was the 'plus' you might receive if people were kind, but you didn't deserve it and couldn't claim it as of right. You could manage without all but the basics.

Aside from this, I was worried about my parents' state of mind. I had sensed their great anxiety in the rushed conversations prior to the evacuation. Could their children manage without them? I was afraid they would imagine us shrinking away into nervous wrecks and did not know how to describe the opposite state of mind, which might include confidence and a sense of wellbeing. In a sort of role reversal, I wanted to reassure . . . 'Don't worry! I am happy, but are you? Are you managing?'

In those two crammed notes sent through Thomas Cook, I had so overdone my happiness that I wonder if they laughed or cried – if they received them.

While I had made great strides in self-reliance and independence, there was still a feeling of life being lived in the double, rather like the parallel panels of a radiator. The front one was visible, warm and seen to function, while the shadowed one behind was doing its work of circulation, joined, but obscured. Dust was settling in the darker hidden places, which no one was concerned with, as long as the system as a whole was working.

If the outer and inner areas failed to synchronise, a valve might be shut down to make life tolerable. A few girls exploded or seemed unusually reserved when the expectations, values and behaviour in their billets differed widely from that of their own homes, and tensions mounted. It might be too risky and rude to resist and, without the maturity to cope, some vented their resentful feelings in school. "The bitch told me to . . .", "I can't stand the way he chews his food", "How could she start the cooking without washing her hands?" Something had to give.

When Mrs. Keating noticed that I was particularly subdued, she would tease mildly and quote a sermon text which had once made a great impression on her. 'Put off thy sad countenance.' I gathered one was supposed to rejoice no matter what. If I had known the Old Testament more thoroughly, I might have dared to quote from Ecclesiastes, 'By sadness of countenance, the heart is made better.'

\* \* \* \* \*

As Christmas 1941 approached, the term ended with a concert which included a Nativity play. Margaret Palmer, as Mary, swathed in the traditional blue, flung her arms wide open and asked incredulously, 'How can these things be?', but the pièce de résistance was Molly Frampton's majestic Herod, who raged imperiously with thwarted anger. It was frightening in its intensity and carried in its resonance the expression of real emotion, which none of us dared to voice directly. Did Miss Winifred sense this too and encourage her to channel her frustration into a form that could be contained? She had Molly rehearse the scene far more often than was strictly necessary.

As the innkeeper's wife, I had to say to Joseph when he discovered there was no accommodation,

> *'Ah: Thy good lady looks but poorly. Get thee to the stable. There is straw there and the beasts will keep thee warm.'*

Elizabethan-style language seemed obligatory. Miss Winifred had probably made up the words herself.

The afternoon of December 16th was the great occasion. £25 had been raised by the sale of tickets and donations. Uncle and Aunty arrived at Champness Hall rather late and had to sit on the front row. Mrs. Neaven was there and Mrs. Keating. We opened with Sarnia Cherie and carols such as 'Minuit Chrétien' and 'Good King Wenceslas'. Then we listened to the two Misses Roughton play various violin and piano pieces and we danced in 'Hungarian' dress (mainly blackout material and crêpe paper streamers). The L VI[th] presented *The Amateur Astrologer*, a short play I had depicted on a poster. Whoever drew the curtains for the Nativity scene I was in failed to pull them back far enough and I doubt whether I was seen or heard.

I rushed back to my billet as Aunty and Uncle had been invited to tea, so that the Keatings might meet them. Mrs. Keating was there to greet them when they arrived, but it was with some amusement and embarrassment that she explained how she had walked all the way up the hill with a minister and his wife and it was only at the last minute that she discovered they were the wrong ones and not her guests!

One of Mrs. Keating's memorably wry comments after attending one of the earlier school concerts was focused on Miss Roughton: "I wouldn't allow one of my daughters to walk on to a platform looking so down at heel."

I wondered how many other people had been sizing up the

Roughton shoes. And Mrs. K. must be a game old bird to go. I saw there could be merriment in social observation.

Before breaking up for Christmas 1941, we gave a similar concert for Castleton school and they gave one for us. Their tap dancing was excellent, but their sketches came over in such a broad Lancashire dialect that we failed to grasp much of the content. The enjoyment offset the dismal experience of being grabbed by the boys in the dinner room and kissed forcibly under the mistletoe.

When I went to Summerseat for the holidays, Uncle was optimistic. Hostilities would end in 1943, he predicted.

Some shared his view. People were elated by America's entry into the war. The damage done to their fleet during the bombing of Pearl Harbour by the Japanese earlier in December had stunned them into action. This augured well for Britain, but the scale of operations was rapidly escalating, for Britain declared war on Japan, and both Germany and Italy on the USA. There lay unpredictable dangers in the Far East as well as nearer home. Much was in the balance, although, for us, the detail and challenge were obscured. In the nature of things, the newspapers carried only what the public could be told and few of us saw them or read them, but we heard the news on the wireless and most of us were quite well informed.

Ruth and Jean did not come to Summerseat for Christmas. By that time, Ruth was working and she had only one or two days off and was to stay with the Hebdens where she was still living. Jean's billeting hostess would not allow her to join her sister. She had made other arrangements, she said.

Ruth had been at Turner's, the large asbestos company, since September. She had left school after due consultation with Uncle and Aunty and with Mrs. Norris, who had become almost like a guardian to the sisters. In retrospect, Ruth is glad that, as a clerk, she was assigned to the Export Office, since this underground complex was separated from the main works where a fine layer of yellow dust covered everything. This was where firefighting suits, asbestos brake linings and such items of wartime apparatus were made. While today the hazards to health are banned, in those days people who coughed unduly or felt ill were merely thought unfortunate. All the entries in the ledgers were done by hand and Ruth was fascinated to be dealing with correspondence from Australia, the Pacific and S. Africa. Such far-off places had previously been only names in the atlas.

Wages for school leavers were low and after she had paid for her lunches in the canteen and given the equivalent of her billeting allowance to Mrs. Hebden, there was very little left for clothes and other essential requirements, sometimes only two shillings and sixpence. Naturally she was disappointed.

I was glad to spend holiday time with Brian and I knitted him a Balaclava helmet and gloves for the windy moors of Derbyshire. John, Aunty's nephew, was positioned in the midst of cables, screws and knobbly chunks of metal, intent on constructing a wireless set out of all the pieces.

On Christmas Day, we all listened to a lunch-time broadcast by Channel Islanders. There was a real hope that the folks at home might hear it. Someone's Red Cross message from Guernsey had got by the German censors with the phrase 'Listen to Big Ben'. Since this famous clock struck just before the news bulletins, we deduced there must be some people in Guernsey still hearing them. Now, on the air, the familiar strains of Sarnia Cherie came from 'children in the west'. Wartime mystery had to shroud their whereabouts. Muriel Lucky, a well-known Guernsey soloist, performed and a Jersey woman explained how she used to make butter.

The winter was very severe. Snow fell for days and the school playground had a lovely thick layer of whiteness. It did not take long for the Castleton boys and the older Intermediate girls to get into an all-out scuffle. Islanders who had thought a few snowflakes were special, pummelled snowballs into ammunition. The trodden areas turned black, people got wet, some slipped, ice slithered down necks, laughter and shrieks pierced the neighbourhood. Miss Roughton was appalled. She called the older girls to account for their undignified behaviour and messy appearance. They ought to have set a better example. The honour of the school was at stake. Mr. Wilson was urged to restrain his pupils. No one was allowed to pick up snow. For days, Miss Roughton's expression was forbidding. Everyone moved within an aura of utter disgrace. It was not a good phase in the relationship of the two schools.

At home, the bathroom cistern was frozen and I was sent to get paraffin for the lamp to thaw it out. The snow had to be shovelled from the gate to the front door and bundles of kindling wood fetched from a little shop to light the fires. Much of the time was spent in dealing with the weather conditions. At school, when the rain finally indicated the start of the thaw, water trickled down the inside of the walls and flooded the floors. We were sent home.

In spite of the difficulties, Miss Keating managed to get a party from her school to the Opera House in Manchester, and I was included. We saw John Gielgud and Gwen Ffrangcon-Davies take the lead parts in *Macbeth*. It was a wonderful experience, where the interplay of the macabre and evil ambition advanced the tragedy. I was intent on mastering the details of the plot. Shakespeare was still new and held to be important, so I must know the plays.

Soon afterwards, I was back at the Opera House when Miss Warren took me to see the Tchaikovsky ballet *The Sleeping Princess*, in which Margot Fonteyn and Robert Helpmann were billed in a Pas-de-Deux. As I knew the story already, I felt freer to absorb the beauty of form and movement.

As older girls left the school, Miss Roughton was seriously worried about its perpetuation. To her relief, she was allowed an intake of fourteen or fifteen scholarship girls to swell the small core of twenty-seven Juniors who remained after parents and friends had claimed the rest. The first batch of new girls had arrived in the autumn (1941), a year late, and came from Alderney and various Guernsey Parish Schools scattered throughout the country. The second quota came in February (1942). Among the newcomers were some I knew: Betty le Page, whose father worked at Milestone but was now evacuated to Stockport, Muriel Blondel, who had attended the Forest Sunday School and Joan Watson, whose father drove the buses which regularly passed Rue des Landes. As it was, there was little chance to see them, as the Seniors did not go to Greenbank and the Juniors seldom came to Castleton.

I was delighted that Jean was among the twelve Juniors transferred to the Seniors in January. Now I could see her sometimes in break to have a chat. After much emotional distress, which she told us little about at the time, she had been moved from her original billet and was now living with Ruth at the Hebdens. At last the sisters were together. There were only occasional signs of the spirited little girl, full of energy, bounce and sparkle, whom we had known in Guernsey. She had lost the ability to concentrate and had fallen behind with her school work. Through all the turmoil, she had felt herself to be in God's hands and an inner strength, together with confidence in her absent parents, brought her through. Her father, Uncle Arthur, like mine, was a Methodist Local Preacher with a firm faith and strength of purpose and her old home influences, combined with new kindnesses, stood her in good stead. The time came when she looked thoughtfully out of the window and, today, remembers saying to herself, "Now I'm going to be alright."

Staff continued to cycle to and fro between the two parts of the school, except for Miss Johnson who remained firmly positioned at the younger end. She had a bed-sitting-room in a private home and so did not share the communal life of the rest of the staff, based at 13, Edmund St., 34, William St. and Boothroyd. Someone said she had been due for a major operation at the time of the evacuation and there were periods when she was ill and absent. She worked hard for the Guides, later becoming a Captain, and recruited many girls into their ranks.

To me she remained rather remote and inaccessible throughout the whole of the war and although I had been in her Transition Class in Guernsey at the age of seven, all personal recognition seemed to have faded away. My prevailing image of her is of a dominant figure in a navy blue skirt and cardigan, with a satin white blouse stretched over an ample bosom. She had short dark curly hair which was greying and puffed out over the ears and, on her, contrived to look old fashioned. She seemed always to be trying to put kindness into a rather piping voice, which sought primly to keep everyone under control without lapsing too often into the asperity of a clipped command. She was well liked by some and deeply resented by others. Her talent for creating percussion instruments out of discarded and broken oddments was much appreciated and she taught some girls to conduct the others with zest and prepared them all for the many concerts so loved by the Roughtons.

Those who had a crush on Miss Brittain, the Games and P.E. mistress, had felt the wrench when she left in November 1941 to join the WAAFS (Women's Auxiliary Air Force). Since the beginning of that year, when staff numbers were drastically reduced, she had come to the school only once a week. The rest of the time, she was deployed to other schools. We had always responded vigorously to her cheerful instructions and could run a mile after her lessons. Her smiles and blushes had won her many devotees, who liked a sign of vulnerability in their heroine. Every fleeting expression was avidly analysed and taken to heart. "Did you see how pink she went when you asked her for her autograph?", "Let me see her signature!", "Do you like her writing?"

With some, she attempted a few 'human reproduction' lessons and one class remembers the course being broken off with two worms lying side by side on the blackboard, presumably in some state of expectancy.

One day, the replacement for her arrived in the hall where we were waiting. Her navy tunic dress, with the low waist of the twenties, suggested the lacrosse-playing school ma'am of pre-war comics. In movement, it revealed angular knees and bony legs bowed slightly outward. She wore soft black dancing shoes with the laces crisscrossed around the ankles and her grey hair was flattened down by a hair net and band which encircled her head. Yes, Miss Roughton was to take us for Eurhythmics, a term which she thought might suit the slow movement to music which she was to direct. As she sprang with pointed foot outstretched, broad grins spread contagiously. No one could hide them. We dared not catch another's eye. Her sister interpreted her commands on the piano, and the Castleton pupils carried on regardless behind the closed doors of the adjoining classrooms.

By this time, we were getting used to Miss Reed. She had arrived the previous autumn (1941) to take over Biology from Miss Brown, whose health had broken down. I had felt her departure keenly. As the leader of my group when we were evacuated, she was the one on whom I had at first depended. Her lessons were nice and her drawings neat.

Miss Reed was also to take some Games and the Geography teaching at Castleton, thus relieving Miss Naftel to spend more time at Greenbank.

If we wanted to remember Miss Naftel by a motif, it would surely have to be the outline of Africa with the equator drawn below the bulge. How could we ever forget that shape which she chalked on the blackboard in nearly every lesson?

In a brisk and business-like manner, Miss Reed set out to tackle the backlog of work. We had alarming gaps to fill if we were to cover the School Certificate syllabus in time. As she stood before a class, tall, slim and dark-haired, with a 'victory' roll so typical of wartime styling, her no-nonsense manner and high expectations made her popular with many. She brushed aside any demonstration of a school girl crush and kept us all at arm's length like a working force that needed shaping.

Those who baulked at her methods soon found themselves smiled on with sardonic amusement, quickly reinforced with reserves of sarcasm. Molly Frampton was the one in our group who found her Achilles heel and liked to take her on. She enjoyed the element of entertainment. The bait was laid before the lesson began and the collusive scene was set. In that classroom, there were individual desks each with their seats attached. Molly slouched sideways with one knee drawn up to her chin in mock comfort and relaxation. She would be 'deep' in a novel. Although she couldn't see without her glasses, she would have them dangling from a corner of her mouth for greater effect. The charade had begun.

"Molly! If you can bear to give attention to your surroundings, you will notice that we are about to start on the respiratory system." . . . "Time to set aside the jolly little story." . . . The tone got sharper and more demanding till Molly moved an arm or leg to signal she would be sitting up in discreetly regulated stages. The big waste-of-time had happened.

If someone smuggled into school *No Orchids for Miss Blandish* or cheap paperbacks of gangster exploits, it was Molly who'd be the first to read them.

\* \* \* \* \*

Concerts often seemed to come in spates, one following close on the heels of another. Sometimes they were given at the invitation of the Salvation Army or a local church. Before each one, the timetable was disrupted for practices. The songs were always of Miss Winifred's choice, in line with the cultural values of the old traditions which the Roughtons cherished. 'Orpheus with his lute made trees. . . .' It made about as much sense as that. We performed it beautifully. Never once did we sing a wartime song or any of those made popular by Deanna Durbin or Gracie Fields.

The playlets and sketches Miss Winifred produced for the senior concerts were childish and undemanding, appropriate for a nine year old. Their value was confined to getting us accustomed to the stage. It was all very safe, because the audiences were well disposed and never critical in our hearing. When she had overcrammed the programme, she pressed on through much scraping of chairs and swinging of doors. People had to catch buses and get up early for work the following day.

Some girls responded well to the stimulus of the public occasion and the thrill of drama took hold. A few were keen to develop their singing techniques. Marian le Tissier and Frances Hemming were two of the most gifted soloists and could hold an audience enthralled. Marian's clear soprano voice blended well with Maureen le Page's alto in 'Santa Lucia' and Frances perfected 'Where e'er you walk', 'O for the wings of a dove', 'The Blind Ploughman' and 'Swanee River'.

When Miss Winifred wanted us to learn a few Guernsey French songs for the concerts, we copied them from the blackboard. She said she had consulted someone who knew the patois and she explained their meaning. She did not think to ask anyone of us who spoke it, but, as it turned out, the vocabulary of the songs she unearthed consisted of many old fashioned words no longer used and the patois speaking girls did not know them. I had never heard the songs at home or at Summerville or Milestone. They must have been older than my grandparents' generation and not in general use anymore. If she realised this at all, it did not seem to concern her. We were never asked about the patois songs we did know and they remained buried in childhood memory, unwritten and unsung. It was unthinkable that the school should use them. We sang carols in Latin instead and so it was that through their beauty we were conscious of a longer continuum. Here was the form and stuff of old-age praise.

In Guernsey, I was used to attending church services in French. The congregation sang the hymns heartily and I knew many of them well. So French was for the old? It didn't matter. I got the gist.

Now, we had to concentrate on formal ways of learning the language, by the step-by-step traditional methods. Miss Roughton's lessons were far from systematic and so progress was erratic. In accent and pronunciation, her French was very different from my father's. We had to copy her.

One day, she set us to work on writing a story in French. My vocabulary was limited and we had no dictionaries. In sheer frustration, I threw caution to the winds. The words flowed and covered pages. I was Frenchifying patois words and tailoring their verb endings to look orthodox. The bell rang. There was no time to check or change anything. I gulped hard and gave the sheets in. It was a case of the turkey voting for Christmas.

When the next French lesson came round, Miss Roughton bore down on me. How could I forget all that she had taught me? Here was the familiar approach. It was personalised. I had let the side down, her side. What I had written didn't make sense. (It didn't to her.) How could I be so careless? It was out of character. My embarrassment grew. How could I tell her that the basis was patois? Eventually she turned away from my incoherence and the lesson proceeded. She hadn't guessed.

There were always wide variations in the pronunciation of Guernsey surnames on the island, depending on the speaker's parish. Near my home at the Forest, the most common way to say my name Brehaut, was Breho (with a short 'e' and with the 'h' pronounced and a silent 't'). In one of the surrounding parishes it might become Brehaut (with a silent 'h' and 't') or Berhaut (the same with the 'e' and 'r' reversed) or Berow (as in 'cow'). Other versions, more common in town were Brayo and Brayho. Miss Roughton insisted on Bréhaut, adding the acute accent, when no Guernsey person used it. In her version, the 'h' was pronounced as if anglicising the name, but the silent 't' was retained, as though its French origin must be recognised. To me, her addition of the accent indicated that she saw the form of my name as deficient. There was something wrong with it and it had to be corrected and made to look respectable. Somehow, the various ways my name was used reflected our situation in a nutshell. Here was epitomised the relationship between the patois nuances on the one hand, the anglicised versions, and the English interpretation which was partly French! On the wider cultural front, we were all positioned somewhere in this threefold pattern of interconnection.

For me, one or two of Miss Roughton's impromptu lessons are among the best remembered. Late and breathless, she placed on the easel an illustration torn from a magazine. What did we think of the colours used, the composition, the impressions the artist was trying to convey? The picture acquired a life of its own. Another time, we were left to learn two passages from *Hamlet* which she scribbled on the board. "Remember them all your life," she said. I have.

> *This above all, – to thine ownself be true;*
> *And it shall follow, as the night the day,*
> *Thou canst not then be false to any man.*

> *The friends thou hast, and their adoption tried,*
> *Grapple them to thy soul with hoops of steel;*

# Chapter XII

## *'Tomorrow When the World is Free'*

It was during 1942 and 1943 that I felt closest to Miss Keating. Slowly a relationship had been developing, which was looser than a family bond, yet based on mutual recognition of each other's place and role. When I was out with her, I tried slotting my arm through hers. I felt her stiffen. This was evidently not the thing to do. If we met someone she knew, she would say, "This is Lois, my Guernsey evacuee." The tone said, 'She's not mine. She came from somewhere else, so I'm not fully responsible for what she's like. She's not here to stay, but I'm looking after her for the time being.' It sounded quite positive.

I was no longer just struggling to hold my head above water, but could recognise more realistically that she cared about my welfare. Her commitment was no less real for being undefined and indefinite. It meant for her certain restrictions on privacy and personal freedom. How could she let her hair down when I was there? Would I go and tell her girls what she was 'really' like?

Who was the middle-aged man in the photo on her chest of drawers? He was always there. "A friend of the family who died some years ago," Mrs. Keating had explained. So why was he in her daughter's room? There was so much about their past that remained enigmatic. I had grown up not knowing their story and had no part in it. What reason had they to tell me of their griefs and loves?

I had modified my view of them since my arrival and had come to admire Miss Keating for the caring effort which she ploughed into her work at school. Towards the end of the summer holiday, she would spend many days creating the following year's timetable. A rubber was in constant use. "Damnation!" she allowed herself to say. This, I deduced, was a softer version of "Damn!" which would have been bad for children to hear and too forceful for your mother.

She made her Speech Days memorable by inviting special guests to present a challenge to the girls. One such was Mary Stocks, then the Principal of Westfield College (evacuated from London to Cambridge) and later to become well known as the cigar-smoking radio panellist with no dress sense. When she came to the house for supper, I was most surprised that she seemed to take a personal interest in my Guernsey story. What could it mean to her? I had expected to stay quietly unobserved in the background, as girls did.

With Miss Keating, it was easy to tell when a major event was looming. The Saturday before, she would dash into Manchester on the Yelloway bus and come back waved. The straight hair drawn back from the forehead into a chignon had been set. Some wondered why she considered the concertina effect to be an enhancement.

Occasionally, when Mrs. Keating was away, I would return from school to find myself shut out. Miss Keating had gone to a meeting and forgotten to leave the key under the appointed stone at the front of the house. I would stroll up to her school and sit at the desk in her room and feel the importance. "Come in!" I would mouth to a phantom secretary and hand her a pile of letters for typing. I saw myself in the head's black gown ready to walk up the crowded hall for morning assembly. I had seen the girls rise for her entry. She had hunched her shoulders upwards as if to add height to her slight figure. Then with arched back and books clasped in front of her, she proceeded ceremonially to the platform, walking quickly but deliberately in her dainty shoes, the archetypal feminine don, exuding full authority.

Once, I found a pile of Picture Post magazines on her window sill. I spent a pleasant half hour enjoying the new art of photographic realism. Later, she told me these were the very copies she had taken out of circulation, because they were unsuitable for the girls. I tried hard to visualise what items merited a ban and only can-can girls would spring onto the pages.

She provided background support for my homework without doing it for me. With her degree in History and long experience of teaching the subject, she could explain the setting for the reforms of the nineteenth century or the Irish Question. If I asked for the spelling of a word, she would focus on the Latin derivation, a habit carried to the point of irritation.

My reading was monitored, but not controlled in an obtrusive way. I kept raiding the library cupboard at school for John Buchan, Charles Dickens, Victor Hugo, the Brontës and later, John Galsworthy and Thomas Hardy. She herself introduced me to the thriller via Dorothy Sayers' *Clouds of Witness*. Occasionally she took me to the cinema and we saw Charlie Chaplin in *The Great Dictator* and that poignant story of a Welsh mining village *How Green was My Valley*.

When I had a long series of sties and boils, the doctor recommended poultices. He turned to Miss Keating and assumed that she would apply them as though she'd been a mother. I was most surprised when she did. The boils were painful whether I sat or moved, but because of their hidden positions, few people knew I had them.

I no longer saw the formalities of the daily routine as a hurdle and had got used to them. 'A lady always uses the butter knife, even when she's alone.' When I had understood at which times such a practice could be waived, I had arrived. In the dining room, the little brass hand-bell now stayed on the trolley and contented itself with being an ornament. No more would its tinkling summons bring in a maid to clear the plates and serve the dessert. The old ordered existence had changed.

The daily help, Mrs. Neaven, had left to do war work. She was on night shift, inspecting bombs. Her replacement, after a gap, was Mrs. Pomeroy, who was often ill. Like Mrs. Heaume in Bolton, she was among the thousands of Channel Islanders adrift in northern towns, flotsam on a wavering sea of insecurity. She was always trying to be in work, so that she could pay the rent for her meagre rooms. Then she would be laid low again with pleurisy and have to give up, only to start the search for work again before a full recovery. She had, I think, three sons in the war, but it was the one on a minesweeper who gave her the most anxiety. Although she had lived in Jersey for many years, she came from Guernsey and knew my family. I went to see her sometimes when she was sick.

When no help was available, Miss Keating and I did all the household tasks ourselves. A good team spirit developed. I cleared the grates and laid newspaper, sticks and coal ready for lighting the fires. The kitchen one heated the back boiler which warmed the water for baths. These were always carefully regulated. Wartime restrictions allowed only a few inches. I went on errands, fetched medicine and library books for Mrs. Keating, washed up, dusted, made beds and prepared vegetables.

Miss Keating set aside Saturday mornings for baking. She had done little since she was a young teacher and stuck to well-tried recipes. I was not allowed to do much, as the rations might be wasted, but I could run into town for fresh yeast for the teacakes, weigh ingredients and peel apples. Pained calls from the drawing room showed how strongly Mrs. Keating was reacting to the thumping in the kitchen. "Essie!" Her daughter was bludgeoning the air out of the pastry. So why did it usually turn out so well?

A wartime cake had to last a week, so we had only thin slices for tea. In the absence of refrigerators, the meat and pies were covered with muslin cages and placed on a shelf over the top of the cellar steps. There they would stay cool and free from flies.

Food rationing, which had started before we left Guernsey in 1940, by now covered bacon (4 oz.), sugar (8 oz.), butter (2 oz.), tea (2 oz.), margarine (4 oz.), and cooking fat (2 oz.), these being the amounts for each person for a week. Meat was rationed by its value rather than its weight and, in the early stages, an adult was allowed a weekly one shilling and tenpence worth (1/10). The Keating cat lived mainly on lites. In the summer of 1941, cheese and eggs had been put on ration. The eggs were in short supply, partly because there was not enough feed for the hens and millions had been killed. Most people had about one egg each week. (Kathleen Cochrane who was sent to fetch the allocation for her billet, went back one day with the eggs stashed in her coat pocket!) By the end of 1942, people had got thoroughly used to the points system, which had been in operation for a year. They could use their allocation of sixteen a month on a few items selected from tinned fruit, preserves, rice, cereals, biscuits, dried fruit, syrup, treacle and other things.

Stung by the comment on a previous school report, I was still trying to discover more ways of showing initiative. One of my more obvious experiments had taken place during one of our rare school walks across the moors. I had glanced up at my companions as we trudged along a valley path and then, without a word, I'd branched upwards to the left. Soon others did the same.

Now I decided I would learn to swim. While at the Intermediate School in Guernsey, I had been permanently 'excused', because I so frequently got cramp in the sea. The debarment was remembered by Miss Roughton and somehow carried over. Since the water in the Rochdale baths was slightly warmed (in spite of wartime fuel restrictions), I was determined to join my class for lessons and find out how I fared. Miss Keating lent me her old red bathing costume. I was dismayed when it stretched in the water and hung in revealing limpness when I climbed out. I borrowed a bathing cap from the school stock and if there were not enough to go round I passed it on to someone else for half the lesson. Soon I could swim and spring head first into the water. I was freeing myself of my father's inhibitions.

I disliked sewing to order in a regimented school setting. Somehow, I hadn't got over the daunting experience of early Needlework lessons in Guernsey, where we all had to make voluminous navy knickers too old fashioned to be worn. But now I grasped the creative opportunity which arose. Sometimes, we made soft toys for wartime charities or for playgroups in munitions factories. For one such venture, Molly Frampton and I were partners. Inspired by Disney cartoons, we decided to make Minnie Mouse, and in two sections, so that we could each take a bit to work on at home. Next day, I arrived at school, excited. Would my section join up well with hers? But I had dropped the head on the bus and she had lost the body!

When the school asked us to make toys for the Aid to China Fund, I was carried away with visions of a cuddly cat and started sewing. Mrs. Keating was worried that I hadn't finished my homework. "Work first, play afterwards!" she advised. "Often", I thought, "there is no clear limit to the reading, writing and learning I have to do for History or Divinity. I always feel I could do more. The task is never finished as with peeling potatoes or making a bed." I felt a bit resentful. And then I overheard Miss Keating talking to her mother ". . . she's a good natured girl and she thinks it's her duty to do something. They're under a certain pressure at school to respond to the appeal. . . ."

Now I felt I had a champion and that someone understood. I was encouraged. My willingness to adapt and Miss Keating's non-confrontational manner prevented many a situation from getting tense.

Once, when I felt too swamped with homework, I complained. There was little chance to do other things. "You have all the time there is," Miss Keating said. (How true.) Listening to the girls skipping in the street outside, I strained at the leash. I was not allowed to join them but sometimes I went for walks in Falinge Park or on the moors with friends from church.

When no one came to do the housework, I did my own laundry. The black line round the cuffs and collar of my white blouses admonished like a wagging finger. But I had washed my neck and arms with care. Why was it that Miss Keating's clothing looked so unaffected by the grimy atmosphere?

At school, for fifteen clothing coupons, some of us received a new raincoat from a stock which came from the USA. Sadly, they were showerproof only, but looked fashionable enough in a pale neutral colour. The snag, as always in the north, was the neckline, which quickly became ringed and needed scrubbing. Perhaps it was my thick long hair which added to the problem. Miss Keating thought I might not wash it very well myself and, for a time, I had it shampooed fortnightly at the hairdresser.

Then on July 16th 1942, it was shorn, another step into mid-adolescence. Carefully, I tied the sweepings into a long tail and wrapped it in tissue paper ready to pack inside my case to show the family. It was like the burying of a much-loved pet.

One day, when I was still fourteen, I realised that I was no longer thinking in Guernsey French, but all in English. The long process of translating before I could speak had ended. Only a slight hesitation suggested the old panic: I was still wondering whether I would get things right.

The patois was displaced and it no longer mattered.

In my thoughtful moments, I warned myself to be careful. If I modelled myself too closely on the Keatings and became too English, I would find it difficult to fit into my Guernsey home again. What would my parents think about that? The confused outcome was painful to consider, but the longer I was on the mainland and growing up, the greater the problem would become.

The companionship with Mrs. Keating grew during her long periods of heart trouble. I had come to recognise that along with her strong sense of duty and correctness there were very kindly and caring traits. During the months when she felt weak, she would stay in bed for the morning. I helped to carry breakfast for three up to her bedroom. She had hers on a tray while Miss Keating and I sat at a small round table, eating our oatmeal porridge and toast with marmalade. I had an extra slice because I was 'a growing girl'. Miss Keating read out the headlines from the newspaper, which was propped against the teapot. I hurriedly did the washing up before running down the hill to catch a bus for school.

Once, I was shown a little bottle of brandy. Was it brandy? If Mrs. Keating had an attack when there was no one else in the house, I was to give her this stimulant. "How much?" I asked. The reply was vague and open ended. I deduced that they did not know themselves. It was an area where you had to rely on commonsense. I checked occasionally that the bottle was still in the cupboard and was very glad to be so trusted.

Paradoxically, I knew I was at home (rather than in someone's house on a temporary basis) when Miss Keating explained that I might have to leave. If her mother's health got worse, they might not be able to keep me. I saw they could have used the illness to be rid of me. They did not do so. I felt more firmly rooted.

One afternoon, I sat on the settee next to Mrs. Keating, so that I could hold a skein of wool for her to wind. (It wasn't sold in balls.) I plucked up courage and asked her about her childhood on a farm in the Isle of Man. In expansive mood that day, she took me skating on a frozen pond and told me stories of her

sisters. One had settled down in Florida and I was always given
the US stamps when letters came. I realised how lonely she must
sometimes feel, cut off from such a distant past, which only she
remembered. (She was eighty in 1942.) Perhaps she missed out
on having grandchildren and I would have to do instead.

As a memento, she gave me a little canvas purse I have kept.
She had cross-stitched it in diagonal stripes of green and brown
stranded cotton. She made a lot of these for Red Cross funds.
When the coupons could be spared, Miss Keating bought her a
length of woollen material and she sewed herself a cheerful dress
of blue or crimson.

While I watched her quietly dozing among the cushions, I
sometimes wondered if she would ever open her eyes again. She
might die quietly in her sleep with the cat still curled up neatly on
her knee. For so life ended with the elderly.

\* \* \* \* \*

My visit to the home of Jean Adams from Stretford High
School in August 1942 was by no means an unqualified success.
As my appointed pen-friend since our days at Roylelands, she had
written me a series of rather scrappy cream coloured letters. Now
it was arranged that I should spend a few days with her family.
The bombing of Stretford and the rest of the Manchester
conurbation had stopped and it was judged safe to let me go. The
siren went only once when I was there.

I soon found that much of her attention was focused on
maintaining the brilliance of her red nails, which she assiduously
manicured into long points. Her bushy girlish hair style, white
socks and Shirley Temple shoes fell far below their level of
sophistication.

It rained a lot and we went to the cinema. The Keating
eyebrows would have questioned *Honky Tonk*. When we were
joined by Jean's friend, the talk was usually of boys I didn't know,
dancing in the park and film stars I hadn't seen. A trip to the
local fair landed me with a prize packet of cigarettes, which I did
not know how to dispose of till Mr. Adams said he wanted to buy
them for a shilling.

The family belonged to a nearby tennis club and we got in
some practice. Jean was the better player, I thought, till her shot
hit the head of a woman on the adjoining court and we watched
with fascination as she slowly folded her legs and passed out.

In preparation for this visit, I had packed into my familiar brown suitcase a dashing pair of secondhand pyjamas, dyed crimson, which I had not worn before. They were in a batch the school had received from the USA. It was very hot at night and Jean and I shared a double bed. When I got up the first morning, I was mortified to find that the bottom sheet on my side was tinged a light rose. What should I do? I felt a freak as if my own skin had exuded redness. I apologised profusely to Mrs. Adams, who was kindness itself. The colour would most certainly come out in the wash she assured me and coupons would not have to be used to replace it.

It wasn't just the good meals and the trip to the theatre to see *Lilac Time* that I appreciated, but the total experience of being in an ordinary small suburban home. While having no hankering after red nails myself, I was a bit envious of Jean's freedom to experiment and not only with her appearance. She had a very firm base from which to roam a little. I sensed the difference in our situations and even more so when we were taken to the swimming baths by a friendly neighbour. While he was bouncing his young daughter in the water, he drew us into a round of splashing and romping and soon I found myself trailing behind a very wet masculine back.

This was the first and only time in my youthful experience when an adult ever jumped around in the water with me and for the fun of it. He wasn't treating it all like a childish waste of time.

It began to dawn on me that this was what I expected: to be someone's waste of time, while their attention should rightly be centred somewhere else. This was hardly fair, I realised, since I was, in fact, receiving a great deal of encouragement and interest, not as personal as a parent might give, perhaps, but that couldn't be helped. I didn't want or need an engrossing, intrusive sort of attention and made sure I didn't get it. I was still trying to distance myself from the unwanted elements of my mother's influence and to feel a separate independent personality. I tended still to hide behind a quiet facade, till I was confident enough to take the next step forward.

* * * * *

CHANNEL ISLANDERS
NAZI DEPORTATIONS

Such newspaper headlines in October 1942 drew attention to the plight of 800 or so men, aged sixteen to seventy, and their immediate families, who had suddenly been uprooted from their

Guernsey homes and taken to German internment camps. More, perhaps a thousand, had likewise been deported from Jersey and all because the men were English and not born on the islands. Non-residents inadvertently caught there when the Germans arrived were also removed. It was rumoured that they would be used as forced labourers on the Continent.

Later information indicated that the deportees ended up in three camps, one for men at Laufen in Bavaria, one for families at Wurzach and the third at Biberach near the Swiss border and about twenty miles from Munich.

It was hard news for everyone at school and not just because we all knew people who might have been deported; it shattered the image of the German Occupying Force as one that respected civilians' rights and customs.

The Channel Islands Refugees Committee, located at 20, Upper Grosvenor Street in London, was trying to list the names of those deported, relying on Red Cross sources.

I wondered if Rev. R.D. Moore would have been taken had he returned to Guernsey in July 1940 as he intended. I thought of him often as my parents were living in the house that he and his wife had occupied. Other Methodist ministers or Anglican priests might be in the deported contingents. The minister of my church, Rev. Henry Foss, could well be one of them.

As we passed the newspaper cuttings around at break, we thought of Miss Roughton, Miss Sayer and others like Miss Ellershaw, Head of the Ladies' College, who had not been born on the islands. If they had stayed in Guernsey and the Germans had included unmarried women on their list of deportees, then they too would have vanished into Nazi camps. Why should the Germans think the place of birth was of such significance? Did coming from the mainland make you the greater enemy? We were all British after all and tarred with the same brush. No rational explanation was forthcoming. A far-fetched report suggested an element of retaliation in the German action, connecting it with the Allied raid on Dieppe in August (fiasco though that was).

We were not to know if the Germans construed that particular raid as the prelude to the Second Front when the Allies would invade the Continent, but they were certainly preparing for the worst and they were fearful. News came that they were importing massive numbers of forced labourers into the islands to turn them into impregnable fortresses. Poles, Russians, Dutch, Norwegians, Spaniards and Algerians were working in droves, under duress, to construct innumerable fortifications along the coast lines. The men were in poor shape and treated badly. Many were dying. In the next few weeks, estimates of the total numbers used rose to 25,000. The suffering and waste must be appalling.

We hoped fervently that the gun emplacements would never come into play, but with a German garrison of an estimated 10,000 troops in Guernsey alone, any spark could light the tinder. If the islands did become a battleground, the effects on our families would be disastrous. Even without bombing and bloodshed, we wondered how long it would be before they felt the brunt of greater deprivation and harsher regulations. What would happen next?

Would those who had fought in the First World War be deported also? The rumours were very worrying. Civilians with military training and experience might well be seen as threatening: the spine of a future rebellion. My father's maimed hand, injured by a bullet in the First World War, had been for us a constant reminder of war's danger and damage. He had always said that if the shot had been directed a few inches further along, he would have been killed and we would never have been born. So much in life seemed fortuitous. Uncle Art had also been in the war. Would ex-soldiers like them be rounded up and sent away to Germany?

Red Cross messages from Guernsey, dribbling through, gave a picture of everyday life which, to our relief, was still mainly reassuring. The tone of other people's messages corroborated my own. By the summer of 1943, I had received twenty-two. They were surprisingly informative, when we tried to read between the lines. It seemed that my parents spent quiet evenings by the fireside. They must have a fire and were probably burning wood. Coal supplies from England must surely have been exhausted during the first winter. My mother was mending and knitting socks. She'd always kept a good supply of wool, but perhaps she was unravelling old jerseys and using the better sections. John was wearing Brian's cast-offs and mine were going to Marion, Uncle Ces' little daughter.

My mother went to town every Friday. This was her routine ever since I could remember. She had made the twenty minute journey by bus from Rue des Landes. Now from her new home on the outskirts, she must be walking or cycling. I imagined her making her way along the pavement in the High Street. What would she do if a German soldier approached? Would she have to step aside, give the Nazi salute or carry on regardless? Would she chat with acquaintances in Guernsey French or was it banned in public places? The Germans could hardly forbid its use altogether, even if they didn't understand a word. There must be things in the shops to buy or she wouldn't go.

Cooking at home was done by gas and with a haybox. This would keep the food hot and prolong the cooking time without using fuel.

My father was growing vegetables at the manse where they were now living. I thought he would find the garden rather small after being used to Rue des Landes, but I didn't really know its size. He was also growing potatoes and other things at Summerville and enjoying the fruit. I thought of all the apples, the luscious loganberries and blackberries that ripened year by year. They must be profoundly thankful to have this continuing supply. John liked his chocolate ration. Perhaps this was imported from France.

On the face of it, they didn't seem too short of food, but the phrase, 'Helene, Miriam, John gleaning after reapers Anneville' suggested harsher conditions. But perhaps they were relying on handfuls of wheat to make their own bread. This was family property.

They were attending the Methodist church at Brock Rd. on the edge of town not far from their new home. John went to Sunday School and had contributed a basket at Harvest. My father was taking preaching appointments. This was a sure indication that many churches on the island had been allowed to stay open. Presumably services were conducted much as before, since Methodist Local Preachers like my father were taking them. He was cycling there, so this showed that his car and lorry were out of action, perhaps taken over by the Germans. Or was it just that petrol was not available to civilians? He had acquired a bicycle since the Occupation. Perhaps it was one left by a family who had evacuated to the mainland.

At 5 ft 3 inches, I was now slightly taller than my mother. I pictured standing next to her and seeing her from a different angle. I measured John's 3 ft 9 inches against the wall and found that he was 4 or 5 inches higher than my waistline. How he had grown! At five, he was doing well at Kingsley House school, could read small words and tell the time. He spoke mainly in English. I wondered about that. Why wasn't he chatting in Guernsey French when he was at home as we had done? I expected my parents to speak to each other as always in the patois and to change to English only to help him learn it.

He remembered his brother and sister well, but clearly he was no longer the much loved little toddler I had played with and looked after. There was a growing gap between us.

My father took John to school and then went on to his workshop. He must have found another one. He couldn't be working at Milestone or Rue des Landes. Both were very likely to be occupied by the troops. Small pointers confirmed this impression; for instance, the piano and my bedroom furniture were now at Courtil-a-Paix, one of the old homesteads near Summerville where Aunty Helene lived with old Uncle Tom. It was a large old granite house with many outbuildings and there would be plenty of room for extra things.

My father had brought back primroses from the Forest. It was so unlike him to pick wild flowers, that this must have special significance. Had they come from our Rue des Landes hedgerows where they grew in such prolific beauty? The large greenhouse that stretched along the field, which I had once used for somersaulting, had been demolished. The message said, 'Ground cultivated where big span formerly stood'. The other two greenhouses on the premises must still be intact, but the last of the ones at Milestone had gone; it was blown down by a gale. Perhaps they were using the wooden framework for fuel. There was a message from Gran of Milestone, but it made no reference to where she was living. My father and one of his older workmen, Mr. le Couvey, were painting the manse. So some of the stocks from Milestone must have been salvaged.

The saddest news was of the death of my beloved grandmother from Summerville. After four weeks' illness, she had died on May 22nd 1942. She was seventy-two. Uncle wrote to me when he heard and I had the news later in my own message received on September 11th.

The house with its lovely garden would never be the same without her. I thought of the memorable times we had shared, the trips to her little conservatory to see the begonias, the long rows of colourful sweet peas, the Christmas gatherings, the old family photo albums and the bowls of loganberries, sprinkled thickly with crunchy sugar. The emotional warmth of her welcome seemed to emanate from house and garden.

In that setting, Uncle Eug and Aunty Helene had seemed to me to be like transient holiday-makers or English strangers, yet I knew they had Guernsey roots going back too far for me to know. What I could remember vividly were the annual farewells at Summerville. We had all crowded round the back gateway, as my

father headed the car for home. Uncle had waved his arms round
and round at windmill speed . . . 'Les grands moulins'. How
different that was from the uncle of war-time Lancashire. The
vigour, the energy and the sense of occasion had gone. He was
older. Things were ordinary. He filled the coal scuttles.

I didn't know how to share my grief over Gran and my
separation from the childhood that had become so detached
from my life in the north. I kept it to myself. One had to be
'brave' and get on with things. This word 'brave' now seemed old
fashioned, smacking of passé Sunday School lessons, which
tended to focus on the heroes of long ago. When my mother had
used it at our departure, even then it seemed out of place and
inadequate. Perhaps she thought she might never see us again
and wanted to convey a mixture of being 'determined' and
'courageous', 'confident' and 'ready to take things on'. That was
how it must be, I thought. There was more to life than
endurance. There must be a sense of moving forward. I felt that,
already, I might have gone ahead further than my parents had
bargained for. So much time had elapsed.

I often wondered how they were really bearing up and tried to
gauge the mood behind their cryptic words. How trivial my
concerns and anxieties must be compared with theirs, but they
evidently maintained their faith and the confidence in the future.
One of their messages referred to 916. I looked up this number
in the Methodist Hymn Book. The familiar words took on a
greater personal meaning now that we knew they were being
sung on both sides of the Channel. The hymn summed up a spirit
of caring, prayer and commitment:

> *Holy Father, in Thy mercy,*
>   *Hear our anxious prayer;*
> *Keep our loved ones, now far distant,*
>   *'Neath Thy care.*
>
> *Jesus, Saviour, let Thy presence*
>   *Be their light and guide;*
> *Keep, O keep them, in their weakness,*
>   *At Thy side.*
>
> *When in sorrow, when in danger,*
>   *When in loneliness,*
> *In Thy love look down and comfort*
>   *Their distress.*

*May the joy of Thy salvation*
  *Be their strength and stay;*
*May they love and may they praise Thee*
  *Day by day.*

*Holy Spirit, let Thy teaching*
  *Sanctify their life;*
*Send Thy grace that they may conquer*
  *In the strife.*

*Father, Son, and Holy Spirit,*
  *God, the One in Three,*
*Bless them, guide them, save them, keep them*
  *Near to Thee.*

*Isabel Stephana Stevenson.*

I had seen little of my cousin, Vernabelle, since we were evacuated. She was a little older and moved around with another set of girls. We had Gran from Milestone in common as she was the daughter of Fredena (my father's surviving sister). Every now and again, we checked to find out if the other had news of the families in Guernsey. Vernabelle had a brother in the Army and three in Guernsey. An early Red Cross message announced that one of them had married. But who was the bride? She would dearly like to have known.

She left before it was time to take School Certificate and went to live with her sister-in-law's mother in London. A course in typing had been arranged.

\* \* \* \* \*

On the evening of April 24th 1942, some of us were dangling gym slip girdles down our backs, trying our best to make them look like pigtails. Miss Roughton wanted us to present a Chinese playlet called *The Emperor's Carpet* which she had produced for school concerts. People in the small audience had seen it before and didn't seem to mind. They called themselves the Guernsey Club and had been meeting every Friday evening for a year at 6, Hunters Lane, in the premises used by the Rochdale branch of the National Union of Girls' Clubs.

The ones who attended regularly were those who had a close association with the school. They were the Maplesdens, Mrs. Ball, Mrs. Palmer, Mrs. Weekes and Mrs. Spiller (all parents). The

Buckley family came and Mrs. Yabsley who had a little daughter.
Her husband was away in the Forces. Then there was Peggy
Mallet, who had found work as an accountant at the Rochdale
Town Hall. She had been evacuated with the school as one of the
young helpers and had previously worked for the Guernsey
Education Council. Now she was entrusted to audit the Club's
accounts, which recorded the sums spent on lemonade and
biscuits and the fees for the use of the room.

Inevitably, Miss Roughton was the President and Miss Naftel
her staunch lieutenant, the one who acted as Secretary and
Treasurer. Members of staff and older girls made up the numbers
to twenty-five or thirty each week. People brought mending or
knitting to do, but some undemanding social activities provided a
pleasant interlude in the week. Winners of Bedlam, charades or
guessing games could expect a badge for a prize. This was the
special creation of Mr. Maplesden, who was a dental mechanic.
He shaped the material used for plates into a shield which bore
the imprint of a Guernsey crest. Miss Naftel kept at the ready her
own compilations of proverbs, jumbled names and a quiz on the
island. Sometimes there was country dancing or community
singing with 'Cherry Ripe' and 'John Peel' showing how much
the Roughton influence predominated. Meetings always ended
with Auld Lang Syne.

Occasionally, Miss Roughton had a small batch of Red Cross
messages to distribute. Many relations and friends in Guernsey
had only the Roylelands address and so, officially, she was the
initial recipient. The Club became a place where concerns could
be shared, whether about island conditions or current day-to-day
problems of accommodation, shopping and employment. Mrs.
Ball, whose husband was usually at sea, had to endure long
stretches with no news of him. She knew others would recognise
the anxiety. Some came to the Club because they felt like exiles
or strangers in the north. When in company with other Guernsey
people, the burden of waiting for the end of the war was
lessened.

By the close of *The Emperor's Carpet*, onlookers were supposed to
know how slippers came to be in use. We went through our parts
with a tongue-in-cheek, slightly supercilious attitude, as if we were
saying to the parents and friends, "We're not taking this soppy
stuff too seriously, but you know what Miss Roughton is like and
even if we seem to be having quite a nice time, you'll know it's
not our choice. We're not really like that." And we knew that they
knew. Some things didn't have to be said. Besides, by this time,

everyone had learned to make allowance for the others in that inevitable three-tier system: girls, parents-and-friends, staff.

The effect of Miss Roughton's presence was to neutralise the quiet gripings which might emerge, however healthy. No one wanted to be 'shown up' in front of her. There was something about her accent and bearing which commanded attention, even 'set the tone'. It suggested a social and cultural background which could still, in those days, incline people to elevate the few on grounds of class, rank or attainment. She was where people set her, occupying the place she was accorded. This did not stop the quiet, amused whisperings behind her back. . . .

"I heard the other day that she was passing an icy pond when she saw some boys trying to get their dog back to the bank. It was stranded in the middle. So she waded in waist high and rescued it. Her clothes were all dripping, but she got on to her bike and went back to Boothroyd as if nothing had happened."

Similar stories were told of Miss Winifred: "She's crackers! She was standing in front of the class, when she caught her skirt on a nail. So she looked at the rip, took it off and taught the rest of the lesson in her slip. As if that made things any better. We were all looking out of the window to see if anyone out there would notice."

On a broader front, the urge to bring new life out of the ruins of the great evacuation upheaval was given expression in *The Channel Islands Monthly Review*. This publication grew out of a slender leaflet, the brainchild of members of the Stockport and District Channel Islands Society, who wanted to publicise personal news gleaned from Red Cross messages and to relay information and announcements.

Within a few months of its launch in May 1941, it had become so successful, that it broadened its aims and changed its title to reach islanders in the Forces as well as those scattered all over the country. Uncle subscribed, so I was able to read back copies in the holidays.

Rev. R.D. Moore was the first to use its pages to suggest that a concerted effort should be made to link together all the Channel Island Societies which were mushrooming everywhere. In January 1942, he was saying that tough times lay ahead, both within the islands under German rule and after the war when those evacuated would return. He wanted to see set up a properly constituted organisation which represented the interests of islanders in Britain, so that they could liaise with Government at any time or be ready to further the work of reorganisation on the islands when peace came. He foresaw the possibility of economic and financial chaos and the difficulty of blending the needs of the returning refugees with the interests of those who had stayed on the islands. The former might find their homes occupied by others or in ruins; their belongings might have disappeared and their businesses would have to be started up again. Vast problems concerning insurance and compensation would have to be faced.

The cry was taken up. A Federation of all the separate Channel Island Societies could be formed to pool ideas and put forward the views of those on the mainland. Proposals were bogged down in a morass of discussion on aims and procedures. The regional societies of which there were at least fifty by the end of 1942, were mainly loose groupings with no defined membership and little funding. They could not evolve any cohesive policy and no one could provide authoritative leadership. The best known and most influential grouping was The Channel Islands Refugees Committee, which was geared mainly to welfare work. No satisfactory way could be found to unite the disparate ad hoc meetings.

Miss Roughton was one of those who went to London in July 1942 to attend a conference of Channel Island representatives from all over the country. It could only take note of the divergent suggestions about the future and had no executive power.

The would-be Phoenix had flapped its wings without lift-off.

# Chapter XIII

## 'Red Sails in the Sunset'

On March 7th 1943, I was received into the membership of the Methodist Church. This could be seen as a step in the long process of growth in the Christian faith, but I was fourteen and had reached the age when the church expected an explicit acknowledgment or decision, marking the development of trust in God's promises. I didn't know exactly where I stood. What was there to go on? There were no rules to apply as with much of school work and no way of measuring one's responsiveness or understanding. I knew that much still eluded me, but this was a decision I would have to take on my own. No one else was in a position to say 'Go ahead' or 'Wait'.

I attended preparation classes along with a few other girls. The minister at our church in Spotland, Rev. George Jobling, spoke about prayer, reading the Bible, the Lord's Supper and the fellowship, history and caring work of the church. Through these, and in other ways, God would work in our lives and in all our concerns. The Holy Spirit would guide and strengthen.

During the service, he turned to our little group:

| | |
|---|---|
| <u>Minister</u> | *In this high moment, do you now confirm your response to His gracious call, confessing Him before men, taking up your cross, and engaging yourself to continue, through good report and ill, to be His faithful soldier and servant to your life's end?* |
| <u>New Members Together</u> | I do so confess Him and pledge myself to Him. |
| <u>Minister</u> | *Do you now resolve, trusting in God alone for strength, to be sincere, pure and upright in thought, word and deed; to hallow your life by prayer and frequent meditation upon God's Word? Do you resolve to give attention to the means of Grace and Fellowship, to further the work of God by the dedication of yourself and your possessions, and to hasten by your service and sacrifice, the coming of His Kingdom throughout the world?* |

New
Members            I do so resolve, God
Together           being my helper.

I already knew the Creed and many of the Church's collects by
heart. Miss Roughton used them in Assembly, and, on a rainy
Sunday or when Miss Keating felt rushed, she would drop into
the Anglican Church of St. Edmund's just up the road and take
me with her.

As the cadences of the liturgy began to take on shape and
meaning, I became more aware of the significance of the words.
In the psalms and prayers, I recognised the expression of truths I
had heard from the pulpit, but they had a different ring. Words
were unfolded like a roll of fabric revealing more and more of
the pattern of God's action, at once both familiar and new.

| | |
|---|---|
| Blessed be the Lord God of Israel, *for he hath visited and redeemed his people* | He comes |
| O God, who art the author of peace and lover of concord *in knowledge of whom standeth our eternal life . . .* | We know |
| We bless Thee for our creation, preservation, and all the blessings of this life; but above all, for thine inestimable love in the redemption of the world by our Lord Jesus Christ, for *the means of grace and for the hope of glory.* | It is a life-giving process |

These words gave expression to something live: a working
relationship with God. He and His people were actively experiencing a partnership, each giving and receiving in a vital two-way
communion. This was an integrating process echoed in the
phrase 'the means of grace and the hope of glory'. Together they
made a 'oneness' and 'wholeness'.

Something along these lines I had sensed strongly enough to
be convinced of it, although I would not have known how to
express it. I knew my faith needed strengthening and deepening
and that I was just at the beginning.

Kathleen Cochrane and Kathleen Frampton had been
attending the Parish Church and were confirmed there in April.

\* \* \* \* \*

It is impossible to think of the Castleton school premises without the tarmac playground making a strong impact. The largest area lay between two main blocks of buildings. Its capacity to separate was retained in spite of the marriage of Mr. Fred Wilson, the headmaster on our side, with the headmistress of the Primary School on the other side. The nuptials were announced by Miss Roughton and treated with one of her enigmatic half-smiles, halted before it became a chuckle. Few of the girls wandered over. It wasn't our territory and we had been officially deterred, because large girls rushing round might have proved intimidating to the infants.

In the summer, the tarmac was hot, so hot that we could not sit on it without a protective book or cardigan, but at the beginning of the afternoon, the wall of the school building was lined with squatting girls who had wandered back from their billets early. I was often fleeing with defiant Scottish lairds through windswept heather, or trapped with helpless prisoners in the Tower of London.

We no longer played marbles or skipped. We didn't play at all. Mostly we chatted, but when Gwen Damarell came along, humming a popular tango or foxtrot, we were soon swept off our feet, gliding with her into paradise. She expected style.

> . . . *The heartaches I cost you!*
> *No wonder I lost you,*
> *'Twas all over my jealousy.*

The words of Patience Strong (to use her later pseudonym) matched the rhythm which was made exciting by Gwen's flair for timing.

In turn, we became Ginger Rogers to her Fred Astaire.

> *Red sails in the sunset, Away out at sea,*
> *O carry my loved one home safely to me.*

No one liked the toilets which were outside at the far end of the other playground behind our building. On rainy days, you got wet before you reached them. Often the doors were unhinged or the seats broken. They easily got blocked or were left in a smelly condition. It seems that the authorities could not find ways to combat negligence or maintain a proper standard of daily care and so counteract this repellent underside of school life.

In the playground area not occupied by air raid shelters, we played netball. With sides of only seven, there was a chance of assembling a team good enough to compete with other schools. We did well in the local Netball League, coming third in 1943. Marion le Page was expert at notching up goals and when my eye was in, I added more as Attack.

For a long time, playing was a challenge. Although I was agile and quick at dodging, I was hampered by hidden boils and an extremely stubborn verucca on my right heel. Defying all medical attacks on it, it grew and grew and forced me to place my weight on the ball of my foot and on my toes, and, of course, to give up swimming.

Even the thought of 'Firgrove' leaves me out of breath. This is where we chased after a disappearing ball during the hour which the timetable labelled 'hockey'. Most of the time, even with the combining of classes, there were too few of us to make up the twenty-two needed for two sides. After the keen and athletic older girls had left, there were few of us with much experience. We had no stamina and were continually puffed out or doubled up with a stitch. Winning was no achievement, since little skill was needed to get past the thin defences of the opposing side. There was little artistry in the pattern of exchanges. "Come on!" Miss Stewart would shout to a flagging player, "Tackle!" and the ball would shoot into the distance where no one wanted to retrieve it. The ground was either hard or muddy and most of us were really cold. If there were exhilarating times, I have forgotten them. Firgrove was right on the edge of the moors, so much part of them that we had to chase off the occasional sheep before playing. Why couldn't we have gone for a brisk walk instead?

Later on, we were allowed to use the playing fields near the Dunlop factory within easy walking distance of Castleton.

The opportunity to play tennis had opened up in 1942. The Rochdale Lawn Tennis Club offered the school the use of its courts in return for our doing weeding and gardening jobs in the grounds. With coaching mainly from Miss Stewart and Miss Reed, many of us became more skilful. Audrey Hamel, Head Girl from 1942–3, was one of the star players, combining strength with accuracy. (By the summer of 1944, I had improved enough to win a doubles tournament along with Doreen Nicholson.)

\* \* \* \* \*

*He is the lonely greatness of the world –*
*(His eyes are dim).*
*His power it is holds up the Cross*
*That holds up Him.*

*He takes the sorrow of the threefold hour –*
  *(His eyelids close).*
*Round Him and round, the wind – His Spirit – where*
  *It listeth blows.*

*And so the wounded greatness of the World*
  *In silence lies –*
*And death is shattered by the light from out*
  *Those darkened eyes.*

This visionary poem by Madeleine Caron Rock with its arresting qualities of paradox fired my imagination. It was included in one of the set books for School Certificate, *Poems of Today* (*Second Series*). Much of the collection reflected the feelings evoked by the First World War.

I responded to the haunting melody of the poems by learning over fifty of them by heart. At Summerseat, in the holidays preceding the exams, I would sit up in bed before the rest of the household stirred and memorise one before breakfast.

At first glance, it is difficult to see why I, a school girl in Rochdale, identified so closely with the spokesman in William Noel Hodgson's 'Before Action', but I recognised in the heightened reactions of a soldier before certain death an intensified expression of my own more ordinary feelings. I loved the music and the beauty of the words:

The laughter of unclouded years,
And every sad and lovely thing.

### BEFORE ACTION

*By all the glories of the day*
  *And the cool evening's benison,*
*By that last sunset touch that lay*
  *Upon the hills when day was done,*
*By beauty lavishly outpoured*
  *And blessings carelessly received,*
*By all the days that I have lived,*
*Make me a soldier, Lord.*

*By all of all men's hopes and fears,*
  *And all the wonders poets sing,*
*The laughter of unclouded years,*
  *And every sad and lovely thing;*

*By the romantic ages stored*
  *With high endeavour that was his,*
*By all his mad catastrophes,*
*Make me a man, O Lord.*

*I, that on my familiar hill*
  *Saw with uncomprehending eyes*
*A hundred of Thy sunsets spill*
  *Their fresh and sanguine sacrifice,*
*Ere the sun swings his noonday sword*
  *Must say good-bye to all of this; –*
*By all delights that I shall miss,*
*Help me to die, O Lord.*

*William Noel Hodgson.*

The brilliant imagery of a glowing sunset, such as I had seen over the fields at home or reflected in the sea at Cobo, added poignancy to the soldier's last recollections of the scenes once so familiar. His realisation that all was to be snatched from him prematurely, the need for courage, the appeal to God and the utter dependence on Him; these perceptions had some affinity with my own.

Suddenly, into the mire of the trenches and the scenes of wistful grief, broke the exuberant joy and defiance of Siegfried Sassoon's outburst depicted as the song of birds:

*Everyone's voice was suddenly lifted*
*And beauty came like the setting sun*
*My heart was shaken with tears, and horror*
*Drifted away . . .*

The longing for places once loved, which were a niche for the soul, emerged in 'Little Waves of Breffny' by Eva Gore-Booth and 'Corrymeela' by Moire O'Neill, but always interspersed with these was a reminder of slaughter and waste and the paradox of the new life within it and springing from it . . .

*The year's pale spectre is crying*
*For beauty invisibly shed,*
*For the things that never were told*
*And were killed in the minds of the dead.*

*Laurence Binyon.*

*We that have known the heart-blood*
*Less than the lees of wine*
*We that have seen men broken*
*We know man is divine.*

William Noel Hodgson.

The respect for English literature which the Roughton sisters created was imbued with the quaint aura of their dominant personalities and coloured by their eccentricities. They filled the lessons in such a way that questionings would not arise and nothing that was said could be gainsaid. As a girl, you could be forgiven for thinking that they knew a lot. The chances are that they knew as much or as little as any teacher, who, like them, has qualified in a subject other than literature. The bandeau, the accent, the studied poses and, above all, the implicit suggestion that it was shameful if you couldn't see what they saw, all these masked the fact that many lessons had little content and were often unrelated to each other. The sisters were not very interested in imparting information. They were performers.

If you cottoned on and entered their world, you stopped thinking it was funny for Shakespeare to make his characters so stupid that they could not see through the most obvious disguises. You even looked on seriously, as Miss Norah Roughton stood on a chair to declaim a famous speech. She made you feel that this was normal practice.

When Miss Winifred Roughton vanished as she did every now and again, she might have been spotted on a train trying to manage large Elizabethan characters cut out of cardboard. She was on a panel of visiting lecturers (perhaps organised by the WEA but no one knew for sure). She went round presenting Shakespeare and the music and instruments of Tudor times. Once, she took Frances Hemming to sing her illustrations. The fees must have been useful, since she remained on the school staff over and above the LEA allocation and so without a salary. It was part of the Roughton mystique to hover within imprecise suggestions of unspecified, but limited private means. Only the very rude would have dared to probe. Labelling her 'a good old stick' would have been far too familiar. So much was left unsaid.

In June 1943, two of us were promoted from sub-prefects to prefects. At Assembly, Miss Roughton called Kathleen Frampton's name and mine. In turn, we stepped forward for the treatment.

Solemnly, she pinned the badge on to my tunic and with the great flourish which she kept for such occasions, she drew up her hand till it reached waist level, then swung it in an overriding curve in my direction. The arching twist of the body and the presentation of the hand for shaking would have been a fit model for Malvolio.

"I place the honour of the school in your hands," she declared . . . and things went back to normal.

Afterwards, the girls clustered round. "Open your hands, then! Let me see the honour!"

"Get out of bed, you bleeting seaupies!" At Boothroyd, Miss Norah Roughton used spoonerisms to wake the girls. Perhaps she herself had once been roused by such stairy fory calls.

After the billeting operation in the winter of 1940/1, the house had come to resemble a small hostel, allocated basically to those older girls who did not want to go into local homes or those looking for work. The billeting allowance was paid to Miss Roughton while they were of eligible age. At any given time, there were one or two members of staff in residence, usually Miss Roughton herself, and Miss Clayton or Miss Mahy. When the house really settled down, parent/helpers such as Miss Platt, Mrs. Spiller or Mrs. Tattersall did most of the cooking and cleaning. The tensions of overcrowding were reduced after the number of girls accommodated had dropped to about sixteen (sometimes fewer). Miss Mahy, when it was her turn to mastermind the preparation of a meal, turned to her Gert & Daisy wartime cookery book which guided her through all exigencies:

How to make gravy

a)  with stock
b)  with nothing

It was the advice in the second category which proved to be most helpful.

Occasionally, the telephone brought news of a distressing problem in the billet. In one home, a girl flouted the house rules when she made toast. It proved the straw which broke the camel's back. Miss Roughton might ride off to discuss the problem, laugh and relieve the tension, or the girl might possibly be brought back to Boothroyd till a new billet could be found.

In the holidays, when there was more space, those few girls doing further training might return for a while if they had nowhere else to go. Cautionary tales are still circulated about the diversionary tactics used by the inmates, so that Miss Roughton would not notice that one was slipping out to see her boyfriend round the corner.

At the back, a few male hopefuls clutched at greasy newspaper. Female faces peered down from upstairs windows, and soon a rope of knotted girdles and dressing gown cords lowered 'a suitable receptacle' to receive their welcome sacrifice of chips. A few of the boys even accepted Miss Roughton's formal invitations to tea and sat round a cloth-covered table making polite conversation with the residents. Frances Hemming was thrilled to be taken on a tour of the streets in a converted charabanc by her current boyfriend's father, who was appealing through a loudspeaker for newspapers and saucepans and virtually anything which could be recycled to help the war effort.

A few of the girls at Boothroyd were younger than the main core. Sometimes they were there just for short spells because of sickness in their billet or changed circumstances. Others stayed longer and for special reasons. The two Colognoli residents, Margaret and her sister, Rose, attended school at Greenbank. Their parents had evacuated from Guernsey and were managing the Devonshire Private Hotel in Stockport. At weekends, the girls joined them there. As Margaret had asthma and was often unwell, perhaps it was thought she would have continuous company and oversight at Boothroyd. The sisters had previously been in a billet where the hosts were Roman Catholic like them, but they'd had to leave. It was, apparently, hard to find other billets of that denomination. Whatever the reasons, the two girls stayed on. Margaret's art and needlework skills developed and when Miss Clayton's niece wanted a christening robe for her new baby, it was Margaret who made it. She created artistic posters for the Junior concerts, which might feature the Raggle Taggle Gipsies or Rumpelstiltskin (played by Janet Nicholle, whose brother, we later learned, was one of the commandos to make a raid on Guernsey. We weren't supposed to know at the time.) "You can't be a rat!" one girl was told. It was her punishment for a small offence, when Miss Johnson was producing *The Pied Piper*. In the run-up period, the girls' poster illustrations advertised the play by scattering the rats over town.

Anxious as always to perpetuate the school traditions and create a sense of occasion, Miss Roughton arranged that the annual Commemoration service be held in the Parish Church. There had been one in 1942 and others were to follow till our return to Guernsey. In the subdued atmosphere, male voices expressed the familiar cadences of Anglican worship. This was the invitation to praise. We were to join in what was going on.

> *'Let us now praise famous men*
> *And our fathers that begat us.'*

The age-old reading from Ecclesiasticus, chosen by Miss Roughton, carried us from one year to the next. Who knows now what it meant to rows of inconsequential schoolgirls, still reaching towards maturity? We didn't seem to amount to much in the scheme of things and sat on the edge of other people's worlds in the shadow of war.

Conducting worship was what the clergy did and they were not caught up in the pressure to go and fight. The nation saw their work in the civilian world as important. They were encouraged to do it. But they didn't try to stop the fighting. Seemingly, they were not against it. Their work and that of the Forces was somehow two sides of the same thing and all for God and the country. The two seemed to be enmeshed. But must it be so? Wasn't our faith about harmony and peace?

> *Praise, my soul, the King of heaven;*
> *To His feet thy tribute bring;*
> *Ransomed, healed, restored, forgiven,*
> *Who like thee His praise should sing?*

However was I going to sort out all the issues? I felt we were expected just to go along with everything happening around us. So what if there had been great and famous men who knew what was at the heart of things? I left them all to it and went home.

\* \* \* \* \*

Many now remember their billets with great affection and feel grateful for the loving care and support they received. They had a very solid base. A few had moved away from Guernsey homes where there were problems, an alcoholic father or a low income. They might be placed in homes that were better off or ones with wide community connections.

Some, while evacuated, lived through painful experiences which they have been able to use as learning points in later life. But traces of scarring from childhood events may remain in spite of attempts to rid them of their power to wound.

At the time, poor nutrition, deprivation or personal strain

might show themselves in physical distress, such as much blinking, stammering, failure to concentrate or assimilate school work, lack of self-confidence, traces of asthma or tummy aches. In one case, the unusual course was taken of sending the girl away to a Special School, but after a short while there, it was found to be totally unsuitable to her needs, since it catered mainly for those who had difficulty with reading and writing. In those months, she was separated from all her school friends, her parents were in Guernsey and she had no close contacts on the mainland. It was hardly a recipe to restore a better equilibrium.

In a few billets, there were times of great tension and nervousness. Girls might be hesitant to speak of their fears in case they were ridiculed, disbelieved or thrown out in disgrace. They felt trapped and did not yet have the self-assurance to deal with the problem or confide in others. One remembers the dread of Saturday nights, when the man of the house returned home drunk. Young as she was then, she realised how vulnerable she was. She listened tensely from behind her bedroom door which she had locked, while he lurched his way noisily upstairs. It was only when she judged him to be asleep that she could relax. He had not battered his way in. Other emotional stresses in the household had their effect on her and her school work went to pieces till she felt able to tell Miss Naftel and she was moved.

Another remembers one of the sons in her billet, who was rapidly growing into a strident teenager. While they were children, they did their homework on the same kitchen table, but the time came when he tried to interest her in cardboard figures which he made to prance around in suggestive poses. Long descriptions of kisses he had seen in films at first made little impression. She thought of it all as sloppy nonsense. Her Guernsey home had not prepared her for any adult understanding of sexuality and it was only slowly that she grasped the significance of his threats, which became so intimidating that she lived in daily fear. After school, when she approached her billet, her hands would shake with apprehension and she sat white-faced before her homework unable to give it her attention. When she tried to alert her host and hostess to her plight, she was cut short in disbelief and had to invent a reason for the cut in her lip. One evening her host found her riveted to a chair in her bedroom, paralysed with sheer terror, because his son had announced he was about to enter. Quickly the father took in the situation, asked for her forgiveness for past neglect and took control. The girl was found another billet and she now remembers the healing encouragement of an older friend, who helped with the move. "Darling. You've learned a bit about life. Everybody does. Forget it now and go and live."

We were a closely knit group of friends, those of us preparing for School Certificate that summer. We liked each other. We were determined to get through and were sometimes earnest. ('We won't let the war spoil our chances.') We rarely went to each other's billets, but out of school hours, might meet up at the Guernsey Club or occasionally the cinema.

Marie Bisson, whose parents were in Guernsey, sometimes seemed very lonely, but she was used to being an only child. She had no close relatives on the mainland and depended heavily on her billet, which was a small terraced house with no bathroom, very typical of those occupied by millworkers. Water was heated in the cellar and baths were taken there. The daughter, Bertha, was rather older than Marie, but became a valued friend and stayed on in the family home when her new husband was sent abroad in the Forces. This wartime home contrasted greatly with the large Guernsey granite homestead and greenhouses she had left behind. Her parents were Methodists like mine and had grown up alongside all the Robins not far from Summerville.

Marie was tall and slim with straight black hair. The wartime utility gym slip that she wore looked well enough on her trim figure, but on plumper friends the shallow pleats would seat and bulge and bag in an ungainly fashion, only to spring back into a tighter concertina at the knee. She was the only other one in our small group who'd known the patois and kept this as a very private matter. We never used it when we chatted together. It had become, irrevocably, the language of our parents' generation, only to be spoken back home.

Ruth Robilliard was tall and strongly built and seemed to use her body to add weight to her persona, exuding something of the masculine. She wore her light brown hair in a semi-circular roll in line with wartime styling. We heard little about her billet, but knew she'd been given a bicycle and went away on holiday with her host and hostess, who seemed better off than her own parents, who were in Guernsey. Smoking a fag or two well away from school scrutiny seemed to harness her more aggressive tendencies and no one knew how she had managed to get hold of them. She would toss her head as if little mattered more than this pose of sophistication. Her work was fairly solid, but she seemed to find in it little to stimulate her interest or inspire her to greater effort. She left the impression that she could achieve more if she so chose or if the system was more to her liking.

Margaret Palmer, with her fair hair and lovely smile, stood tall and gave out an aura of self confidence which often made her seem older than her years. Miss Winifred Roughton found her very responsive in the drama roles she was assigned, so that she made a successful Rosalind in *As You Like It*. We knew, also, of some vulnerable areas where she must have felt the precariousness of her mother's position and the threats to her health. After her sudden arrival in Wales in 1940, Mrs. Palmer, a widow with no formal training, had had to find employment to support herself. She had gone to Harrogate as a cook and general help in a large 'establishment' household, where the nannies in the vicinity were apt to meet in the grounds to exchange confidences. The next move was to Rochdale to be near Margaret and the work that she found was in such a noisy, boisterous young family that she was left exhausted. She had not fully recovered from a major operation in Guernsey. Eventually she found quieter work as housekeeper for elderly people. Margaret was allowed to live in the same house on the understanding that the billeting allowance went to the householder. Wartime pay for this work was very low and financially Margaret seemed no better off than the rest of us. Mrs. Palmer found companionship at the Guernsey Club and among other Channel Islanders in the area.

Kathleen Frampton was shorter than the others and her mass of thick springy mid-brown hair had to be flattened through the slides which kept it down. Her blue eyes and merry smile revealed an even temperament, always ready to press on and make the most of her circumstances. Good marks rewarded her hard work. In the holidays, she would go and stay with her mother and younger brother who had been evacuated to Bradford. Her father was still in Guernsey, but the family had a network of members on the mainland and they kept in touch.

Her cousin, Molly Frampton, also in our class, was more enigmatic about her holiday visits to Stockport, where her mother had been evacuated. It seemed that she was out at work and hard-pressed when Molly went and they had little chance to be properly together.

Molly wore dark rimmed glasses which accentuated a troubled facial skin. Her straight brown hair tended to escape in lank strands from the clips which held it. By the end of the week, a scuffed blouse collar or ink blotches on the sleeve, gave the tousled look she liked to achieve. Sometimes she moved with deliberate slowness as if she couldn't be bothered to act briskly. She was loath to let on that she was quick on the uptake and more streetwise than most of her contemporaries, lying low like a motionless tiger biding its time. Mundane work was something she could manage without; she could well afford to waste school time since she was quick to assimilate what was important to her, knew how to get by and shrug off criticism for her inattention.

When she challenged Miss Mahy as to the value of doing so much geometry and algebra which, she reckoned, would never be used in later life, she was (wisely) taken seriously and we all had a comprehensive answer to our unvoiced question.

If her temper was sometimes on a short fuse, she had learned to control it, but her magnificent raging Herod showed the hidden vehemence which she kept in check.

Kathleen Cochrane's beautifully modelled face was crowned with wavy chestnut hair which matched her deep brown eyes. She was calm, not easily fazed and seemed cheerfully able to set limits to what she could do, and work well within that framework. Her parents were in Guernsey, but a sister of her mother's was in Llandudno and every holiday she went to stay there and met up with a number of other relations and a circle of Guernsey people in that area. With them, she went frequently to the cinema. At the Odeon, the cashier in the foyer kiosk was a Guernsey person, a Mrs. Falla who used to work in the fish market in St. Peter Port. When she recognised a fellow islander arriving, she would tip off the organist, who then included 'Sarnia Cherie' in the interval medley.

Kathleen found it hard, sometimes, to adapt herself to the situation in her billet, but was allowed a hot water bottle in the cold weather, always a boon when there was no central heating and when coal for the living room fire was in short supply. She saw this as a luxury since her own mother, in a rather spartan way, had thought such things unnecessary.

Hazel Maplesden, almost seventeen, was the oldest in our group, and the only one to have both parents on the mainland. She lived with them in rented accommodation which they had found in Rochdale a little while after the evacuation. They had arrived, initially, in Bitterne near Southampton, having left virtually all their possessions behind. Their dog had been hurriedly put down, so that it would not suffer from becoming a hungry stray. Mr. Maplesden's work as a dental mechanic (near Oldham) provided the family with a measure of security which few others could rely on, but when it came to clothes, food and leisure, she seemed little better off than we were, not because her parents were slack (quite the reverse), but because, by that time, the others of us had found quite a lot of backing from various sources and were managing to hold our own.

In our small circle, Hazel was often the first to be in the know when there was something afoot. Her parents who met the staff at the Guernsey Club and joined in all the activities related to the school, picked up straws in the wind.

Except for me, the youngest, all were fifteen or sixteen, and so old enough to leave school and move on. Some were planning to go as soon as exams were over.

I had been entered for eight subjects for School Certificate: English Language, English Literature, History, Divinity, French, Maths (Arithmetic, Geometry and Algebra), Biology and Art (Painting, Plant and Figure composition). Shortly before the exams, I had dropped Geography and Latin, which would have brought the subjects over the limit the school allowed. Those who had given up History some time before never did get a grasp of the modern scene and the significance of the two World Wars and they felt the loss ever afterwards.

The front room at Boothroyd was prepared for us and Miss Clayton did most of the invigilating. As we ploughed through one paper after another, we worried that we had not always covered the entire syllabus. Would there be enough questions that we could answer? Several had grave doubts about the French. We all had gaps and blind spots because of the disruptions of the previous years.

We wouldn't know the results till after the holidays, but we had five weeks instead of the usual four to compensate for our lost Whitsun holiday, which we had been obliged to forego and work through. Teachers had staggered their own holidays to make this possible.

When I look back to the first week of that summer holiday in 1943, I think of back ache and sore hands. I went away with a party of Miss Keating's girls to pick peas near Wigan. Many from other schools could be spotted in distant clusters of forty or fifty like moving ants on a ribbed green background. Rows of peas stretched to the horizon. After exams, the outdoor work proved a salutary experience.

The orientation took the form of a severe thunderstorm, which started rivulets through our camp site. On this our first evening, we had just spread out our bedding for the night. We were told to dig trenches round the tents, but only a few forks and spades could be found. An assortment of kitchen knives proved useless in loosening the hardened earth. I got soaked through to the skin and my Wellingtons filled with water.

The next day we were up at 6 a.m. to do the chores before being tipped from a lorry into a field of turnips. The peas were not ready. We had each weeded four very long rows when the rain drove us back to our tents to attend to stinging hands and blisters.

It was with relief that we saw peas when we were unloaded the following day. Someone showed us how to uproot the plant, turn it upside down and strip off the pods from the root downwards. Soon we gathered speed and in four days, I had filled 13½ sacks each bulging with 42 lbs of peas, thus making a grand total of 567 lbs. Pay was at the rate of one shilling and fourpence per sack, so my earnings amounted to eighteen shillings. To this was added a small amount for the initial turnip weeding at eight pence (8d) per hour. This might have been regarded as very acceptable pocket money for a schoolgirl. It exceeded slightly the sum I had brought from Guernsey. When, however, it was offset by the camp expenses of £1, then the financial result was very disappointing. The positive benefits of fresh air, communal living and the camp concert could not completely outweigh the lingering feeling of helplessness and futility. I looked at the millworkers with new respect. However hard they worked, there could be little experience of reward or improvement in their position. Their gaunt white faces and their clothes bespeckled with cotton fluff which floated about everywhere inside the mills, conveyed the impression that they were constantly losing out. They were caught in the long-term effects of repetitive work with little prospect of better conditions, higher wages or of altenative employment. There was no choice and no exit or so I felt. I saw what it was like for myself some time later when I was taken over a mill. The noise of the machinery was overwhelming.

I remembered my parents' maxim to do your best, work hard and save hard. It applied well to people like themselves, who were not tied to fixed wages and hours of work. If, in propitious times, they ploughed in enough time, money and skill, they could develop a thriving building or tomato-growing business. They reaped the reward of their extra efforts. Not so the millworkers.

But, I reasoned, they must have learned to accommodate themselves to those rigid patterns, otherwise they would not grow mellow or genial like Mr. Livsey.

I thought of Miss Winnie Davenport, my Sunday School teacher with her pallid, pinched features and thin legs. She was a most perceptive, intelligent person, who gave us interesting things to discuss. Yet she was tied to routine mill work and an overcrowded home where she had to cope with the sharp demands of an older generation and make a contribution to the rent. She had never married. I was filled with admiration of her stalwart character and faith.

My observations were simplistic and ill-informed but I was trying to fit them into the wider picture of poverty and social reform which had loomed large in Miss Stewart's more graphic History lessons. There was still much to be done to improve conditions. Sometimes, I watched children skipping in the narrow cobbled streets between the blackened terraced houses. "One of these days," I muttered to myself, "I must do something about all that." (As if I could!)

After pea picking, I spent the rest of the holiday with Brian at Summerseat. It was always important to us to talk of home, discuss our various concerns and show each other the things we had acquired. The rest was very matter of fact, I would do much of his mending, turning a shirt collar or patching his pyjamas. I passed on the brown blanket I had brought from Guernsey for use in the cold nights on the Derbyshire moors. The boys had to sleep with their windows open and sometimes the rain and snow blew in.

Brian had moved in September 1942 from Gt. Hucklow to join the ninety or so boys in the senior section of the school, which was accommodated at Whitehall, a large house with accompanying lodges and chapel set in grounds of 39 acres, obtained on lease. They were three miles north of Buxton and about thirteen miles away from the fifty to sixty Juniors, who stayed on in Gt. Hucklow.

Groups of boys ate, had lessons and spent their spare time in the same room and took it in turn to sweep, serve meals and do the chores. They chopped wood for the fires and fed chickens and some helped the local farmers in the holidays, especially the few who had nowhere else to go.

Aside from this, the traditional grammar school curriculum was maintained, interspersed with long, rigorous cross-country runs in all weathers. It seemed these were part of a deliberate policy of 'toughening up', closely associated with the goals and activities of the JTC (Junior Training Corps) in which boys were prepared for the gruelling life of the army. In line with the traditions of the school, this was accorded much prestige and boys were often

expected to follow their comrades into war, as if dicing with death
was the best option their world could offer.

It was later estimated that over 500 Old Elizabethans served in
the Armed Forces or the Merchant Navy during the Second
World War and that at least forty-six lost their lives. It seems a
disproportionately high percentage and draws attention to the
type of pressure placed on the boys to volunteer. As Channel
Islanders, they were exempt from military service and were not
called up. If they believed fighting was a futile way to resolve
problems, they were considered 'pansy'. Any of the parents
trapped on the island must have dreaded the day when their sons
reached an eligible age, in case they enlisted without their
knowledge or consent and bad news followed.

That summer, we set aside Monopoly, which had begun to pall,
and switched to ping pong on the long-suffering dining room
table. Our walks took us to places where we could get peat or leaf
mould to improve the soil for Uncle's vegetables, and along the
Irwell which smelt so strongly of chemicals from the mills. I liked
to pick bluebells, catkins, harebells and any wild flowers in season
and we found our own câches of blackberries for tea. Grants'
Tower was a favourite landmark to encircle. Its falling rubble was a
growing danger to the public, but dismantling it seemed far down
the list of wartime priorities. Besides, it was arguably worth
preserving, since Charles Dickens had modelled the Cheeryble
brothers in *Nicholas Nickleby* on the real-life Grants.

I read many of Aunty's books. One has left me with the
lingering memory of a treacherous bog which could suck in
people – *A Girl of the Limberlost* by Gene Stratton-Porter.

I sat in a field near the house and sketched the scene which
spread before me: Holcombe Moor, crowned by Peel's Tower
which dominated the surrounding landscape with its scatter of
mill chimneys and villages. We had come to know each one by
name although they had shed all their identifying plaques and
signposts. Later, I used indian ink to give a crisp definition to the
outline and added a wash of paint to suggest life and warmth.
Now it lies in my case as a memorial to talent that was never
developed to the full. It was one of the few drawings I did during
the war, which was not instigated by someone else. The effect I
produced on paper was an etherialised expression of the
thoughts and feelings I had about the neighbourhood. I had not
captured the mood or the pain or the courage. I was dimly aware
that one could and I set aside the resulting sense of frustration.

In contrast, my heavily shaded pencil drawing of my own face was soulful. One day, at Edmund St. when I was in a thoughtful mood, I had tried to express what I saw in the mirror. After a quick glance, Miss Keating told me to throw it away. My look had by-passed the normal mode of communication between us. I felt that there must be something too revealing or too distorting in my effort. It's as though she had said, "We can't have that now." Such in-depth views must be postponed, till everything returned to normal. The family was the setting for that kind of exposure. But what would they see, when they looked at me? I realised all too clearly that, at home, the old patterns of relating could never be resumed. Too much water had passed under the bridges. I was older and had adapted myself to my billet. I had come to understand Miss Keating's 'language', the way she expressed her personality. It was perfected to an art form. In comparison, my newly acquired skills were, like the crust on an apple pie, applied. But processes of identification and integration were taking place and, viewed from her side, I was more acceptable.

While in Summerseat, Brian and I did the errands, fetching the bread from Mrs. Davenport's and some of the rations from the Co-op. It was while I was queuing up at the butcher one morning that I was riveted by a lively conversation. A grey-haired customer wearing the usual shawl and clogs was holding forth. Was it the sight of slabs of meat around me, which gave special vividness to her story of someone's searing pain, the tearing up of draw sheets, blood and people being fetched? There must have been a dreadful injury or death. We were down to stark realities.

And then I knew. So this was birth. I was relieved. For much too long, it seemed, the people round me had been hesitating. "Is she old enough to know?" – as if the experience was too awful, harmful or frightening for young psyches. Now I knew otherwise. I could be told and all was well. It was an initiation far more natural and helpful than the oblique references in novels and the text book diagrams of reproduction I had seen.

"Brutes!" Cousin Cyril announced. For a full hour, he had been struggling with the theorems in my geometry exam paper. He and his family were staying at Summerseat for a short holiday. His wife, Florence, was Aunty Helene's sister and he himself came from that large family of Robins at Les Longs Camps near Summerville. He taught French in S. London, but the bombing had driven his school to a country area in Hampshire. They were both exhausted from acting as wardens to a group of lively evacuated boys and Cousin Flo had frequent palpitations and needed respite.

Their teenage son came with them, another Brian. He was tall, with masses of jet black hair, sultry good looks accentuated by thick lips and bushy eyebrows. His hearty laugh, good humour and energy enlivened everyone. His mother took care to explain he was off to visit his girl friend's home.

When we were back at school and the School Certificate results were announced, we were pleased that our little group of eight had done so well. Inevitably, there were disappointments in the French. Despite a last minute push, Miss Roughton had not given enough time for the subject. Perhaps she had too many irons in the fire and was trying to do too much. Those whose patois might have given them a headstart were not placed to do much better than the others. The 'oral' had been abandoned. We hadn't had enough practice.

The overall results gave three of us matriculation exemption. Although I had credits or distinctions in every paper, I felt I had it in me to do better. Was I rating myself too highly and being pompous? It was hard to tell where we stood in relation to other schools. Some, like Stretford, had been demolished or badly disrupted too. There was no way of judging whether I might have done better at Miss Keating's school. And did it matter anyway?

She must have thought so, for she asked Miss Roughton once again if I could be released to attend her school. Predictably, she was refused.

By that time, I had become absorbed in the development of ideas, tracing cause and effect and following their interplay and trying to understand differing goals and motivations. I liked to know what made people tick. My writing skills were improving, I had a good short-term memory and was better able to assimilate assorted material.

It was arranged that I should stay at school and take Higher School Certificate in two years' time with History and English as main subjects and Geography and Art at subsidiary level. There were virtually no other subjects on offer. No choice.

GROUP **A**  Miss Naftel
Mrs. Steele
Mrs Underdown

**B**  Miss Clayton
~~Mrs Harwood~~

**C**  Miss Mahy
Miss MacPhail

**D**  Miss Brown
Miss ~~Little~~ Mallet

**E**  Mr Blicq
~~Mrs Blicq~~
Miss Sayer

**F**  Miss Brittain
Mrs. Miles

**G**  Miss Stewart
Mrs. Chisnall

**H**  Miss Ogier
Mrs. Le Patourel.

**I**  Miss Hubert
Miss Wendover

**J**  Miss Simpson
~~Mrs Morgan~~
Mrs Watson

**K**  Miss E. Johnson
~~Mrs Robert~~ Mrs Blicq

{ **L**  Miss P. Johnson
Mrs. R. O. Falla
Mrs Morgan
Miss Hazell
**M**  Miss Gavet
Mrs Leeder.

In draft, Miss Roughton's listings of the leaders due to escort the school groups at the evacuation.

Norah H. Roughton

Roylelands, the Reception Centre, which housed the senior girls. (In this post-war view, there are newer windows.)

Horse Carrs, the Reception Centre, where many of the juniors lived for six months (taken many years later).

A group of older and younger girls taken soon after their arrival in Rochdale. Standing on the left is Miss E. Naftel and kneeling near her is Mrs. Nellie Ogden.

The senior school at Castleton,
taken when the shelters in the
playground had gone.

Miss Norah
Roughton

Salvation Army

The King
Sarnia Chérie
Chorus All through the night
      Fisherman's Evening Song
Solo Angels ever bright and fair
Chorus Lord at all times I will bless thee
Recitation Upper IV A + B.
Chorus Venetian Gondola Song
      Polish National Dance
Dance Mountain March

Solos Maydew
      Hark hark the Lark } Joan Adams
Violin Solo Miss N. H. Roughton
Chorus Verduronette
Dance Varsouvienne
Recitations Overheard on a Saltmarsh
      The Twins } H. Bewey
              G. Damarell
Song Rolling down to Rio
Dances Polka Piqué
      Clap Dance
Violin Solo Miss N. H. Roughton.
Folk Song Ho, Ro my nut brown maiden
      Solo Verses Gwen, Joan, Joyce
Dashing away with the Smoothing
        P.T.O.    Iron

Sample
Concert
Programme

Mrs. Jessie
Keating
in 1950.

My billet at 22, Edmund Street,
Rochdale (taken years later
when the windows had been
replaced. My room was the one
over the door.)

Miss Essie
Keating.

*Saturday April 18th 1942.*
I helped to do some jobs in the morning and
I washed my gloves. Then I went to get the
bread and went to town with Miss Keating
and Mrs. Keating. It was sunny, but cold.
I finished my Art, when I came back and in
the afternoon I went to the High School to do
some gardening. Miss Keating had an appointment
for the first half hour, so she showed me
what I had to do and said "Dig as deep
as you can". I dug till she came and she
said that I had nearly reached New Zealand,
but that the deeper the better for the soil.

Extract from
my diary.
'Dig for
Victory'.

## Chapter XIV

### *'I'll Be Seeing You in All the Old Familiar Places'*

A sea of 3,000 faces receded into the distance. Those of us in the school choir were perched high in a vast arena and feeling like little dots ourselves. We were at the King's Hall, Belle Vue in Manchester (adjoining the Zoo) and all eyes were fixed on our navy figures. In the hush of anticipation, we knew great things were expected of us. It was Sunday afternoon, September 19th 1943, and these Guernsey and Jersey people had come from all over the north for a reunion. The rally had been organised by the Manchester and District C.I. Society and the London based Channel Islands Refugees Committee (as a follow-up to the first one on June 19th which I had missed). Now, our voices sounded thin and ineffectual, but the loud applause for our songs showed us how much the feelings of solidarity mattered.

The Jersey Chairman, Lord Justice du Parcq, praised the achievements of Guernsey's new VC, Major H.W. le Patourel, and spoke with pride of the 10,000 or so Channel Islanders who were serving in the Forces, most of them there 'without compulsion', he added.

Referring to those still on the islands, he said, "They don't get much food, not much more than just enough." They were not starving, he assured us, merely finding the diet rather monotonous and they were cheerful. "I can tell you some were very cheerful at the beginning of the Occupation, but they are not so cheerful now and those are the Germans."

In the maelstrom afterwards, and over the plates of meat pie and a very rare tomato to remind us of home, there were cordial exchanges. "Hello! I thought you were still in Guernsey. Where are you living?" "Is your husband over here?" "I think the Germans have got our car . . . we heard Morris had moved, but we don't know any Morris." "Do you know what it's like in Biberach? I think John was deported there." Fragments, but enough to renew the sense of belonging and shared hope. Alfred le Page, who had worked at Milestone, was there. He thought Rue des Landes had been 'laid to rest'. Did that mean our house was flattened? I didn't take this too seriously. Wouldn't I have heard if that had happened? Anyway, it didn't seem to matter all that much anymore. It would just be one more factor to take into account later on when everything came to light. Now it was swallowed up in the dark inner context of all the severe disruptions.

One of the best of the Red Cross messages trickling through at this time came from Gran of Milestone. It said, 'Nature very beautiful. Sunsets remind us you. Hope you will soon enjoy them with us.' I knew she must be thinking of a painting I had given her, awash with crimson and orange, my streaked effort to capture the breathtaking qualities of a Guernsey sunset. Conventional greetings could not have matched this for a moment of shared appreciation and mutual understanding. (Did she still have enough 'eucalyptus' for her handkerchiefs?)

When Miss Roughton announced that we were to have a week in October to find out more about Rochdale, it seemed a novel idea. The word 'Project' had not yet been applied to such freelance activity and those at our stage always followed a set syllabus or guidance by the staff.

Strenuous efforts were made to assemble books and maps of the town and its environs. VIPs came to give us talks on education and, inevitably, on the Co-op, since we were on its home ground, where it originated. Mr. Fred Wilson illustrated the local dialect. The sharpness of 'Lancashire wit' was so strongly emphasised that we hurled the phrase at anyone of our number who made a mild crack.

As I pick up my wallpaper-covered notebook, my eye travels along the trail of billowing smoke which curls out of a tall mill chimney. It spells out 'Rochdale'. My turgid notes give text book outlines of the lives of leading citizens: John Bright, Gracie Fields and John Collier, a poet whose epitaph I quoted:

> *Here lies John and with him Mary*
> *Cheek by jowl they never vary*
> *No wonder they so well agree*
> *John wants no punch and Moll no tea.*

I drew a creditable representation of the Town Hall from a photograph and made sketch maps which located places whose names I'd seen on buses. Now I knew where they were.

After the predictable questionings ("What about your proper school work?"), Mrs. Keating had come up trumps. One or two postcards of old scenes were produced and today I see, stuck in my book, a shallow river Roch being crossed by horse and cart. Dotted around are loosely scattered mills with trees and fields still evident.

Is it a little strange that no one asked us what we thought of our discoveries or how we were reacting to our stay in the town? The approach was very academic and impersonal, but it provided access to outside sources and allowed us to cross the usual subject boundaries. The speakers must have thought it was worth while coming and gave our efforts greater credence. Investigating our surroundings had become an acceptable activity for the classroom and we felt 'special'. In small measure this experiment made up for our immense ignorance of any national development of the previous fifty years, whether literary, historical or political. Such 'recent' topics were not usually dealt with in schools, since, it was alleged, you could not get an impartial view so soon after the events. On that showing, it was a risk to take history as far as the First World War. (But we were behind with the syllabus and did not get that far anyway!)

The few sporadic current affairs lessons we had left us feeling outdistanced and outclassed. They had usually taken the form of a quiz on political figures. 'Who is Home Secretary?' 'Who lives at 11, Downing St?' How were we supposed to know? "Read the newspapers," they said. But how would these provide the answers to such selective factual questions? Articles always assumed previous knowledge. The task seemed formidable, hopeless and unrewarding.

One October day, Miss Roughton received a message from the Infirmary. Miss Reed and Miss Sayer had been admitted after being knocked over by a district nurse's car as they were cycling to school. Fortunately the injuries were not too serious. Miss Reed's head was hurt, requiring a few stitches, while Miss Sayer had grazes and bruises, mainly on her legs.

Our class quickly clubbed together to convey our good wishes:

> *Dear Miss Reed,*
> *We hope you're not bored*
> *With the look of the ward*
> *Or with reading in bed*
> *With your poor bandaged head,*
> *But we hope you will soon*
> *Walk into our room*
> *To see that our homework's well read.*

> *Dear Miss Sayer,*
> *We were sorry indeed*
> *For you and Miss Reed*
> *When we heard of your plight*
> *You gave us a fright!*
> *But we were relieved*
> *And we fully believed*
> *That doctors would soon put you right.*

When I went to Summerseat for the autumn half-term, Uncle said I could have a copy of a photograph of Brian and me which had been taken at the end of the summer holiday in the hope of getting it to Guernsey by a new channel. Direct communication was still through Red Cross messages only, and ordinary letters and packages were not allowed. But now there could be another avenue of contact through the Channel Island civilian deportees, whom the Germans had interned on the Continent. These were allowed to write occasionally, both to the mainland and to the islands. Perhaps they could be used as intermediaries to relay news between the sets of relations separated by the Channel in 1940. It was worth a try. Among them was Cousin Harold Robin (brother to Cyril, from the large family at Les Longs Camps). He was in the men's camp at Laufen and we assumed he had been taken there because of his experience in the First World War. My parents had asked Uncle Eug in a Red Cross message to send them a photo of Brian and me through Harold.

Uncle wanted to comply, but had no film because of wartime shortages, so, before the start of the autumn term, he had taken the two of us to a scruffy little shop which, no doubt, had done passport photos in its heyday. A nondescript middle-aged man emerged through an inside door. He had no idea how to make us feel at ease. "Now smile!" the two men insisted. If one of us did, the other couldn't. The situation had got too fraught. We must look our best for our parents. The man lost patience and clicked.

Now, as Uncle handed me the print, I saw for myself the sorry result. My hair had refused to be coaxed and tamed into shape and I looked cross-eyed as if hit on the head and poised to sink to the floor. Brian, beside me, was attempting a smile, but looked nervously uncertain. Memories of the whole upsetting episode came flooding back. . . . Now Uncle's voice obtruded. It sounded casual enough . . . "and I put in a covering letter to say we were all well. . . ." I ran upstairs and flung myself on the bed in tears of impotence. How could he send that *awful* picture? How dare he? What a ghastly impression they would have in Guernsey. There was no way of getting it back or of explaining. I hoped it would get lost, drowned, burnt . . . (much sobbing). Small resentments fuelled the fires. I was angry and upset and tired of trying to go along with everything and 'fitting in'. I wanted to differentiate myself from others. I challenged some of Uncle's assertions on the war, on European history and theology, all areas that seemed to be his special domain. He was annoyed. He told me I was echoing Miss Keating's views, but I knew I wasn't. She would have taken a different stand. Secretly I was pleased my ideas were accorded so much status. They could pass for hers. Fortunately an ingrained reticence saved me from being continuously bombastic.

For months, I often found myself crying into my pillow before falling asleep. I had little idea why and yet there was some sense of release in the experience. At last I was allowing myself a chance to let go. It had seemed imperative to be 'brave' and this I had confused with being restrained, tightening my belt and holding myself in.

\* \* \* \* \*

It was November 23rd 1943. My face fell as I picked up my brand new School Certificate from the tea-trolley at Edmund St. It was smudged with fresh paw marks. I was greatly relieved that the worst effects rubbed off when they were dry. That day, our Prize-giving (Speech Day in the north) had been marked by having actual prizes. Someone had given money for them. I flicked through the pages of my new books: the Complete Works of Shakespeare, an anthology of verse and Cruden's Concordance. Those in our class received our School Certificates and Audrey Hamel (ex-Head Girl) was congratulated on getting Higher School Certificate. With teaching in mind, she had begun courses at Salisbury Training College.

The guest speaker was Miss Cowell, Head of Hulme Grammar School for Girls in Oldham. She had been of great help to the Ladies' College in the first days of evacuation. Now, she spoke of the adventurous spirit of Marie Curie and others. As she urged us, likewise, to be constant and enduring in our efforts, she could not have foreseen how soon her words would be applied (if scaled down in their scope and rigour!). For it was just three weeks later that we, as prefects and sub-prefects, found ourselves stranded in the dark at an Oldham bus-stop. We were returning to Rochdale after a party which she had organised for us at her school. Her senior girls had entertained us with games, a treasure hunt, dancing and a sumptuous tea (outstanding in times of frugal rationing). After an hour's wait for the bus, our feet were freezing on the snow-covered pavement. A pea-souper fog thickened and all the traffic came to a standstill. Our escorts, Miss Roughton and Miss Naftel, decided we should have to walk home to Rochdale. Those whose billets could be reached by telephone crowded round a kiosk and soon we were off, holding each other's hands in a long unbroken line as instructed. Suddenly a disturbance at the front brought us all to a halt. Miss Roughton had tripped over the pavement and cut her lip and Miss Naftel, close behind, had fallen over her. Fortunately they were not badly injured and we trailed into our billets round 11 p.m. The seven mile walk, inching our way along, had taken three hours, but only three hours. That, as much as anything, made us realise later how close we were to Oldham and yet so far removed from the Intermediate brother school. Why didn't we see them sometimes? The witty speeches of the Boys' headmaster, Mr. Fulford, on his occasional visits to Rochdale were much appreciated, but did little to bridge the gap. We heard little news and knew next to nothing of other Guernsey schools scattered over the country.

Apart from that Oldham outing, the Seniors had few privileges and the duties could be irksome. Collecting money for National Savings, bus tokens or dinner was routine enough, but shooing out the obdurate at break was galling. In the cold and icy weather, the resistant sandwiched themselves behind blackboards and stonewalled all attempts to prise them away. They held their statutory third-of-a-pint milk bottles to their mouths and sucked at empty straws. As prefects, we were appointed to make Miss Roughton's system work and it was a measure of her authority and our deference that we felt compelled to try – against all odds.

For much of the winter of 1943/4, our days were spent huddled in overcoats. We were given permission to keep them on, since, through shortage of fuel, the radiators were barely lukewarm. A few of us lingered on at school, uncertain of the future and how to prepare for it.

Kathleen Cochrane and I perched side by side on stools in the old lab. Science teachers had evaporated, absorbed in the war effort. Ageing rubber tubes curled into bunches on top of cupboards and residual crystals clung to dusty jars on shelves.

Kathleen barely spoke. She was immersed in Tolstoy's *War and Peace*, tossing aside one volume for the next. Lessons were few and far between. I sat with a Geography or History textbook taking copious notes for later indigestion. The lab air we were breathing had the smell of limbo. We were the dregs inside a jar, left over without structured purpose.

What next? We could not make the war come to an end and we were tired of waiting. We knew we must buckle down to more. The directed effort which had carried us through School Certificate had not been harnessed into other things. Now we knew, that like waves of girls before us, we would have to decide on a job or a career and start the training.

Kathleen and Marie took to sketching female figures, whose sleek forms were clothed in smart practical dresses or the full-skirted glamour of post-war fantasy when clothes rationing would end. Could they prepare for careers in art? Miss Sayer made enquiries at the Manchester School of Art and thought so. Olive van Bodegom who had outstanding talent and a highly individualistic style had got in easily. A benefactor was paying her fee. Perhaps Kathleen and Marie could get backing from the Scholarship Fund which Miss Roughton had been building up from the proceeds of our concerts.

That year, there was an atmosphere of finality about our Christmas activities in Summerseat. It was the end of childhood. Brian, Jean and I marked it by one last fling at indoor Hide and Seek, crouching in tea-chests or climbing into wardrobes. Then feeling this was silly, we walked to Rochdale. A mile in Guernsey had seemed a very long way, but now with a revised sense of distance, we found we could easily get to my billet in half a day. Brian had not seen the house before, but we couldn't go in because the Keatings were away.

The highlight of our holiday as a threesome was to be the Grand Concert presented by the Brobins (an amalgam of Brehaut and Robin). Besides a charade, a quiz and a competition, there was to be a play where Brian and Jean (always a good mimic), would be transformed into Mr. and Mrs. Ernie Greenhalgh, a Lancashire couple recovering from 'flu. I was to be their son, Humphrey, returning home from college . . . 'our 'umph'. His mother, with curlers protruding from her turban and an old apron and mop, would stuff the conversation with as many 'ee-by-gums' and 'reet-to-do's' as she could manage.

Because the advertising agency was so lavish with its posters, those who intended to come must have been overawed by the grandeur of the occasion. They appeared at the top of the staircase with all the dignity at their command and were duly announced as Monsieur et Madame Robin (pronounced for the occasion in the French way and not the customary anglicised Roebin). Madame put forward a silvered foot. (She was wearing her seventeen-year-old wedding shoes.) A carefully preserved shawl was draped over her shoulders and shiny jewelry glittered on her person. Her escort in top hat and tails added the necessary hauteur. As they sailed to their seats, they were handed specially designed programmes and the show began.

Since settling in with Ruth at her billet with the Hebdens early in 1942, Jean had moved twice more, the first time to Mrs.

Hebden's sister, Mrs. Charlton, whose husband was in the Forces, far away, and probably in Libya. They thought Jean's lively personality would help to fill the need for companionship. As they were Christian Scientists, Ruth and Jean felt they could not share their beliefs and they had found a Methodist welcome at the Central Hall. Now, Jean was with the Midgeleys, but preparing to leave school and Mrs. Norris, taking up her role of guardian, arranged a placement for her at Foxlease, the Girl Guide Training Centre at Lyndhurst in the New Forest. There she would get training in catering and domestic work, while helping to look after the guests. Perhaps they were picturing the day when Jean might assist her parents in their own guest house if it re-opened. Mrs. Norris, herself, had warm recollections of her frequent stays there and felt close enough to the family to take on the parents' role in bridging Jean's transition from school to work.

In the meantime, the Guernsey Club was flourishing. It had started on a new phase in September 1943 when it moved into different premises, the ARP Club in Milkstone Rd. The Committee said they could not afford the increase in fee for the use of the original room. Since there was plenty in the Club kitty and no need to make provision beyond the end of the war, it is difficult to see why the alarm bells rang.

The new venue had more facilities. Darts and table tennis tournaments were organised and Lady Turner provided a piano for community singing. A cosy fire burned in the grate and Hazel Maplesden's grandmother, who lived on the mainland, contributed a gramophone and records.

At Miss Stewart's instigation and for the benefit of the girls, it was maintained, three evenings took on an international flavour. People from Austria, Czechoslovakia and Poland came in turn. Perhaps they were not experienced speakers, since they seemed to come from a cardboard world of geographical features, music and educational processes. (They were not allowed to talk of politics.) In my role of secretary to this International Club, I tried in vain to bring a little verve into my flat-voiced vote of thanks. Miss Winifred's face looked rapt with interest.

On entertainment evenings, sections took it in turn to sing or act. 'My Ain Folk' became Maud Bewey's theme song. Although it related to a different part of the British Isles, by its haunting quality, it evoked a moving response in us all. We sometimes sang it together but it was she who interpreted the feelings of separation and the solidarity.

> *And it's oh! but I'm longing for my ain folk*
> *Tho' they be but lowly, puir and plain folk:*
> *I am far beyond the sea*
> *But my heart will ever be*
> *At hame in dear auld Scotland, wi' my ain folk.*

One girl daringly launched into a tap dance. Would that be considered common or ill-chosen? A few popular songs crept in . . . 'Jealousy' . . . 'Yours' . . . 'If I had my way'. These were never heard within the school walls, because they were not of the 'right' period or genre. But in content, were they any different from the ones included in the traditional singing, which we all joined in at the Club? 'Drink to me only with thine eyes and I will pledge with mine' . . . 'Cherry ripe . . . Come and buy!' . . . 'Early one morning'. . . .

I didn't attend on a regular basis, but remember being in a sketch called P's and Q's which was subsequently done to death. It concerned people reaching the end of a queue before realising they were not going to get peas after all, but dental treatment. On one occasion, Miss Roughton forgot herself and wrote, for presentation by the staff and friends, a farcical murder story with an outlandish number of sprawling bodies, looking ghoulish in their greasepaint.

There was a joyous sense of relief when news came that Monica Ball's father, who came to the Club when on leave, was safe. He had been feared missing at sea. By the end of the war, after experiencing many vicissitudes and rescues in the Navy he could say that he had lost three ships without getting his feet wet!

The spring weather of 1944 blew away the sluggishness of winter and Miss Stewart's stock went up. She was organising an away weekend for a few senior girls at the end of the Whitsun holiday. We were to cycle over the moors from Todmorden to a Youth Hostel at Jerusalem Farm near Colne. Most of us could ride already, but few had bikes. We were amazed to hear that members of staff would lend us theirs. So we were not just classroom fodder after all. They thought we were sensible and could be trusted as people. Shackles dropped off and the sense of anticipation and excitement was heightened by the news of the Allied landings on the French beaches. At last it was D-Day, June 6th 1944. Something was happening. New developments could be expected.

Three days later, I set off on Miss Winifred's squeaky bicycle with Miss Keating's knapsack on my back. It was something of a last fling for us all. We had grown close together over the years, but in a few weeks everyone would be gone except for me. The L VI<sup>th</sup>, after taking School Certificate, would find work, the remaining members of my group would disperse and Jeanne Guille and Monica Ball, who were older, were going to Training College. Times were changing. The war might even end quite soon.

Pushing the bikes a mile or two uphill and then freewheeling down the other side together was a heady experience, no matter that we were soaked in clinging mist. Then the brakes of the bike Gwen Damarell was riding failed. It was Miss Norah Roughton's. Miss Stewart insisted on exchanging it for her own and used her foot on the wheel to slow down the faulty one.

Joining with other young hikers and cyclists to do the hostel chores, singing popular songs, dancing, sleeping in bunk beds, picnicking on shared rations, the fresh air, the companionship, the sense of escape, the fun, the exercise . . . it was so light-hearted . . . a wonderful change and release. . . . We made a vow. Never again would we refer to Miss Stewart as 'Stewpot'. 'Stewey' was more friendly. But it proved to be too late. When we got back, she told us she was leaving. She had found a post as second mistress at a school in Aylesbury.

This had been her swan song.

\* \* \* \* \*

"For this is Flora's holiday!" . . . we would tunefully inform an audience of Lancashire housewives . . . "sacred to ease and happy love," we quavered. At least once a year, the ticket money for a concert went into the Old Intermedians' Scholarship Fund, intended for girls who wanted further training. As one of its trustees, Miss Roughton was glad that four of the others were on the mainland, two of them on the staff: Miss Clayton and Miss Naftel. It is perhaps a little surprising that no use was made of the Fund till September 1942. Many able girls had left the school before that date without the benefit of its financial support. It seems that the trustees held back partly because they did not want to touch the capital of £975 invested in War stock. They considered that only the interest (3½%) could be used, together with the sum of £129.19.2 held in a current account. (It was fortunate that deposits in the major English banks, which had been made in Guernsey, could be drawn on in the UK.)

As the fees for a residential college course were usually in the region of £40 to £50 p.a., there was enough available to pay for a few girls, as long as replenishments could be made if the war went on. In a handful of cases, where the girls' fathers were Freemasons and still in Guernsey, sponsors on the mainland were found (usually from among the staff of the Boys' Intermediate School), and grants were made to the daughters for commercial courses or other appropriate training.

In Guernsey, few Intermediate girls had stayed on at school beyond School Certificate. If they wanted to go further, they were usually transferred to the Ladies' College, but there were some exceptions, and on that basis, early on, Miss Roughton had been assured by the Rochdale authorities that she could keep a few older girls on the roll.

As it turned out, only seven were helped by the Scholarship Fund while the school was in Rochdale and four of those not till the autumn of 1944. The pressing need for financial provision had been lessened in 1943, when the Ministry of Health decided to allow the equivalent of the billeting allowance to be paid to a Training College in respect of a Guernsey student's board and lodging. Lady Turner and a few anonymous well-wishers paid all or some of the fees for other girls and Miss Roughton herself may well have been one of the contributors.

Some of the girls, trying to make a life for themselves, were very enterprising and found jobs that offered help and training, whether it was in an office, a bank or as a children's nanny. Others moved away to family friends or relations, who undertook to see them through.

Among the school-leavers who did full-time further training during the evacuation were Phyllis Duquemin and Ruth le Page who did a year's course in pharmacy at Manchester University; Molly Duquemin went to Portsmouth Training College and Marian le Tissier went to the Mathay School of Music and later emerged with her LRAM. Frances Hemming did three years at Anstey Physical Training College at Sutton Coldfield, while Barbara Spiller and Yvonne Robilliard were at Bishop Otter Memorial College evacuated from Chichester to the Old Palace in Bromley, Kent.

Yvonne remembers vividly how her final exams were disrupted by the 'doodlebugs', the V1 'pilotless planes' which Hitler was rocketing across the Channel. These flying bombs exploded on landing and as no one knew when they would reach the end of their journey, they created a trail of apprehension all along their course, 'bomb alley'. The Germans were trying to counteract the morale-boosting effects of the Allied advances into France. As Yvonne and her fellow students concentrated on their exam papers, they were told to ignore the siren. The caretaker of their building would be positioned on the roof to watch the doodlebugs pass over. If he thought they might stop and so drop suddenly and wreak havoc, he would blow a whistle and all the students would duck under their desks. The invigilator noted the time so 'wasted' and added it on to the scheduled exam period!

When this was happening, Miss Mary Keating had been settled back into her London home for some time and Mrs. Keating had gone to stay with her for a while. Suddenly, the shattering of glass brought her to her feet. The front door had been hit by blast. Mrs. Keating did not turn a hair, but the two sisters thought that their mother's heart might not be strong enough to withstand the continuous uncertainties of this new onslaught and she was brought back to Rochdale. Once more the town was to accommodate an influx of evacuees. About 800 arrived and some were being helped by the people at Spotland. Now, we, the Guernseys, were like an earlier wave of immigrants, settled if not absorbed.

Marie Bisson pressed her host and hostess to take in a London boy. She said that she had been so fortunate in having a home, that she wanted the same opportunity for him. The Hindles generously agreed, although it was a squash to fit him in. When he arrived in July (1944) he looked tired and ill. His name was Bill and he was twelve years old and came from Fulham.

Many of us have kept a photograph taken before the end of the summer term, showing the whole school grouped together in the Castleton playground. The Juniors came up from Greenbank on one of their rare visits. In a prominent position was Monica Ball, who had been Head Girl that year and was taking Higher School Certificate. She was due to start on a teacher training course in the autumn at Whitelands, a London college evacuated to Durham. It was the one where Miss Naftel had been a student and where she had been May Queen in 1907, an honour that carried with it the duty of saying grace at meals. Jeanne Guille was also taking Higher School Certificate and would be going to Salisbury Training College. Hazel Maplesden also hoped to go there.

## Chapter XV

## *'And When Your Letters Come, They Bring a Smile, a Tear'*

It was the start of the autumn term 1944 and I was sixteen and so old enough to take over Miss Stewart's weekly round of Red Cross house-to-house collecting. In her footsteps, I headed for the Gas Works, to the rows of small terraced houses curving down a cobbled hill. I stood on the pavement holding my tin as I knocked on each front door, which opened directly into the living area. As likely as not, a woman with a floral cross-over apron and turban would have a contribution ready, a penny, threepence or even sixpence. I was amazed that people, so obviously hard up, could be so generous and cheery. They lived perpetually trapped in the pervasive smell of the Works, whereas I scampered off to a well furnished house in another area. Within a few months, over £12 was dropped into my tin.

I was really glad to be a collector since I had good reason to be grateful to the Red Cross. It was through its good offices that the messages to and from home were exchanged. Then as the winter of 1944/5 approached, there was a growing shortage of food in the islands. Again it was the Red Cross which was to come to the rescue. We didn't hear the details till after the war, but we knew that the Allied blockade in the Channel had stopped supplies of foodstuffs to the islands from the Continent. These were now cut off from France as well as from England. The civilian population in Guernsey and Jersey, as well as thousands of German troops stationed there, were suffering from malnutrition.

Then the cry went up in Guernsey, 'The *Vega* has come!' Just after Christmas (1944) this life-saving ship from Lisbon arrived in St. Peter Port and an unbelievable number of Red Cross parcels were unloaded. Each civilian could have one. There were a few later shipments of the same kind. The parcels had been packed with Canadian or New Zealand prisoners in mind and were crammed with unaccustomed goodies. As we later learned, the Canadian assortment consisted of

| | |
|---|---|
| 8 oz. sugar | 20 oz. biscuits |
| 4 oz. tea | 5 oz. Canadian sardines |
| 4 oz. cheese | 20 oz. milk powder |
| 16 oz. marmalade or jam | 6 oz. prunes |
| 6 oz. chocolate | 10 oz. salmon |

| 14 oz. corned beef | 8 oz. raisins |
| 20 oz. ham | pepper and salt and soap |

In that last year of the war, I was stranded at the top of the school and felt marooned. Having gone through most stages as the youngest in my class, I had the unusual sensation of being a senior far ahead of the others and in detached isolation from them. All my own class mates had left and all those in the class below. They had got through School Certificate and started on jobs, mainly doing office work.

The ones two classes behind me suddenly rose to prominence. Quickly they were given prefects' responsibilities and I was appointed Head Girl and expected to keep them on their toes. The brunt of the shooing-out-at-break operations fell on me and I decided to treat that task as sago pudding which slithered down my throat without my tasting it. "Outside!" I bawled in as deep a voice as I could manage and they mostly slinked towards the door.

Supervision in the dinner hour was now more demanding, since twenty or thirty girls were staying. A new contingent had moved to Castleton from Greenbank and it was too far for them to reach their billets at the other end of the town. Meals had improved, but there were times of potato shortage, when we had bread instead.

On the rare occasions when the two parts of the school came together, I was aware of the nudging and whispering among the younger newcomers. "Look! That's the Head Girl!" "Let me see! Which one?" I sensed a kind of awe. It was the very way I'd viewed the big Senior girls when still in Guernsey, a school generation and a world ago. The basis of authority has been loosely described as what one is and what one is landed with. I missed my friends and worked mainly on my own, positioned in front of a class while lessons went on behind me. These were side-tracked or punctuated by a giggling commentary on the latest victim in boys, who were greedily dissected and the component parts held up for comment. "Nice teeth!" "His hair's too greasy. He should wash it more often." "Did you see the way he looked at her over his shoulder?"

I looked forward to Thursdays when Margaret Palmer came to school. For the rest of the week, she was doing teaching practice at Lower Place Senior School. That way, she would be able to save a little for her fees at a Teacher Training College and hoped to go to Whitelands. Without any preparation she had been pitchforked into a classroom full of children and told to get on with them – all day. She was a resourceful person and did just that and made a success of it. Her day at Castleton was intended as one for refuelling and getting help, but there was little offered. She was obliged to join me while Miss Roughton ploughed through a glossary of Chaucer's English for my own exams.

My two companions in Art and Architecture, Marie Bisson and Kathleen Cochrane, were now attending the Manchester School of Art, financed in large measure by the Scholarship Fund as their parents were in Guernsey. We were grateful to Miss Sayer, who had sometimes complemented our classroom work with a few visits to an art exhibition or to a local church, where, once, we experimented with brass rubbings. Always keen to encourage a greater awareness of form and beauty, she drew attention to the patterns woven into Yugoslav costume at an exhibition in Manchester. I copied one or two designs thinking I could incorporate them into my knitting. My skills had developed. I made a maroon skull cap with a fair isle pattern and two elaborately patterned jumpers which lasted many years. I owe much to her guidance in composing a picture and recognising the need for balance and the harmonious distribution of colour. I have kept my drawing of the aftermath of an air raid where a family's belongings are being salvaged and thrown into a small home-made handcart. This was typical of much of the girls' work sent by Miss Sayer to the Refugee Children's Evacuation Fund in London for exhibition in the provinces, along with that of other refugees.

Now on some Saturday afternoons, I was invited to join her Art Club which she ran that winter for girls who had left school. We sat cosily round the fire at 13, Edmund St. doing lino cuts, and in the spring, we took to the moors to sketch.

Her home there with other members of staff had become more comfortable over the years. This was largely the achievement of Miss Lowther who had previously worked in the late Mrs. Roughton's family household. She would have moved to Guernsey to keep house for Miss Winifred if the evacuation had not intervened. Hers was a short, slight and neat figure, and quickly and efficiently she relieved the others of the cooking and cleaning and provided a camp bed or meal for the frequent visitors.

At school, it was still hard for the staff to cover essential subjects adequately. After Miss Reed left to be married in December 1943, there was no replacement for her, and Miss Roughton had taken over the School Certificate Biology herself. There was no one

available to teach me Geography and a correspondence course
was arranged. Miss Stewart's young successor, Miss Folkard, led
me to the deserted, stale Cookery room, held up my long History
essays and (nicely) branded them stodgy, diffuse and off the
point. "Answer the question," she insisted. I had practice in
marshalling facts, shaping an argument and drawing my own
conclusions. Miss Clayton borrowed books from the local clergy
and I had some most thought-provoking lessons on world
religions. I was encouraged to think for myself and did. The word
'mature' crept into my school reports. I took up an independent
position and questioned things.

Often there was a grey sameness about the days and many girls
were not as robust as they might have been in different
circumstances. Staff just managed to carry on from one day to the
next and no one felt they could go in for long-term planning.

The end of the war still seemed too far away to cause
excitement, but we followed the progress of the Allies. Their
successes were taken to confirm that victory was due and
inevitable. Since Britain was great and right, she would triumph.
This was only to be expected. She was in the forefront of the
winning side. Others were helping, because they saw the
legitimacy of her cause.

However factually and emotionally skewed such assumptions
might prove, many people felt buoyed up just as though their
basis were actually the case. There was more in this outlook than
easy optimism or the need for a corporate sense of security. The
red, white and blue colours of the Union Jack denoted a concept
of international relations which would not allow that Britain could
go under. She had the right to predominate, because she was
honourable. Now that it was Germany's turn to make a bid for
expansion, Britain saw this as an alien cloud overshadowing the
globe. It would soon pass over, because Germany was less worthy.

Britain's position of prestige would once more be
acknowledged world-wide. This outcome was self-evident, since it
derived from her sense of justice and morality and the wisdom
inherent in long experience of democratic processes and
benevolence. The loyal support of Canada, India, New Zealand,
Australia, the 'red' parts on the map of Africa and scattered
places on the globe, all vindicated this inalienable claim to
authority and dominance. The component sections of the
Empire by a process of identification with Britain's goals and by
participation in the struggle, would get the benefits of victory,
peace and subsequent prosperity.

Such a sense of valour and honour which we were supposed to feel somehow got confused with that inspired by visions of the Kingdom of God:

> *These things shall be: a loftier race*
> *Than e'er the world hath known shall rise,*
> *With flame of freedom in their souls*
> *And light of knowledge in their eyes.*

And centrally positioned, as though a mouth-piece, was the figure of Miss Norah Roughton in navy heading up the Guides and leading liturgical prayers at Assembly:

> *Therefore with angels and archangels*
> *and with all the company of heaven,*
> *We laud and magnify Thy glorious name*
> *evermore praising Thee and saying,*
> *Holy, holy, holy*
> *Lord God of hosts*
> *Heaven and earth are full of Thy glory*
> *glory be to Thee O Lord most high.*

This conviction of high-flown purpose was no doubt little different from the aura breathed in by German school children.

Glimpses into the illusory and transient nature of such self-congratulatory attitudes might make us feel a little uncomfortable, but hardly served to deliver us from them. Their immense emotional force could be best experienced if you tried to disassociate yourself from them. You were made to feel inferior, inadequate and shamed. And you couldn't withstand the pressure of being so outnumbered, especially when you were already conscious of your minority status and dependence and had other reasons for feeling undervalued.

Besides, girls like Maud Bewey, Delma Torode and many others had brothers in the Forces. They might have to kill or die for the cause. Billeting hosts had been called up. Some 'Old Girls' were in the WAAFS or ATS. Boys from the Elizabeth College and the Intermediate were in the war. Some might be getting hurt or butchered. Several had been decorated for bravery. You shouldn't let the side down by your questionings or misgivings. It was somehow disloyal and you would again be the outsider and the exile, standing apart and being different and of little worth.

And Miss Roughton, what did she think as she stood in front of

the girls at Assembly? Did she ever realise that she might be taken
to epitomise the national aspirations, patriotic, religious and
ethical? I think she did and I think it mattered a great deal to her
that it was so. On her were focused the projected hopes of all
those faces. The responsibility was enormous: to place herself in
such a position that she could be so used. But to succeed in these
terms she did not have to put on a performance; she had only to
be herself, as she was all the time, and others would do the rest
and emulate her ideals and her standards.

I hung back inwardly from all the flag waving. If Britain and the
Allied countries stood for a form of justice which would triumph
over evil and would prove invincible, why was it that they
seemingly gave themselves up to a bloody contest where the
winners would be the ones who could whack the hardest, and not
those who qualified as 'best'?

All the time I was wrestling with the tenets of the hymns and
the dilemmas, dangers and futilities of war, I was *very glad* that I
was being saved from Hitler. We'd heard he was trying to destroy
the Jews. It was on the wireless occasionally, since the end of 1942.

I knew, too, that if I'd been a boy, I would have been expected
to get myself ready to kill people. The thought was chilling and
revolting. Would pacifism be the answer?

I didn't realise fully at the time what a protected world I lived
in and how untouched by the mighty conflicts raging all around
me. My survival was in the hands of others and I did not have to
take responsibility for it.

Through all this, the Jesus of the homely prayer, the Friend,
lived on.

How were we going to shape the world when peace-time came?
It required a leap of imagination to work out new ways for society
to operate.

> The merits of a Welfare State
> The role of women in the future
> The way ahead for Christianity
> Post war reconstruction

These were among the topics tackled by a series of Youth
Forums and Brains Trusts in the town. They were well attended.
Miss Keating who was on an organising committee encouraged
me to go. "Why don't you speak?" she asked. Me? I was astonished
that anyone should think that I could. The themes were

stimulating and intriguing, since they were not discussed in school and considered beyond the compass of a girl's experience and general knowledge. Most of us had the impression that anything we might say (if we were bold) didn't count, because we didn't know enough to make considered judgments. "How can you be so brash?" "That's just what your father used to say. He had some strong opinions." Whether we challenged or copied our mentors, we were still silly to suppose we could say anything worthwhile. Who would listen anyway?

Now, in Champness Hall, teenagers just like myself were on the platform speaking to a crowd of young enthusiasts from all over the town. One was Audrey Courts, a Guernsey girl, who lived with her parents in Rochdale and attended Miss Keating's school.

'I could be like that,' I thought.

Suddenly, it seemed, islanders in the north proliferated. Everywhere, on buses and in shops, they could now be identified, since, for a shilling, they were wearing the new Guernsey badges, long promised and at last in circulation. Shaped like a shield, they were dull red and blue and displayed the three lions which run (though not rampant) through British heraldry. Even if we got no further than nodding or saying 'hello' to the stranger in the market, there was a sense of solidarity in the experience. We were people 'in the know' with a story in common, that of being a long way from the home base with the exile's feelings of dependence on the reception area's ability to sustain a welcome. Soon, we would have to come to grips with the problems relating to the return home and the integration into island life.

A favourite meeting ground for many was the Rochdale and District Channel Islands Society, which had been formed in November 1941 and met fortnightly on Sunday afternoons in the Pioneers' Hall. For me, the meetings coincided with Sunday School and so I rarely went, but occasionally I was roped in when Miss Winifred recruited girls to sing in a choir. As many as 300 people would turn up to see a Railway Company's lantern slides of the islands' beauty spots or to hear the band of the blind.

There were, by then, well over fifty such societies scattered over Britain. Their activities were summarised in the *Channel Islands Monthly Review*, so we knew of their existence.

In Rochdale itself, groups of islanders met in clusters in people's homes. Some were well known to us. Mr. and Mrs. Courts, for instance, with their daughter, Audrey, had arrived at Horse Carrs in 1940 as escorts to the Torteval Parish School, where Mrs. Courts was a teacher. They had stayed on in the town, when the Torteval children were moved to Cheshire. Mrs. Courts' brother, Tom Buckley, with his wife, had also left Guernsey at the time of the evacuation and had gone to stay with his brother in Hull. There, the nights were often disrupted with bombing and eventually the Buckleys decided to move to Rochdale to be near relations and friends. They were joined by their daughter, Kathleen, an Old Girl of the Intermediate School, who had been a pupil teacher at the Vale Infant School in Guernsey and was evacuated with them to Cheshire. Miss Roughton was able to use financial resources from an anonymous friend to enable Kathleen to go to Gipsy Hill Training College which had been evacuated from London to Bingley in Yorkshire.

When Mr. Buckley fell seriously ill in 1942 and spent nearly a year in hospital, there were many at the Guernsey Club and in the network of relations to give support. In her turn, Mrs. Buckley, as an experienced dressmaker, helped the Intermediate staff and neighbours by making clothes or adapting old ones. They had fun with 60 yards of pyjama material which had been sent by the Channel Islands Refugees Committee. The Buckleys moved into 34, William St., which had, at an earlier stage, been a home-base for the staff, rented by Miss Roughton.

Many homes like these became known points of contact where hospitality was offered to those with Guernsey connections.

Likewise, there was a warm welcome at Champness Hall where the Methodist minister in charge, Rev. J.E. Eagles, invited islanders to the services and to the wide range of activities that took place on the premises. People flocked there for celebrity concerts, talks by Romany on animal life and a variety of lectures. While in Rochdale, Ruth and Jean, Marian le Tissier and others attended the services and some of them acted as ushers at orchestral concerts where famous conductors drew the crowds.

The Champness Hall was the base for the Citizens' Advice Bureau where you went if you wanted to send a Red Cross message home. You might then wander up to the caretaker's flat where the Torode family had settled. Mr. and Mrs. Torode and their son, John, had been evacuated from Guernsey to Bristol and were bombed from pillar to post. Emerging from falling plaster and rubble, they had just escaped with their lives. After moving about five times, they had come north to Rochdale and gravitated towards Champness Hall with its strong Methodist nucleus. It was when John went down into the depths to explore and saw the Heath-Robinson contraption which passed for the boiler, that he spontaneously exclaimed, "My dad knows all about those." Soon Mr. Torode found himself in charge of maintenance and installed in the caretaker's flat.

Here, Mrs. Torode could be found sitting behind a large brown teapot with a home-made slab of Guernsey gâche ready for slicing. A coal fire glowed behind her. A small circle of friends chatted easily in the patois or in English. There was a welcome chance to be 'Guernsey'. (It was sad that Mrs. Torode died before the return to the island.)

The Christmas of 1944 passed off rather impatiently. It was hardly worth making a thing of it. Surely it would be the last on the mainland. Allied advances on the Continent continued. But perhaps we were being too complacent. The latest German weapons, the V2 missiles, were causing devastation. A few came north and one fell not far from Summerseat.

As I was in the school choir, I joined others on Christmas morning for a live broadcast from the Manchester studios. We hoped our singing would be heard in Guernsey. In Summerseat, Uncle had the chance to borrow some lantern slides of the Channel Islands. John (Aunty's nephew) came some of the time.

By now, holidays felt much like the ordinary time spent in a family home. As 'kids', we did many of the chores, preparing vegetables, shopping, carpet sweeping and washing up. In the early afternoon, to conserve fuel, the live coals of fire from the breakfast-cum-living room were scooped up in a large long-handled shovel and deposited in the lounge grate. Brian and I could now be trusted to do this without disaster.

Aunty went to the clinic one afternoon a week to help weigh babies and there was a church sewing party in the dining room. Now and again, we went with Uncle to one of his other churches, for a social, a service or a concert. We saw some of the elderly or infirm he visited at the Robinson Kay Homes. By then we knew many of the Summerseat people quite well. Brian often went for rides on Uncle's bicycle and I did too, but how we wished there was a second one available so that both of us could go together to Rochdale, Oldham or Bolton and the surrounding countryside. Occasional visits to the local flea pit kept us up to date with the latest films: the absurdly stylised *Mrs Miniver* and *The Man in Grey*. (We rarely went to the cinema during the term.) Sometimes, we traced the family tree back several generations, a fascinating task which fizzled out on the edges of Uncle's memory.

Two of the people who regularly found hospitality at the manse were the sisters, Lena le Poidevin and Olive Brouard, whose husband, Cecil, had previously worked at Milestone. She had been evacuated with her young son, Rex, and then joined her sister, Lena, to work in the Guernsey Children's Home, which had been evacuated from the island to Bury. Their young charges, mainly those once orphaned or abandoned, were accommodated in a large house and the staff were very hard pressed to get through all the domestic chores and to give the children the support they needed. The washing started on a Sunday morning and didn't finish till Tuesday. Lena was often exhausted on her afternoon off and fell asleep in Aunty's armchair.

\*   \*   \*   \*   \*

Millions of people switched on their wireless sets at 3 p.m. on May 8th to hear Churchill announcing the end of the war in Europe:

> *'Hostilities will end officially at one minute after midnight tonight, Tuesday, May 8th, but in the interests of saving lives the cease fire began yesterday to be sounded all along the front, and our dear Channel Islands are also freed today.'*

There was a sense of jubilation in the air and Miss Keating and I nearly forgot Children's Hour. In fact, we missed the first ten minutes, but tuned in just in time to hear descriptions of excitement. Then came my voice (pre-recorded a few weeks earlier), speaking on behalf of the school and young evacuated Channel Islanders. For a full minute, I heard myself saying how glad we were to be going home after five years of separation and how we wondered if our parents would recognise us.

The Parish Church in the centre of Rochdale was packed for a Thanksgiving Service at 7.30, and after attending, some of us wandered around. As it got dark, floodlights newly trained on the Town Hall, the Church and the Cenotaph were switched on and there were a few strings of fairy lights here and there, beautiful in their novelty. At last we could see after nightfall. The lights lifted our spirits. Groups of people converged on the Town Centre, but it was oddly quiet, as though the signal for something to happen had not been given. I missed any cheering, loud music and jitter-bugging that there might have been later on. People were just glad to wander round in the unaccustomed glow and some were strolling arm in arm.

At Edmund St., I retreated into the attic. All was quiet. In reflective mood, I gazed over the neighbouring roof tops. The blackout habit of years had been broken and some people were letting the light shine out.

"I must make all my experiences count for something," I thought. But what was there in store? There would be many decisions to make and I felt I needed the hand of God to guide my course.

This was VE-Day, a great celebration of victory, but the war against Japan was still in progress. No one thought that it would delay our return, so when the islands were ready, we would be leaving and changing homes.

When I came to pack my case, there would be only a few of the old things I had brought from Guernsey to put in: my Bible and the photographs. I had outgrown the childhood contents.

### "Yippee!"

My first letter from home was handed to me on May 17th during a country dancing lesson at school. It was addressed to Roylelands.

I tore at the envelope and opened out the letter in my mother's handwriting:

*'Dear, dear Lois,*

*'It is with hearts filled with thankfulness that we sit to write this our first letter after almost five years of silence. Considering the many lean years, we are all still well and can hardly realise that freedom has come at last. So many restrictions have been imposed upon us that it will be some time before we can shake off their effect.*

*We are now longing for the mail that will bring us news of our loved ones. The Manse is still our temporary home. Rue des Landes has been occupied by the forces as a First Aid Station with a doctor in attendance daily since November 1940 and Milestone since July 1940.'*

The words were strangely formal and clearly copied from a draft, but here was the first *proper* letter. They must have saved the thick sheets from a pre-war pad. I hadn't seen the like in years.

So we'd been right to suppose that the Germans had occupied Rue des Landes and Milestone. But where was Gran? There was no mention of her. Presumably she was still alive and staying in someone else's house. The letter went on to say that Grandpère of Summerville had died in his sleep on May 7th, the day before the letter was written. He was very frail after a long illness and he had just missed hearing the final announcement of victory. So I would not see either of my dear Robin grandparents again. There would be simultaneous feelings of grief and rejoicing in our family households.

No one at school was in the mood for work. I had sent my first letter home a few days previously on May 11th, as soon as mail was allowed. 'With oceans of love and a kiss on every wave', I finished. Now, I settled down to write twenty-three pages of detail and pelted them with questions. What did they most need? I wanted to send off parcels as soon as the Post Office would take them. While I waited for an answer, I assembled soap and toiletries, some new underwear, stationery, mending wool and rare coloured pencils for John. Combs were still unobtainable in our shops. Sending food was forbidden. We were warned of risks and delays, so I divided my assortment into seven packages, hoping some would get through.

The Whitsun holidays were upon us and I was off to Summerseat. Brian did not have a break then, since he always had long Easter and summer holidays instead. By arrangement with him, I packaged an outgrown overcoat and suit he had been saving up for John. They were kept carefully mothballed in a box in Summerseat.

Aunty heard that her aged relations were as well as could be expected and we all pooled our news. Grandpère from Summerville had sent loving messages to us all before he died. His funeral service had been conducted by Rev. Beaugié, a well-loved Methodist friend of the family, and my father was the undertaker. He had made 220 coffins during the Occupation, mostly of rough imported wood, although about thirty were made of local elm. Those island trees which had been felled were used mainly for firewood.

At Milestone, the greenhouses had collapsed after the framework had been wrenched apart for fuel. There were rather confusing references to German plans to extend the airport right through Milestone property and across the main road to take in nearly all the land at Rue des Landes. Something had hindered full implementation, but all the Milestone outbuildings had been demolished (no doubt in preparation) and the house there was a ruined shell with the staircase, floorboards and joists all missing and gone for firewood. Gran was living in a farmhouse just opposite her daughter, Fredena, at Les Pièces.

I looked frequently at the two black and white photographs enclosed in one of the early letters. They had been taken in the summer of 1943. One showed my father looking thinner and with a drawn, hollow expression. He didn't usually smile for the camera, so it was no surprise to see him serious. In contrast, my mother's face was fuller and her hair shorter than usual. Her dress was one I remembered well with rust, green and fawn patterning. The most marked change was of course in John, six, when the photo was taken. I would not have known him. He had lost all his toddler podginess and was looking very grown up in a navy suit of Brian's. His hair was cut short with a fringe and he looked well able to fend for himself.

Why were they so strangely reluctant to list the things they needed? When pressed, they mentioned a toothbrush and a pan scrubber. But we'd heard how the shops were emptied in the siege conditions following D-Day. It would take weeks to restock them with the myriad things that were always imported. Were they short of medication, ink, paper, nails, wool, sewing cotton, soap, toothpaste? It was frustrating not knowing what to send. I went by guesswork.

Ruth came. She had heard that five German soldiers had been billeted in her home, the guest house at Les Fontaines, but her parents had not been compelled to leave. She was overjoyed to hear that their dog, Topsy, though now very old and shaggy, was still alive.

Ruth had taken up nursing in the autumn of 1943 and I felt that she was moving in a world far removed from mine, shouldering adult responsibilities and receiving the benefits of regular pay, meagre though it was.

Already her early experience in the Turners' asbestos works seemed distant. At Mrs. Norris' instigation she had taken ten weeks off to do an intensive course in typing and had stayed in the Norris' London flat, a home-base they found more convenient than Bedfordshire when Mr. Norris was promoted to Squadron Leader. On her return to Rochdale, Ruth had worked for a while in the Turner typing pool and stayed on with Mrs. Hebden to keep her company, while her husband was away in the RAF. But she needed more opportunity to develop her skills and Mrs. Norris prompted her to apply for training at the Royal National Orthopaedic Hospital in Middlesex.

Nursing in wartime London and its environs was strenuous and sometimes dangerous. Once, when the doodlebugs were passing overhead, Ruth was suddenly woken by the shattering of her window and the bed and floor were covered with broken glass.

The working day started at 7 a.m. and ended at 8 p.m. with a break of three hours in the afternoon, the only time available for learning the necessary physiology and anatomy. The wards were built as separate units, scattered throughout the grounds and were open-ended to allow for the maximum circulation of fresh air. They were very cold in winter and there were times when snow blew in up to the foot of the beds. Many of the long-term patients were children with tubercular bone disease or crippling hereditary deformities. Some were the victims of air raids, which had left them with crushed limbs and disablement.

· The trainee nurses had to do much of the work of orderlies, sprinkling tea leaves on the floors, so that they could be swept without raising dust. Bandages were in short supply and the nurses washed by hand the ones that were used in the day and dried them on the hot waterpipes!

Among the highlights were the occasional excursions to the West End theatre when grateful patients produced the tickets.

Jean was to have a few weeks at the Hornsey School of Art in London before going back to Guernsey. She was eager to explore new ground.

One of the early letters I had from Guernsey was from Aunty Helene, my mother's sister.

'My very dear darling Loli' she wrote in her old affectionate style. 'I cannot quite picture you all grown up, so I am just going to talk to my little Loli that I knew and loved in those long years ago . . . Do you remember all the fun we had . . . we went for walks, played in the fields, hunted for the first primroses, played bat and ball on the lawn. . . .'

Yes, I remembered all of it.

She had stayed at Courtil-a-Paix throughout the Occupation and looked after Uncle Tom whose house it was. Handicapped by an amputated arm, he needed a great deal of assistance. He had been hospitalised twice under the Germans, but was back to his pre-war self. His brother, Emile, living next door at New Anneville had lost his wife, my great Aunty Millie (Emilie) in April 1942. She was one of Grandpère's sisters. (My father had arranged the funeral.)

"Lois!" Miss Keating called. "This is for you . . . from Guernsey!" She was standing by the telephone in the hall. I felt the colour drain from my face. I thought this might happen when the lines were re-connected. They were like strangers, foreigners, the people who spoke, not at all like the parents I remembered or the ones I had visualised from recent letters. I tried afterwards to recall the words of greeting which seemed to have no meaning and I hadn't known what to say in reply. The call was short. I was acutely conscious that the Keatings in the adjoining room could hear every nuance. The door was open. It was a shock which was not repeated. I liked my old image of my parents better. So what were they really going to be like when I went back and lived with them again?

# Chapter XVI

## *'Cheerio! Here I Go on My Way'*

The man in the boxing ring, who, on June 3rd faced 5 or 6,000 excited Channel Islanders, was already known to most of them. Words like 'sleek', 'dapper', 'popular' sat loosely on his broad well-tailored shoulders. It was impossible to think of him without visualising a gardenia in his button-hole, but who is to say he ever wore one? No patois conversation about him could end without the English word 'reputation' coming into it. He seemed to attract the old Guernsey mistrust of English people and yet even the old country folk relied heavily on his skills. While he could hold all these contradictory reactions in balance, he rode high. He was Dr. Gibson.

Now he was addressing the third of the gigantic rallies at Belle Vue in Manchester. Along with a few others, he had recently been allowed to leave Guernsey on compassionate grounds. He explained that he was one of the eight doctors, who, in 1940, had been asked by the Guernsey States' Controlling Committee to stay behind on the island in anticipation of the German occupation. If he had been Clark Gable emerging from the American deep South where he had 'Gone with the wind', he could not have had a more tumultuous welcome. Deafening applause punctuated every reference to the scenes of Liberation on Guernsey. With eloquence not usually associated with the medical profession, he declaimed:

> *"I have seen the Bailiff of Guernsey from the steps of the Royal Court issue a proclamation to the Islanders, stating that the Germans had surrendered unconditionally, which was followed by a crowd with sobbing voices singing 'God Save the King' for the first time in five years. That was followed by three cheers for His Majesty and three cheers for Mr. Winston Churchill, whom the Islands had been looking upon as their deliverer for the past five years.*
>
> *I have witnessed in the early hours of the morning the arrival of the British Navy and I have been one of a small crowd of about 150 people who broke the police cordon on the harbour and welcomed the first landing of troops. I have witnessed the hauling down of the swastika and the hauling to the mast-head of the Union Jack after five years' absence. I have sat in the Royal Court House of Guernsey and listened to the Home Secretary of England, for the first time in history, addressing the States of Guernsey, and that was followed by his presenting to the States of Guernsey our local V.C., Major le Patourel,*

*who was received with tremendous acclamation. Next Wednesday, I am*
*hoping to have the privilege of seeing their Majesties the King and*
*Queen in the Island of Guernsey. . . ."*

He went on to praise the islanders for the way they had
managed during the Occupation, especially in the siege days of
acute shortages following D-Day, till the SS *Vega* arrived with food
in December. There had been no epidemics and the most
common ailments had been indigestion, chilblains, septic sores
and scabies. Because the children had been well supplied with
milk, their teeth were in good condition.
"For he's a jolly good fellow!" we all bellowed.

Our school's contribution was in music. 'Glad hearts adventuring' we sang as if we now knew the ups and downs of life's
journeying . . .

> *Brothers take to the trail again*
> *Sisters, follow the star!*

It was easy to urge this on so many expectant faces. Miss
Winifred had found that songs relating to separation from the
homeland could be transposed, emotionally, to our situation. So
the words of 'The Road to the Isles' carried meaning for
everyone:

> *If it's thinkin' in your inner heart*
>   *braggart's in my step,*
> *You've never smelt the tangle o' the Isles.*

The strains of 'Praise, my soul, the King of heaven' were accompanied by a hymn looking for forgiveness and we ended with the
customary vision: 'These things shall be: a loftier race. . . .'

When the island had been re-stocked, the missing half of its
population could return and the Government would provide free
transport. But some on the mainland were hesitating. Perhaps
they had nowhere to settle, finding that the accommodation they
had previously rented in Guernsey was no longer available. Those
who had abandoned their own fully furnished houses were
hearing of wreckage and grime left by the German occupants.
Some places had had all their floor-boards and doors ripped away
for fuel and their belongings had disappeared without trace. A

number had made a new life for themselves on the mainland and wanted to carry on rather than go back to Square One in Guernsey. Many thousands in the Forces were being demobbed and no one knew whether they would find work on the island. Young people on leaving school had found congenial jobs on the mainland or were well into training courses which they were loath to interrupt. Some had married.

No one could predict the numbers likely to return for keeps.

Excitement built up as we were all caught in a whirl of farewell visits to friends. The school's departure was scheduled for the end of July or the beginning of August. We all had to go back together with the school, unless taken independently by returning parents when they were given the green light.

Strict conditions were in force. People had to get permission to return. Only a few were granted special authorisation to make short visits on compassionate grounds. Cousin Cyril, for instance, had been allowed in to see his dying mother at Les Longs Camps (sister-in-law to Grandpère of Summerville, my great-aunt Mim). She died on June 3rd without having recognised him.

Miss Roughton was informed that those who had attended the school and left during the evacuation period could return with it. That way they might get back sooner than applying as individuals. Among Old Girls and erstwhile helpers, there were about fifty, including Ruth and Jean, who wanted to join the core school party of around 100. The numbers on the roll had kept to this level as new scholarship girls came in 1943 and 1944.

Some girls would be returning with a real feeling of sadness. In two families the mother had died in Guernsey during the Occupation. Other girls would be sharing their grief over war casualties. The Hartland sisters, Laurine and Pat, early in the evacuation period, had been informed that their half-brother was lost at sea. He was in the Merchant Navy. It fell to Laurine as the eldest to notify their parents in Guernsey by the only means available – a short Red Cross message. Pat Noel, who was with the school for a while, had faced the tragic death of her father in an air raid on the mainland. With his experience of flying in the First World War, he had once fascinated the Guernsey crowds with his aeroplane stunts over Vazon. Now his service with the RAF in the Second World War was abruptly ended.

Jacqueline Pidduck, who was only five when she was evacuated with the school, was billeted with Mrs. Nellie Ogden, a member of my church in Spotland and well known in the town for her work on many committees. She was deeply upset when Jacqueline, recovering from scarlet fever, fell ill with more serious problems. After Liberation, her parents were allowed to come over and see her. Sadly she was considered too weak to go home and died soon after we had returned to Guernsey.

Elated by the Liberation and all the renewals of contact, Channel Islanders from the vicinity of Rochdale gathered at Champness Hall on June 23rd to celebrate and give thanks at a special Remembrance Day service and rally. Some came from Cheshire and Yorkshire. The school sang. Taking part in the service was Rev. Henry Foss, a Methodist, who had been the minister of my church in Guernsey before we were evacuated. He had been on the island till February 1943, when he and his wife and daughter, Dulcie, were deported to Germany. They had been freed from the internment camp at Biberach, when the Allies got there. I was delighted that Mr. Foss could remember me when I spoke to him after the service. Their hardships had not been too severe. The address was given by Rev. George Whitley, also well known in Guernsey. In 1940, he and Rev. Moore had worked closely together to help evacuated Methodist Channel Islanders and had enabled them all to have Moffatt's translation of the New Testament. I had treasured and used my copy over the years.

In all this unsettling bustle and the stir caused by the General Election, it was a real effort to buckle down to exams. There were eight due to take School Certificate. Much of the girls' time was dissipated in chatter, as if they needed its bolstering effect before parting from each other and venturing into the unknown. Their return to Guernsey would coincide with their leaving school, in most cases.

I worked mainly on my own. I'd got through School Certificate Latin at Christmas. Now, Miss Roughton, distracted, popped in for occasional English lessons. She had concentrated too long on the sufferings of Chaucer's poor Griselda in *The Clerk's Tale*. There was no chance to process so thoroughly the selected portions of Wordsworth or of Milton's *Paradise Lost*. Even Anthony and Cleopatra got short shrift. Seated on her burnished throne, the Queen of Egypt, framed in the purple curtaining of her barge, glided into waters beyond my reach. I had little practice in writing essays and had to rely on the skills acquired in Divinity and History.

It was now early July and Higher School Certificate exams grabbed me from the task of sorting and packing my belongings. The books and paraphernalia of the years filled three cartons and the kitbag we were issued with. They had to be taken to school ready for inclusion in a special railway container. My case was partially packed and waiting for the final contents.

In the Geography exam, I found that the specialised questions on the set continent were all related to Africa. I had been prepared in the wrong continent – I'd 'done' Europe!

The three of us in the Keating household went down with a flu-like virus and I battled with the History, feeling ill. I needed to give myself a boost of reassurance. I was just seventeen and had a year to go before I was old enough for university. If I failed, there was time to sit the exams again.

Formal farewells to the people of Rochdale were made on July 24th at a final school concert. The packed audience betokened £42 for the Scholarship Fund. The school had survived to reach its fiftieth anniversary. Miss Roughton's speech acknowledged with warm appreciation the affection and many kindnesses we had all received. Underlying this public expression, we all knew that in our number, there were girls who had grown so solidly into their billets that it would be a wrench to leave. Others had moved many times and sat loosely to each new set of circumstances. A few had found Rochdale boyfriends, whom they wished to keep. There were mixed feelings of loss, anticipation, excitement, thankfulness and misgivings about the future.

Now we had to concentrate on Miss Winifred's over-crammed programme. In her accustomed concert style, some girls did a quaint play called *Dark Betrothal* while others acted out the trial scene from *The Merchant of Venice* (I was Antonio). For the last time, the yearning notes of 'Sarnia Cherie' produced their rows of glistening eyes.

As we walked home, Miss Roughton's dramatic announcement was uppermost in all our minds. The date for our return to Guernsey had been postponed by a fortnight – to the middle of August. By then the Keatings would be away on holiday and I would have to go to Summerseat or Boothroyd. Brian, travelling with his school, would be leaving in a few days' time, at the beginning of August, so now he would be arriving in Guernsey well ahead of me.

In the meantime, friends were giving us a warm send-off. Along with the four other Channel Islanders who had attended the Methodist Sunday School at Spotland, I was presented with a hymn book, which would be a lasting reminder of the caring way in which the Church had taken us under its wing. In passing on their conviction that God was at work, our teachers and leaders seemed deeply rooted in realities. Perhaps I was looking for the unshakeable. Through that community, I had absorbed much of the Christian faith and had become more confident in my understanding of it, with trust in God's grace at its heart. I was grateful for their encouragement and for being allowed to teach and test out my beliefs and skills. I hoped those in my small group of juniors were resilient.

Mrs. Keating with an unusual show of warm feeling gave me the Book of Common Prayer which had belonged to her since she was a girl. On the fly leaf was her Manx name, Jessie Clague, Christmas 1874. This was an inheritance. I was the almost-granddaughter. I felt she had chosen this way of telling me how important her faith was to her and was passing it on to me to preserve and communicate. Through the wisdom of the prayers, I would learn more of life's richness and opportunities and the need for healing and forgiveness. The whole gamut of human emotion was focused in the words of the General Thanksgiving:

> *We bless thee for our creation, preservation*
> *and all the blessings of this life;*
> *but above all, for thine inestimable love in the*
> *redemption of the world by our Lord Jesus Christ;*
> *for the means of grace and for the hope of glory.*

Through the medley of daily experiences came grace. In them was to be discovered the hope of glory. God's redemptive work was in progress. All I had absorbed from the homes I had known I could have available for my life as it unfolded and I would have to learn to avoid the pitfalls. The future held the promise of progress in understanding and development.

Into the confidence of such teenage musings dropped the atomic bomb. August 6th, and Hiroshima lay in ruins. Three days on and Nagasaki was flattened. The full horror and scale of these grotesque acts of American barbarism came to light only later, when pictures of the burning of human flesh penetrated into the newspapers. Justifying arguments were soon assembled to vindicate the utterly cruel massacres inflicted without warning and the wanton spread of radioactive havoc. Apparently, it was all a matter of speeding up the killings and terrorising whole populations out of their wits. Fortunately for the Allies, the Japanese did call a halt. Otherwise the USA might well have damned itself further by repeating the murderous atrocities. Many

of us were sickened at the predatory nature of war and appalled by
the consequences as the press revealed more and more horror.

If I had any lingering illusions that good was all on one side and
evil on the other, then this shattered them. The war, which had been
started to maintain the old balance of power in Europe, had
escalated to assume gigantic dimensions. It was underway long before
Hitler's need to destroy the Jews was understood or implemented.
The declaration of war by the British had not been based on that.
Now, with the victors drooling at the kill, there was no chance of
reverting to the status quo of 1939. Much talk was concentrated on
the Allies exacting heavy penalties from 'the enemy'. The limited
aims of the earlier war efforts had long been superseded. Countless
millions of lives had been lost to sustain a bitter conflict whose
purpose was lost in limbo. And what had been achieved?

I, for one, was left with a profound sense of futility and waste and
I wasn't going to be fobbed off with easy assertions that everything
was too complicated to explain and that the Government, with all
the facts to hand, was there to make the decisions and knew what
should be done. I wanted to know what it was all for.

It was against this backdrop that the next few months of my life
were lived out. Their little ups and downs paled into insignifi-
cance. Thousands like me with the hopefulness of youth felt we
had to do something about the mess and the reconstruction. But
what? We could only start with our own scene. There were no
clear visionary leads and many of us had to shape our own future
before the dust had settled.

During those last few days on the mainland, when I was in
Summerseat, Aunty and Uncle were preparing for their next
move, an appointment in Warrington. Then Aunty left for
Guernsey. She had at last received permission to visit her frail and
elderly relations. Brian had gone back to the island with his
school, straight from Derbyshire. I waited for their news. When it
came, it was factual and impersonal. Perhaps they were not
committing much to paper.

Since I was Head Girl, it fell to me to present Miss Roughton
with a 'thank you' gift from the school. Someone knew where to
find holdalls and handbags which were rarely obtainable in the
shops. We judged these to be just what she would find practical
and useful. Most girls had spent their reserves of pocket money
on sending things to their parents in Guernsey and, sadly, had
little left to contribute, but it was enough to get the bags.

Schoolgirl words could hardly convey the prevailing sense of gratitude and thankfulness for her continuous efforts on behalf of the school, for her sense of responsibility for the girls, for her visionary hope, her sterling qualities and the cachet she had given the school and the way she had held it together. She had given it rock-bottom stability and she and her sister had, largely, given it its public image. Girls were generally known in the town as well behaved and well spoken. If this was so, it must be largely attributed to her influence. And undergirding her work was always the strong belief in God's guidance. 'In his hands He gently bears us. . . .' These were the words of the hymn she called 'our hymn': 'Praise, my soul, the King of Heaven'.

Yet who among us could say that we really knew this woman, who had given so much of her time and energy to the school, sometimes to the point of exhaustion? Perhaps a few who had lived alongside her while she was at Boothroyd knew her best or a few members of the staff, who understood the personal cost and themselves had weathered the storms and were bracing themselves for a challenging year of resettlement. Yet which of us would really miss her? We were all poised for other things. Many would be leaving her behind in their lives. Would she have the physical stamina to reconstitute the school and start again with disparate elements when she returned to Guernsey? Clearly she was so determined.

Members of the staff stood loyally and solidly with her. They must together have felt a great sense of achievement after bringing the girls through such demanding times. I am sure we never showed our appreciation with sufficient warmth and thankfulness. Hopefully, we place a greater value on their contribution now.

News of schooling on the island had reached Miss Roughton through the Education Council and through Miss Brett and Miss Moon, members of her staff, who had remained on the island because of their commitment to elderly dependants. They had continued teaching. Miss Brett, no doubt, was still wearing the same work-worn jacket of brown leather which we knew so well, when she gave us an excellent grounding in English grammar and poetry. Who could think of her lessons without mouthing to themselves:

> *If I were Lord of Tartary,*
> *Myself and me alone*
> *My bed would be of ivory*
> *Of beaten gold my throne.*

The new generations of Miss Moon's Maths pupils would all remember her as we did, seated, with her full figure clothed in a navy dress patterned with regular rows of white polka dots. Its skirt was stretched tautly over the generous lap, made to look wider by the wearer's way of holding the knees apart. The head was topped with straight grey hair drawn tightly into a bun held by an array of struggling hair pins. She shot piercing glances over the top of dark rimmed spectacles and the forward tilt of her head habitually sank her chin into fleshy folds. In a rasping voice, she issued instructions about the long-division sums she had chalked on the blackboard. Nothing missed her attention. Those who were not too afraid of her quite liked her, in spite of the deterring signals she threw out. Was it possible that she enjoyed the role of battle-axe and adopted it to ensure her pupils got on well? Why else did she persist, year in, year out, with the same performance and the herculean task of marking work? "Pass out!" she would say, grim-faced to generations of girls as they filed out of her classroom.

During the Occupation, the remnants of the Girls' Intermediate School left behind on the island, together with those from the Boys' School, the Ladies' College and the Elizabeth College, had all joined forces and, in April 1941, gelled into a co-educational unit, augmented then and later by small drafts of the more academically inclined drawn from the Parish schools. Starting with sixty-eight pupils, the school was named the Occupation Intermediate School and was staffed by part-time teachers and gifted members of the public, who managed with no formal training. Under the leadership of Mr. Peter J. Girard, it functioned two or three days a week (subsequently adding mornings).

The school, at first, was allowed to use the premises of the Girls' Intermediate School in Rosaire Ave, but when the Germans commandeered the building in November 1941, they went through various vicissitudes before ending up in Roman Catholic premises in Burnt Lane in town. The Guernsey educational authorities had somehow managed to devise their own set of exam papers in line with School Certificate requirements and the successes in February 1944, were, after the war, formally recognised by the appropriate University Examination Board in England.

As Head Girl, I was deputed to write to this Guernsey part of the school and send them news and greetings.

During the war, we had heard little of the way those in the Parish Schools were faring under the Germans and did not even know how many children remained on the island till the *Channel Islands Monthly Review* of August 1942 published the results of a German census taken in July 1940. This revealed that, in Guernsey, there were 2,146 children under fourteen (including babies).

Information arriving in dribs and drabs after Liberation, indicated that children cycling to school from a distance sometimes had little to bring to eat in the lunch break, especially when bread was very scarce. The Cobo Soup Kitchen had been opened and nourishing meals were provided, till, one day, supplies were running out. Mr. Theo Allez from my church, who was an administrator on the island's Essential Commodities' Controlling Committee, at risk to himself, engineered the diversion of ten tons of vegetables from fields designated for the use of Germans. Loads were secretly stored in a stable loft, ready to go into the soup. In town, the sisters of the Church of Notre Dame du Rosaire provided a similar soup service.

\* \* \* \* \*

It was on the day that the atomic bomb devastated Nagasaki that I made the journey to Whaley Bridge to say goodbye to the Keatings. We had tea amid the flowers in the hotel gardens where the three of them were on holiday. I heard that I was mature for my age, perhaps because I had lived with adults, that my social life had been a bit meagre, that Miss Keating was sorry that, with her own full-time responsibilities she had not been able to arrange for more out-of-school activities. (In her holiday time, I was away.) She said she would miss having all the errands done. There seemed no way of expressing how things had evolved during my stay. They were not a demonstrative family.

I handed over some books I had bought as a present. There seemed little else in the shops that was suitable. My words of thanks for all the caring of the years sounded totally ill matched to the experience. Soon I was waving through the coach window. Miss Mary Keating dabbed at an eye and they were lost to sight. For me, the war was over. So what had peace in store?

More news of the conditions on the islands was coming through, but how would we find the people? Had morale been at a low ebb? When the excitement of Liberation had died down, would our families have the strength and stamina to build things up and make adjustments to a different world? I felt I could never go back to being the person I had been, the one that my parents seemed to be expecting. There was much about that girl I didn't like, a goody-goody two-shoes, on guard and trying to please. I was more confident and self-reliant. I was getting ready to take on the world, spread my wings and fly.

Would I find at home, the very same influences and circumstances that had shaped the girl I had outgrown? Or was all that changed? I sensed I would have to resist a great deal of pressure to revert to the old norms and ways of relating. No one had prepared us for the personal emotional adjustments or the cultural acclimatisation. It seemed to go without saying that once you were restored to the bosom of your family, all would be well. Everyone was looking forward to reunion. The Red Cross messages and letters always said so.

Miss Roughton had shown little sign of recognising any of the girls' individual and personal anxieties. She was preoccupied with moving the school. I felt that Miss Keating knew that I was apprehensive, but that she would assume it was my sense of loyalty which prevented me from saying so outright. Besides, she did not know my family and could not guess how we might interact.

My relationship with her was about to be severed almost as definitely as that with my parents in 1940. We had always known that it was temporary and now the end had come. I was unlikely to see much of Rochdale in the future, but we would write and stay in touch.

A few days later, I sat fingering a sprig of heather which she had enclosed in a farewell letter, wishing me a pleasant journey and a 'happy landing'. It ended

> *'Goodbye, my dear and love and best*
> *wishes from us all. E.K.'*

There was five years' worth of caring in those few words and I could now read that into them.

At midnight on August 14th, Clement Attlee, the new Labour Prime Minister, announced the war with Japan was over. The following day would be VJ-Day, a public holiday. Most of us knew nothing about it till we got up in the morning, the day of our journey home. I had spent a restless night in Rochdale. The Law family, where the le Gallez sisters had been happily settled, had offered me a bed. When the early coach arrived for the first lap of our journey to Southampton, Miss Roughton turned to me and urged, "You must be the first on board. You're our Head Girl."

I climbed in and took a seat at random. I had said my farewells elsewhere and there was no one who had come specially to wave me off.

# Chapter XVII

## *'When You Come Home Once More'*

I slept fitfully on deck that night. Very early the next morning, everyone was about. We wanted to watch the distant island grow. Not much was said. You couldn't tell from their faces what the girls were feeling. I was still filled with unaccountable dread. It scared me. There seemed no rational explanation.

As we headed south, it was clear that we were not going to approach the harbour on the east by the normal direct route. We were veering westwards and going almost full circle round the island. As we drew closer to the shore, familiar landmarks greeted us, a lighthouse, outcrops of rock and inlets, granite cottages, a church high up beyond the trees. We cheered as we identified the bays. Excitement grew and thankfulness. So here we were at last!

Inserted in the southern coast of cliffs was Petit Bôt. The bay in sunshine looked so marvellously unchanged with its Martello tower still warding off Napoleon. Countless tides had lapped the pebbles since I scrambled over them.

Soon we were gliding through into the harbour. St. Peter Port was beautiful as ever with its banks of houses rising up beyond the forefront of the sea. White gulls swooped overhead. Some dockers stopped to see us wave and cheer. But the welcoming crowd had been kept back. As we tripped down the gangway, no one took much notice. We were checked and counted. Then, tamed in navy coats and berets, we filed along the pier towards the Weighbridge. I swung my case and bag in easy strides.

Dark groups of waving families stood in restraint behind barbed wire, which masked our view of them. Somewhere behind that barricade keen eyes were watching. And my heart sank. To see that screen was intimation of another barrier.

I recognised my parents straightaway and not because of Brian with them. They knew me too and gathered close. I smiled and kissed those short and tired-looking figures. My mother wore her pale green pre-war coat, its shoulders sadly faded. In sunken tracks along the seams, the sunlight had not drained the dye away. Her old brown floppy hat was one I well remembered.

My father looked quite thin and old and John kept smiling through a lot of teeth. He clutched his mother's arm as for protection. And Brian hovered with the air of one who's seen it all before. Already he was one of them I thought, and John was like a new acquaintance. I tried to register his features. I must know him if I saw him on his own, away from all the others.

Now I was being drowned in greetings. "At last, we're all together again!" "What a relief it's all over!" "Did you have a good trip?" "Where's the rest of your luggage?" and, finally, "Give me your case!"

I felt enormously distanced. Here were two people claiming me as if I were theirs already and they didn't even know me. I took refuge in practicalities and, as instructed, went off to get the rest of my belongings. Soon enough, the car was heading home. I knew the route so well, but everything was looking drab and needed painting.

At Rue des Landes, the house seemed little changed, since all was clean and tidy. Rotting floor-boards had been replaced. Aunty Am and Donald had joined a small team to scrub the grease and smoky film from inside walls, which were freshly painted for Brian's arrival. The back rooms were done in beige and pallid green, my mother's favourite colours. The furniture was reinstated in its old positions. No scratch betrayed its hurried flight by horse and cart to scattered wartime quarters. The mahogany stood glowing in its rich brown tones. My mother's damask cloths and crocheted doilies smelled freshly laundered and everything was stored away from summer moths.

The shelves of a built-in cupboard in the dining room, like a museum, still bore the strips of gummed paper labelling in German the medicines and supplies of the First Aid station. 'Medikament' I read. Because some of the rooms had been used by a dentist and some for minor operations such as tonsilectomy, they had been left in tolerable order and were spacious enough for patients to stay there to recuperate.

Outside, work parties of Germans, held back after Liberation to clear away their mines and debris, had carted away some sixty tons of stone dust which their compatriots had stacked in bags against the granite walls of the house, in places reaching bedroom level.

At the back, across the one-time lawn, untidy mounds of earth and rubble spilled on to straggly weeds, besprinkled with surviving daisies. Where there had been grass at the front and an apple tree, there was now a large bare rounded hump, the outward sign of a cavernous underground shelter with concrete roof. Steps down on either side led to the flooded depths below.

As if the seizure of the house by the Germans had not been nuisance enough, there was more to come. As soon as they were gone, it was immediately taken over by the RAF, who failed to ask permission from my parents. In the course of six weeks, they wreaked more havoc than all their predecessors had in their long tenure. They carried lino and other belongings to the hotel opposite which they had also taken over and it was only after much questioning that my father located and retrieved the missing things.

The field where I had somersaulted was flanked to the west by a series of tank tracks which together formed a long broad runway, extending from the airport across the family property alongside Milestone, over the main road and right through the land at Rue des Landes and neighbouring fields, till it ended abruptly against an enormous flat-faced concrete structure called 'The Target'. Its shape was like the enlarged gable of a house or barn and painted to give that illusion from the air. Metal grids were embedded in the muddy tank course and displaced strips were jutting out at dangerous angles. My father had seen a gang of some sixty foreign labourers forced to flatten his earthen hedge which stood as an obstruction. The line of my early somersaults ran parallel.

My pre-war 'treasures' were snuggled in a drawer of the same dressing table which had marked my transfer to the Ladies' College. Now, the pale blue satin handkerchief sachet from Aunty Helene nestled beside the brown ostrich feather from the Gold Coast and I saw reflected in the small green-handled mirror a face with shorter hair and sharper features than its younger counterpart. Along with my cherished stamp album was the little black notebook which recorded the main events of those far off pre-war days. I turned with delight to the pages of *Little Dots,* a well-thumbed present from my mother for my seventh birthday. Throughout the upheavals since, the frilly figure of Nelly Bly had been tripping up a rainbow to a willowy Fairy Queen.

Gone was my cuddly pale blue rabbit with its pink-lined ears. On impulse, my father had given it to a German soldier when he brought out a photograph of his own children. "They were fathers just like us and had their families to think of." I was surprised that people didn't seem to have been afraid of the Germans.

John went round the house with the Union Jack he had draped from an upper window of the Kings Rd. manse at Liberation. He pressed into my hand a small wooden mallet, which a German soldier, one of hundreds, had tossed towards him as his forlorn column marched down to the harbour for final embarkation. Many of the troops looked tired and ill-fed, too thin for their army tunics, which hung limply on their sad defeated figures.

Spread over John's bed was the small woollen blanket of coloured squares which I had knitted for the refugees. I was touched to hear that it had covered him over all those years and reminded him of his sister, Lois.

Wherever I went, John followed. He took a special interest in the contents of my case as if there was more to be seen than the present I had given him.

Among my much-darned stockings was my switch of hair, like horse's mane tied up for exhibition. He held it to his head to test for shade and styling. Long turned brown were the fair curls of the podgy toddler in the photograph I'd had in England. I looked at that again and at the sepia family portrait I had packed when I was someone else in 1940. There were now two segregated sections of my life and I realised I could never again live in the one or the other. I would have to become a new and different person.

So where was I heading?

I handed over to my mother the stack of twelve exercise books, the diaries I had filled, a daunting way of saying, 'This is what I did'. She would have to find out for herself the person I'd become.

"You painted that?" John asked as he gazed at my sketch of Peel's Tower commanding the surrounding moorland. "Have you been up there?" "What was it like at the top?" I had to get used to the myriad questions. This was my brother, who would be around all the time, latching on to us, wanting to do what his novelty older brother and sister were doing. But the eight year gap was wide.

There was more in the case to unpack. I hung up the smart blue costume Miss Keating had bought me to see me on my way. I would use the little purse made by Mrs. Keating and wear the bracelet with its pearly segments, but how could I convey to John how much it signified the warmth and kindness of those who accepted unknown girls into their midst.

Parading in my gas mask was too stifling to enjoy and soon he was matching the twisted Oldham shrapnel with his own collection from St. Peter Port, of greater interest to him than the box of sea shells I had found in Southport. I showed him the hymn book conveying the encouragement of my church and the pre-war Bible always opening to the same bespattered page, recording where I'd dropped it in the Rochdale mud. The marker's silver bell still rang the peel, COME UNTO ME.

These small tokens of my life away would remind me how God's grace is felt in the ordinary event or experience, however enjoyable or painful at the time. Everything would be ploughed into a new and creative process. I needed reassurance that somehow things were going to work out and was trying to make sense of all that had happened, so that something positive would emerge that was an asset for the future. I was acutely aware of my lack of discernment and of the bridging work that had to be done within the family.

When the wind was blowing from the south, I could lie in bed and listen to the sea's distant and intermittent rumbling as successive waves caught the Petit Bôt pebbles in the undertow and rolled them smooth. All through the centuries, while human vitality had made the soil yield forth her produce, primeval energy had kept the ebb and flow of tides to an inexorable rhythm. For eons, the momentum would go on and nothing anyone could do would halt it.

Through my bedroom window, the much-loved face of the church clock was clearly visible between the trees at the end of the garden. The oldness of le Bourg as a place of habitation was evident in the crumbling walls of grey granite still warmed by the summer sunshine. In their crevices grew ferns and pink tipped daisies as though they'd always made their home there. A small menhir, once carried from its ancient site nearby, now formed the end-piece to the wall at the head of the valley which leafed its way down to Petit Bôt bay. It stood unrecognised in such utilitarian guise, its French engraving 'le Perron du Roi' distracting from its earlier purpose.

The camellia which had always dropped its red petals in the roadway in spring still leaned from a neighbouring garden towards the graveyard where our family members lay.

The aura of stillness around the church could not be shattered by the war's upheaval. While foreign labourers dragged their tired feet along the lanes and German troops sang hymns within its precincts, that church had stood in solid witness to eternal truths, its granite foothold sign of timeless permanence.

At 5ft 6 inches, I was tall by island standards and seemed to tower over the short squat figure of Gran from Milestone. She was thinner, but her legs had swollen and she relied on a walking stick to move around the room. She was seventy-seven. A watery look to the eye, a slight deafness and a softness in the voice told of a weakening physique, but a fancy handkerchief and necklace hinted at the former smartness. Her smile was welcoming.

I learned how on July 2nd 1940, just three days after the Germans landed, they had forced their way into her home at

Milestone, while she was out. My father happened to be in the neighbourhood and noticed their vehicles parked in the road outside and went to investigate. Upset by his reception, he hurried towards le Bourg to intercept Gran on her way home and give her warning. When they knocked at her front door, about six Germans in bathing suits clustered round. They refused to let her move her furniture out, but she was allowed to retrieve a few clothes and personal belongings.

"Don't worry," they called out from her own doorway as she was leaving. And to make sure she understood they used French instead of German to add their own brand of cheery comfort, "It's only for three weeks. We won't be here for long. The war is nearly over. England will soon be defeated."

At the time, Gran was just getting over the shock of having her brother-in-law's wife, Alice Brehaut (my great aunt), killed in the German raid in St. Peter Port a few days previously.

Quickly, accommodation was found for her in town, and later, she spent a little while at the Kings Rd. manse with my parents. Then she went to stay on the farm at Les Pièces, opposite her daughter, Fredena. By the time I saw her, she had moved again and was staying with her niece, Nelsie, who was the daughter of Alice, who had died in the raid, and the mother of young Arthur who had been away in the British army and was tragically killed in the war.

As I saw for myself the empty ruined shell of Milestone, I heard that when it was first taken over by the Germans, my father had hired a horse and cart (since both his car and lorry were already requisitioned), and gradually, he wheedled away precious paint, nails and linseed oil from the premises. Gran's framed tapestry pictures which she had worked and a few other possessions were later salvaged. In the meantime the Germans were freely helping themselves to what they wanted. A fierce dog guarded a transmitter in the yard, and, later, mines prevented access.

My father dispersed the rescued stock and kept it in nine scattered places, so that it could not be traced too easily and seized. When foodstuffs became really scarce, it went round on the grapevine that he would be in one or other place at given times and up to twenty people came with their own containers to buy linseed oil for cooking. He sold it at cost price, a modest 10d. for a pint.

Much bartering went on in the island and within the official limits set, advertisements could be placed in the local paper. My father exchanged balls of twine or paint for a rabbit or some jam, and timber or putty for honey or oats. Dan Nicholle, who had formerly worked in the carpentry business at Milestone, had no nappies for the new baby in his family. In anticipation, he went to my father with something to offer and returned to his home with a large roll of coffin lining material. Just the thing he had hoped for!

It wasn't long before I was taken to Summerville. There was a tousled look about the garden, but untended splodges of brilliant colour emerged from former flower beds. Hydrangeas and sweet-scented roses had bloomed on from year to year, ignoring the invader. Sorrow at the absence of beloved grandparents and the sense of loss were soon overlaid by the warmth of the greetings and all the bustle. There was something irrepressible about the place as though it breathed the older generation's welcome and the essence of the island life they'd lived together.

Aunty Am had hardly changed in looks or manner and a dated dress hung loosely on her fragile figure. "My word! You've grown," she said in English. 'My word!' It sounded so intensely Guernsey. I smiled to recognise her well-used exclamation. Its frequent interpolation in the patois had been so normal that I'd grown up thinking it belonged there. Its use in English was outmoded, but in patois it lived on, expressive of a different way of seeing life.

Uncle Ces, shortsighted like his eldest sister, Am, had been settled at Summerville for a while. Together with his wife, Ada, and their daughter, Marion, much changed at nine, they had kept things in order and helped Aunty Am to look after Grandpère when he was ill. The Germans had ejected them from their own home at The Poplars and after a temporary stay elsewhere they had found a home at Summerville. Uncle had grown crops on the surrounding land and my father had cycled up from town to dig and weed and do the maintenance jobs. The relations had been most fortunate to have the Summerville field and greenhouses and, in the siege conditions following D-Day, they had relied heavily on the produce. The fare might be unvarying SOS (Same Old Soup), but it was nourishing and there was linseed oil for frying potatoes, much prized when the flour for bread ran out towards the end. At the time, many townspeople without gardens had been forced to queue for just a few parsnips perhaps, and some had relied on emergency soup kitchens and were in a very weakened state when the *Vega* arrived in December with its life-saving Red Cross parcels.

One of the Summerville outbuildings, where a pony-trap had once been kept, was home to my father's car for most of its

Occupation life. Unaccountably (or perhaps because they had damaged it), the Germans returned it to him in January 1941 and there it stayed, both banned and useless. When pushing his bicycle up hills or trundling coffins on a hand-cart, it had irked him to have German drivers pass him in his own new lorry.

I was shown Gran's treasured tea service, its brilliant whiteness edged in a delicate pattern of gold leaves. Now, blotchy discolorations marred some of the pieces, the sorry result of life underground. The set had been buried in the garden, in case the Germans raided the house and confiscated her most cherished belongings.

All the generations, those who went and those who stayed, were invited to a feast at New Anneville. It was to be the first and last time such a crowd of relations would gather. The 'children' would disperse and some would leave the island altogether; the older ones would die and their properties pass on. It was a delight to visit the old adjacent homesteads again, so clearly etched in memory. Uncle Tom at Courtil-a-Paix, sat amid the stuffed birds and shells as if he had not moved. Soon we were scrambling all over the premises, absorbing the old-world smell of the ancient granite barns and stables and admiring the ferns and pots of red geraniums, set brilliantly against the whitewashed walls. Hens pecked at morsels in the yard and an ageing cat called Nico strolled by in stately indolence. Old Mac at Summerville was dead. Aunty Helene had prepared some lovely baskets of fruit for us to take home – peaches, medlars, figs and nectarines. We hadn't seen the like since 1940. "So long!" she called as we drove back home.

It would take a long time to catch up with all the Occupation stories. My mother, not wanting the family camera to be confiscated, had sewn it into a cushion with a partly used film still inside. After the war, this had been rescued and developed and there was John, a toddler, sitting in a little boat and waving. It seemed, in retrospect, a poignant symbol of the last goodbye.

Uncle Ces had defied the German demand to hand in all wireless sets in 1942 and when he and his family were turned out of their own home and they settled temporarily nearby, he hid the set among a pile of unused furniture. At BBC news times, he found some reason to withdraw to this spare room and his wife (Aunty Ada), who was very deaf, had never guessed what he was doing.

Uncle Art, who worked at the Potato Depot, one day, was bending over a heap of stored potatoes, listening intently through his earphones to a voice emanating from the middle, where his crystal set was buried. He froze as he felt the presence of

Germans approaching from behind. Thoroughly used to chasing ferrets in our Christmas romps, he now frantically poked around for 'rats'. The Germans were taken in by the diversion and offered to assist his search.

I was surprised to hear how my parents had continuously been given the BBC wartime news by cheerful neighbours and relations, who had hidden their sets when they were banned. Always they had the British bulletins with which to evaluate the German version in the newspapers and so they kept up their spirits. They had been thrilled to hear Brian's broadcast message in October 1940, before their wirelesses were banned.

Around the islands, German bunkers and fortifications had already been abandoned for some months and had begun to smell of the litter of curious visitors. We went on a few car rides to see the most conspicuous. Every monstrosity could tell the story of inhuman suffering. I heard how many of the forced labourers from the Continent who had built them were ragged, ill-fed and badly treated. They had to make do with strips of sack or tyre to protect their bare and blistered feet. A member of our church showed me some niches in the hedgerow near her farm, along the lane which skirted my father's field. When there was no one around, she would press in some bread or vegetables and cover them up with overhanging grass and leaves. If the workers-in-the-know managed to escape the notice of their German guards, they grabbed the food in passing. Punishments for givers and receivers were severe.

I was shaken. Some were the very hollows where I had searched with Aunty Helene for the first sign of peeping violets and primroses in the gentleness of early spring.

Those lanes near the Forest Church had seen much poverty. The old cottages had crammed their large dishevelled families into small damp rooms. There was dirt and drunkenness and misery. But the deliberate cruelties which the Germans inflicted on the foreign workers were far more disconcerting and showed a callous disregard for those compelled to give the army of their strength.

The atrocities in the worst concentration camps in Germany were being shown on film at the Forest Parish School. Everyone was urged to go. The rest of the family had been, so I went on my own. Seeing the emaciated bodies and unspeakable wastage of human life made us all realise how fortunate we were to have escaped such evil. How superficial and trivial our own little differences and strivings for adjustment seemed and yet they were disturbing and they claimed attention.

There was over the island a pall of tiredness. Like a sea mist, it had descended imperceptibly and was only briefly dispelled by the thrill of Liberation and the prospect of new beginnings. People's energies had been drained away, leaving them too listless to tackle everything at once. Those affected hardly seemed aware that they were sapped and inattentive. Some faced returning islanders with a deflecting blankness, discounting hardships on the mainland, and digging in. Entrenchment, as a response, had served them well when face to face with Germans, but needed modifying now. In some instances, returning islanders were viewed with some suspicion, as if they were yesteryear deserters, dribbling back and expecting everything to fall into their laps. On this showing, it was the ones who stayed who had held the fort and shouldered responsibility and thereby proved themselves the stalwarts.

Altercations could be bitter when an Occupation survivor confronted an evacuated family wanting to return, "Yes! Alright! We know we're in your house, but that's because the Germans threw us out of ours and we had nowhere else to go. We've looked after all your things. Be glad of that! Just give us time and we'll move out. We've got to get things fixed in our own house. The Germans left us nothing and all the woodwork's gone. How can we pay for new just now?"

Such resentment against the evacuated, even when it had no specific target, could be wounding: 'What do you know about conditions here?. . . . what it was like . . . all those years we were cut off, ignored. You've had an easy time of it. We suffered more."

Whenever I came across this deprecating attitude, I hardly knew how to handle it. It was absurd to construct a kind of competition with points for those who had lost the most or worried more. I sometimes felt I was expected to apologise for having been evacuated, eating adequately and coming through safely. If I had been older, I could have understood better the need for recognition and support which the trapped islanders had missed. Some felt abandoned by the British Government. When the Allies cut off the islands from France after D-Day and near-starvation followed, it was the Germans, we were told, who appealed to the Red Cross to come to the rescue and feed the islanders. Although this proved to be a rather one-sided story, there were some who felt that Westminster would have left them to their fate.

On the domestic scene, some of the emotional difficulties arose from the unresolved conflicts which had torn the family apart in 1940. My parents were still feeling ambivalent about the best course to have taken. The return of their evacuated children confronted them with the consequences of one course of action, the one they had taken and which had proved irreversible, since the arrival of the Germans prevented them from changing their minds. But would things have been better if my mother had left with John or if we had all stayed, for instance? For her the 'Don't be Yellow' warnings had done their intended work and, on the point of leaving, she'd been sick with indecision. Who had plastered those posters in the town and why? No one could say.

It was the conversations about the most ordinary things which sometimes pointed up a lack of connection between us and the difficulties in communication. At home, to achieve a healthy mutual understanding, we all had to evolve a style of 'give and take' newly tailored to suit each other's change of roles. In this unfamiliar context, Brian was almost as much a stranger to me as were the others and he had his separate aims and expectations and a different set of friends.

While relationships were being explored, individuals could feel isolated and anxious, not knowing what to expect and unsure of the outcome.

SCENE: THE KITCHEN.

My mother and I are preparing vegetables. I have been topping and tailing beans, which now fill a large saucepan, so that we can all have a generous helping. I had never dealt with such large quantities before.

*Me.*   How much salt do these beans need?

    (Silence)

*I think: 'She probably just tips the salt in from the jar and sort-of-knows through practice how much to put in. If I do the same, I'll probably tip in far too much.' I suggest answers:*

*Me.*   One spoonful or two?

*I think: 'If she doesn't usually measure it in spoons, why doesn't she say so? She must think I'm undervaluing her methods and forcing her into something she's not used to. Perhaps I'm pushing her. I start to feel guilty. She's not feeling on top of things. Shall I ask again? I wish she'd give a straightforward answer.'*

*Me.*   I've put in one spoonful. Is that enough?

*Still hesitating, she comes up to see, takes the jar and pours some in herself.*

I leave her to it. The problem about the amount of salt has not been resolved. Next time, we are likely to repeat the same uneasy process. I feel I've been too overbearing and demanding to suit her and that she has resorted to passive means of control. She must feel resentful about my attitude but doesn't want an open conversation about it. She doesn't like the way I go about things, but wants me there recognising her ways. In her eyes, I mused, I ought to be fitting her picture of me and I wasn't doing so.

How were we going to arrive at the big decisions, when even the trivial ones were fraught and difficult to make?

An envelope stood on the mantelpiece in the living room at home. It had been there for days unopened. My father had made enquiries in town and found details of a job in an office. "Here! This is for you!" he'd said. I would not look at it, since it gave out a very plain message: I was to leave school.

He was used to the old farm homesteads where the daughter of the house milked the cows and packed tomatoes or flowers for export. Even the boys would often work without cash payment. When old Uncle Tom was first married, he was kept so dependent and short of ready money that he had to ask his father for a few coins to put in the church collection on Sundays. The old island traditions died hard. My father was making a concession in allowing that I need not work at home, but could get a job in town as befitted someone with a good education. He saw the responsibility for my future as being in his hands.

"You must do something useful with your life," he urged, "Help people." He stood so solidly within his world and thought so highly of it that he had not noticed that others in the family circle might not readily fall into the same pattern and yet have a sense of responsibility. "Teaching?" he queried. That would cost a lot and mean going to England. (There were no training facilities on the islands.) I could see that he would find both hurtful, the financial outlay and the further distancing. He expected that his children had come home to stay. "A degree?" What would I do with that? He could see little utilitarian value. Surely it would be a waste of time if I got married. "History?" He might be thinking of his old school textbooks, tight with stodgy detail, of no current relevance. I wondered.

One day, when he made reference to Russia's role in the war, I judged it to sit loosely to the facts and to lack balance. He always seemed to go for black and white or right and wrong in all things. With the arrogance of my age-group, I spelled out the system of alliances I had learned in school and challenged his position. Too late, I realised there could be no meeting ground in 'academics' of that sort. From then on I would steer clear of undermining tactics and cheap victories.

In no way could he envisage how I had got to the point where I wanted a university career. Indications in Red Cross messages had been too slender to be convincing and for over a year they had not been getting through. Later letters had likewise made little impact. My life on the mainland was still an enigma, a blank only partially sketched in with personalities such as Eug and Helene, whom he knew a little, and Miss Roughton and Miss Keating, whom he did not know at all. The gap was called THE WAR. He had not yet read my diaries and why indeed should he plough through the morass of that detail? Where would it take him? That life was gone. He would see it overstuffed with headmistresses. If I went the same way, I would be leading a comfortable middle class life, cushioned with domestic help and far away in England, separated from my Guernsey roots and upbringing and absent in his old age. The evacuation had been a hiccup, an unwanted interruption in the general continuity of things. I was trying to turn it into a lasting break away. He was shaken. When his father and brothers all died, he had vowed to continue the family business on his own. 'F.M. Brehaut & Sons' would be perpetuated through him and the effort of the years brought to fruition. It came, therefore, as a double blow when Milestone's ruination by the Germans was followed by the State's decision to complete their policy of flattening it into the airport. The third blow might be imminent – if his children turned away from the business which he was trying to revive and relocate at Rue des Landes. He was transforming the old coach house into a workshop and could already visualise the sign over the door: 'B.P. Brehaut & Sons'. He expected Brian or John to follow in his footsteps and was full of good intentions.

"Give her time to settle and things will soon be back to normal," I could hear him thinking. He took me into his office and pointed to a drawer in the old pine desk his father had made. That was where he kept the stamps. "Now, if there's anything you need, just ask." The idea of giving regular pocket money had not occurred to him. "I want everything to be the same as it used to be," he went on confidentially. He was appealing lovingly to my old self, as though my larger size were an irrelevance and bore no hint of maturational change. "If you have any little troubles, you can always come to us," he added, not noticing the ones I'd posed already. And off he went; his brusque and kindly self was heading for the workshop. He'd said his piece and, in his terms, it was a generous overture. With pride, he stood solidly in the centre and he would help others to find their feet and take up their positions around him. That was the way of it. His world had gone to pieces but now it fell to him to integrate the parts. People admired him for his fortitude. He was a good old boy and sometimes he would laugh. His rough edges could be forgiven, because he went round meaning well. It was so plain to see. When someone knocked at the back door, he would glance at the man in cloth cap and navy knitted 'Guernsey' and already he had 'read' the situation: 'She's gone.' He knew the family and there was no need of words. He would grab his cap from the hook and the rule from the office table and by the time he had felt for the opening in the back pocket of his overalls and slotted it in, he was up the yard and off to measure the body.

For a long time, I wondered why there were no condolences or a friendly grip of the arm. And then I understood. It was the way the old country folk related to each other. Death was treated as a very matter of fact occurrence. People were used to it. Facing its finality brought out all that was hardy, dour, stolid, silent and determined about the Guernsey character. Those were traits which did not normally stop the same people from grumbling about the costs and the inconvenience. The disgruntled could be both sullen and sardonic. For generations, they had been shaped by the demands of the land, and their relationship to it was their relationship to each other. Pride, a sense of achievement, an urge to economise tempered with bursts of generosity, a deeply felt and underlying sense of gratitude which rarely found expression, all these were the outcome of the country people's hard work on the land. Their identity was usually defined by their relationship to it: Bazil Brehaut of Rue des Landes. That said it all. I never heard anyone say: Miss Keating of 22, Edmund St. In Guernsey, they took their colour from their habitation. And it had honour.

It was no wonder that the Germans had made little impact in the country areas. Their orders in the Press, their foreign money, their impingement on housing, their fortifications, their military presence . . . everything was just externally imposed, a superficial nuisance like the flies on cattle.

As usual, the cows would be milked, the patois spoken and the old buried – no matter what. Sod them!

A story is still told of the old self-sufficient country woman, who was asked by an English visitor to the island, "And how did you manage on the rations in the Occupation?" "Oh!" she answered, "We never bestirred ourselves to go and fetch those. . . . You want to know about the Germans? We took no notice of them. They never came round here. They didn't bother us."

When I saw myself in this setting, I recognised the unshakeable stability of the island and its power to hold. How extraneous my Rochdale life must seem. So that was why it was always described by my parents in terms that seemed relevant to them – the separation. Now it was over. I was like a soldier coming home from the war and the onus was on me to settle and resume old ways. There was little sign of middle ground where each could meet half-way.

I was afraid that my wanting to go to university would be construed as lack of loyalty and ingratitude, a rebuff and rejection of my parents' needs and expectations, a cruel blow to their hopes of reuniting. If I ever did get their emotional backing, it would be too late for the entrance exams. I would have to 'go it alone' and rely on the notes Miss Keating had promised to send, giving me the addresses of universities I could approach for a prospectus. As soon as the time came, I would set to work on the list. She had been supportive, reassuring and generous. If Guernsey education was too disrupted to provide proper facilities, I could go back to Rochdale, she said, and stay with her for another year and take the necessary exams from her school.

It seemed that Brian had been at home for months, but in reality, it was a mere three weeks since he had filed through the barbed wire at the harbour and passed the waiting crowds unrecognised. It was on the second 'parade' that he was spotted and identified and there was much shaking of hands through the barbed wire.

I realised early on that he was approaching the future differently. Unlike me, he had come to stay. At fifteen, he still had a considerable time to do at school and did not have to choose a career just yet. Already, he had gone the round of relations, met up with his friends and got the feel of things. He was settling into a pattern of home life which seemed so comfortable compared with the rigours of a wartime boarder's life on the moors of Derbyshire.

I felt that the five year period of absence would not colour the making of decisions about his future so much as it would affect mine. There would be time for adjustment and the growth of mutual understanding. I would be the one to open up the way and reach for new horizons and with more pain.

# Chapter XVIII

## *'Follow the Star!'*

While adjustments were being made at home, a letter came from Miss Roughton for my parents. Her school could no longer make provision for me. The authorities had decided that I could take up my scholarship at the Ladies' College once more. With Higher School Certificate behind me, I could apply for university entrance from there.

My parents wrote a nice letter to thank her for what she'd done in the war. "Oh!" they said, when I explained that she had considered herself bound by a special promise to them to watch over me throughout and how she had made it all a point of honour, effectively blocking my prospects of rejoining the Ladies' College on the mainland and of attending Miss Keating's school. They were most surprised. They had no recollection of expecting such an undertaking from her or of receiving one. On that fateful day in June 1940, they said, they had approached her personally only because it was necessary to have her permission for me to be taken with my old school. Otherwise, they would have followed the set procedures like all the other parents and merely registered my name at a staff table. Yes, she'd done a good job. It must have been very hard work. They were grateful to her as they were to all the people who had helped us. But thankfully, that was in the past, though, and now there was a lot to do.

Somehow I found myself walking through the gates of the Ladies' College ready to start the new autumn term. I had the curious sensation of one who is attending two schools twice. It was to give me a much needed sense of detachment and free me from the pressure of all-out loyalty. I could sit loosely to the new; it was temporary; a means to an end.

The building was in fairly good shape as it had been used mainly for office purposes by the States' Essential Commodities Committee which dealt with allocations of food, fuel, clothing and other rationed goods during the Occupation. Many of the school's belongings had been kept in order by its bursar, Miss Adèle Lainé.

Time went quickly. The school made a surprisingly cohesive start considering the administrative and staffing problems. There were 157 girls on the register, forty-two of whom had been with the College in Denbigh. Sixteen were, like me, rejoining the school after leaving it in 1940 and ninety-nine were new. Consolidating such an amalgam would be an achievement in itself. During the war, the staff had been whittled down to four, because the number of girls fell to sixty. Now those four, who included only Miss Bateson from the pre-Occupation era, came to Guernsey, intent on rehabilitation. A few others were appointed. Miss Ellershaw stood, a stately figure in academic gown, on the platform of the panelled hall with stained glass windows. The aura of traditional values gave weight to the doughty pilgrim hymn:

> *He who would valiant be*
> *'Gainst all disaster*
> *Let him in constancy*
> *Follow the Master.*

We were on our way, carrying on and heading forward.

It was a small sixth form. Some were aiming to get into Training Colleges. I was the only one with university in mind. The timetable allowed for some diversity. I was made joint Head Girl with Mary Chapman, who after a few weeks at Roylelands, had been transferred to the Ladies' College. She represented the Denbigh strand and I the medley of other 'new' ones.

As the staff had not seen my previous work, they did not know what I was capable of achieving and I did not know what standard was expected. I would take Latin and Geography to more advanced levels and practise writing essays. I had a few dummy runs under examination conditions: 'In the kingdom of the blind, the one-eyed is king.' As I tried desperately to outline how to be visionary when blinkered, I was voicing how I felt in a world of conflicting emotions and values.

I was even more fascinated than before in finding out what made people tick, their goals and modes of relating. I asked probing questions about the Sociology and Psychology courses on offer at the universities, but received little encouragement. It seemed they were new and Cinderella subjects, accorded little status and in themselves not leading to jobs without other training or experience. Social workers, especially women, were very overstretched and underpaid. If I wanted to teach or had to, the courses were of little use, since they would not appear in a school curriculum and would not equip me to teach the subjects that were.

I decided that to get to university, at all, I would have to use history as a backbone subject and then see if the field would open up. Perhaps teaching was the answer. I veered towards it partly because I could see its value and partly because it seemed the only viable way to proceed. The Ministry of Education was offering grants for tuition to those willing to commit themselves to this course. Such financial backing would relieve my father from feeling the pressure to pay.

I thought deeply about the need to help others and wondered how best to shape a career which would take this into account. I was greatly distressed about the situation at home, where I seemed to be doing the opposite of helping: I was acting hurtfully towards my parents in planning to leave the island for training, shunning much of their accustomed life style and failing to settle in the expected emotional niche. It was disturbing to them when I was not under their tight control. Did they think I would end up a wastrel or was it just that they felt I wasn't their sort? The conflict of interests worried me. Wasn't that just what wars were about? And we were trying to construct a more peaceful world.

When my self-confidence was at a low ebb, I remembered some of my school reports which had pointed to a good analytical mind and a developing critical faculty. Perhaps these were gifts which God could use. But how and in what area?

I was facing great competition in the rush for university places. Men were pouring out of the Forces and trying to make up for lost time. In Liverpool, I heard, there were 600 applications for sixty places.

After exams and interviews on the mainland, I was offered places at Bristol and London. I decided on Bedford College in Regent's Park and was admitted to the hall of residence, where students who had shown promise were assigned. I accepted a Ministry of Education grant which would cover my tuition fees and was delighted when the Clothworkers' Company made available to the Ladies' College a new exhibition of £80 p.a. for three years in higher education and I was nominated as the first holder. The sum would pay for residence and leave a little over for books and my journeys back to Guernsey. Clothing was likely to be rationed for some time to come and would therefore not be an expensive item. It looked as if I could be self-sufficient and I was immensely relieved. I could go ahead without initial financial support from my father who was finding the question of making such an outlay a difficult one to face. His income during the war had been negligible and now he had to use his savings to set up his workshop at Rue des Landes, buy new equipment and supplies for his business and purchase Summerville. My grandparents wanted it to stay in the family and the Robins looked to him to make that possible. Tricky problems over compensation for Milestone might take several years to iron out and he was disappointed that many obstacles seemed insurmountable. He stood to lose a lot.

I had realised, early on, that if I was to take a degree and go on to teaching, I would not be able to have any steady boyfriend for years to come, especially as Local Education Authorities did not normally employ married women teachers or even those who were engaged. Such appointments were deemed to be short-lived and inadvisable. Marriage for the experienced teacher usually ended her career. There had been exceptions in the war, but it was likely that in a very competitive field, the old conventions would apply. I would have to do without a special person and avoid making close attachments. For me, the choice involved much soul-searching. I had no experience of teaching except in a church setting and had no means of judging whether I could make a success of it. I was also positioning myself outside Guernsey, perhaps for always. There was little prospect of finding work with grammar school objectives on the island. The only schools taking pupils to School Certificate or beyond were the two I had attended (leaving out of account any future provision that the Roman Catholic Church might make). The boys' schools did not take women teachers in the mainstream subjects.

By my actions, I might be disinheriting myself, making myself into an exile once again, though of my own volition. There was little sense of security when it came to the future, unless I fitted into the accepted roles. There were very few openings for women graduates in History unless they taught or abandoned their subject to work as librarians or secretaries. I knew I was taking risks. There would be much gruelling work ahead. The memorising of historical data, which had to be mastered before developmental processes could be understood or evaluated . . . all this was just hard slog. Could I spend the next few years on this?

In the end, I decided to use my head to find my feet and hoped I would not lose my balance in the process.

Now there was energy for life, growth and adventure . . .

Follow the Star!

The rousing song learned in school re-emerged later on in my own synthesis:

*Be wise! Look up!*
*Just where you are;*
*We'll meet at journey's end*
*By light of a star.*

My father had always promised that when Brian and I were fourteen, we could have a bicycle. Now, much later than intended, he'd produced them. I sped downhill through the lanes, furiously ringing my bell to advise the hens around the corner I was coming. I loved the wind in my hair as I soared along the coastal roads invigorated. I shook off the sedate constraints of school and home and billet and was freed from the scrutiny and comment of the passengers on the island bone-shakers, those well-used buses rattling on at 30 m.p.h. The whisperers in the seats behind me must have thought I couldn't understand the patois.

"Who's that tall one who got on at le Bourg?"
　*"She must be Bazil Brehaut's daughter. . . . You know, the under-taker. . . . He did Madeleine's funeral."*
"Ah! yes! . . . The one who built the bungalow for Mr. Martin."
　*"That's right. His workshop was at Milestone, but nearly everything's gone. He'll never go back there now."*
"Who does she look like? Can you see her face?"
　*"No, we'll have to wait till she gets off."*
"Weren't there two boys?"
　*"Yes. The youngest one was only a toddler when she went away. The family lived in town during the Occupation, but they're back at Rue des Landes now. I noticed the curtains were up when we passed."*

I felt uncomfortable in such a closed community. It was one thing to be privately rooted, another to be publicly pigeon-holed. I wanted to be anonymous as in a town and free from claustrophobia. When someone asked me if I liked the island, I said, "Yes, but I wouldn't want to live here!" It seemed too constraining.

The first time I came riding up behind an army truck, I was hailed with shouts and wolf-whistles. Completely taken aback, I slunk behind and veered into a lane, for they were Germans. I'd been face-to-face and paralysed, not knowing what to do. Parties were still clearing mines and obstacles from cliffs and beaches.

If such an incident had happened in the war and I had smiled or waved, would that have counted as collaboration? Some local girls who'd 'entertained' the troops were labelled 'Jerrybags' and there were growers who had been forced to produce vegetables in their greenhouses for the Germany Army. Were they disloyal? I heard of a few who vowed they wouldn't give the Germans something for nothing and, eventually, they made a tidy profit out of the arrangement. Was it the amount of remuneration they received which made the practice questionable? And, ethically, was there a difference between obeying a German order to grow potatoes or to vacate your house? In each case, you were responding to their authority.

Many members of the States advised islanders to adhere to the regulations which the Germans imposed, without defiance. The provocation would get them nowhere, but could well provide a ready excuse for reprisals and deportations. Feeling helpless, most people preferred a recognised state of coexistence rather than risk a fear-ridden futile life of petty resistance and the consequent clamp-down.

Those who broke German rules by selling milk or giving out rationed food on the quiet ran the risk of being blighted as black marketeers and many trod a tightrope amid conflicting laws and loyalties. At one time or another, everyone benefited from acts of kindness which ignored German restrictions and vigilance.

The RAF raid on the island airport, which we had heard about on the Summerseat wireless in August 1940, had damaged the slates and glass of our Methodist church at the Forest. A nearby greenhouse had been hit. My mother and John were only a few hundred yards away at Rue des Landes when it happened and my father was cycling along a lane when he saw the bombs actually falling from the aircraft. After that, the Methodist and Anglican authorities had felt their churches at le Bourg were too susceptible and closed them, although, later, the Germans had used the Forest Parish Church exclusively for their own worship.

In July 1945, just a few weeks before I arrived, services were resumed in our Methodist church. Mrs. Heaume, whom I had met among the bales of cloth in the Bolton market, was settling back in her homestead with her two evacuated sons and the husband she had not seen for five years. As we now know, the rifts made in such split families were not always properly healed. Growing together could take years of time, patience and goodwill.

As more children returned, our Sunday School re-opened. I was back in the small Primary room, where I had once been taught by the 'grey' and the 'brown' ones. Now, I was a teacher myself. The same dog-eared Bible pictures were still rolled up in bundles, ready to unfold again their familiar depictions of 'The Good Samaritan' and 'The Sower' to a fresh semi-circle of small faces. War restrictions on paper and publishing meant inevitable delays before they could be replaced with newer images.

Les Adams, Sion, Torteval, Carmel, Galaad. These names featured in my father's conversation whenever he was preaching in these island chapels. In spite of the demands of his business, he spent much time in preliminary reading and his sermons were thoughtful and rock solid at heart. During the Occupation, when he had free access to Rev. Moore's wide range of books, he had spent many a quiet evening reading. There was little else to do when it was dark and curfew restrictions kept people in their homes. On his return to the island, Rev. Moore had been delighted to find his library intact and every volume dusted. I was to find that my mother had also read more widely than I realised, for she was not given to discuss impressions or ideas from books. The works of Jane Austen, Victor Hugo, John Bunyan and many others had been carefully removed from Rue des Landes and stored.

As time wore on and we became more used to each other, I saw how strong a role the church had played in my parents' lives, not only in building up their faith, but in widening their horizons. Frequently, there were speakers from the mainland and overseas, inspiring large rallies with their own insights and their vision. In response, local people had gone out as missionaries to the Ivory Coast or India and Ceylon. I found out too, that most families had connections in Prince Edward Island or the far-flung parts of Canada, Australia and New Zealand. In my grandparents' youth and before, there had been times of great economic hardship on the island and the younger sons, under the strict rules of primogeniture then in force, had no prospect of inheriting enough land to make a living, and had emigrated.

Our evacuation experiences had revealed that many Guernsey families had members in England and that connections between the island and the mainland were closer than we had realised. (It is likely that those with no close contacts across the Channel stayed at home, since, as evacuees, they would have no one to act as anchor.)

My parents were loath to see me go back to England now, mainly because they had seen the reintegration of the family in terms of all its members being in one place as a single unit. I was a challenge to this hope which had helped them through the Occupation. To me as a young adult, their compulsive need to hold things together in this way, seemed unnecessary. I didn't intend to break away and their possessive hold felt like a tight constraint. I understood (I thought) their fear of further loss and disruption, but resisted the pressure. They seemed to think that if I loved them, I would relate to them with ties that felt the same as pre-war ones. If I was no longer the dependent and dependable little girl I had been, then it was proof that I had grown away from them and did not want to create or respect a bond.

I saw that it might take many years before I could be my own person without seeming to provoke their anxieties. Sometimes, I thought the only way forward was for me to make decisions on my own, since there was so much anxiety about making joint ones. And then I felt sorry and guilty when this course seemed to be so hurtful. It would take a long time for mutual confidence to grow. I had lived for five years without them and no longer needed to have them available to consult. They felt I did not value their judgment enough. They had been brought up to defer to their own elders and found my independent attitude difficult to come to terms with.

For my part, I had worked hard and shown initiative, according to the precepts given. So where had all that got me?

It was a time when we all felt uneasy. Back on my old stamping ground, I was once again the outsider and the exile, the one appearing from a different stable. I'd lost the sure foothold of the legitimate as if, in growing, I had damaged what had given me a valid place. Some things had gone 'awry' and now it was too late to straighten them and push them back on course. What lay ahead was first-aid patching, damage limitation and the salvaging of opportunities for new development. It was worth treading carefully and trying to forge some strong relationships.

One of the great surprises of the first year back related to the use of the patois. John, who had grown up in a house where it was used all the time, did not speak it. It was not expected of him. Children used English at school and everywhere else. Even in the hard-pressed isolation of Guernsey, when people were striving to maintain their feelings of solidarity, the patois had virtually stopped being the langauge of domestic intimacy between the generations. It was still freely used by the middle aged and old who had grown up with it, but thousands could not understand it, especially among the Townies, those who lived in the vicinity of St. Sampson's and St. Peter Port.

Now, few of the returning younger children could remember it and those in my age group from patois-speaking homes made no attempt at fluency. I was no longer freely bilingual. At Rue des Landes, our parents chatted to eath other in the patois, even when we were present, as they knew we could follow every word, but when they spoke to us directly, it was in English. The patois was fast dying out and no one seemed too bothered. John, the one who had not been away, soon picked up a Lancashire accent, which, for a time, was all the rage among his schoolmates.

The formation of a Youth Club at our church was one of the signs of a buoyant expectancy. Brian and I were quick to join in the cycle trips, games, and discussions. Some of us took torches, so that we could ramble along favourite cliff paths afterwards. In the moonlight, the stark silhouette of branches against a silvery sea created sets of breathtaking beauty. How hard it was to return for my parents' bedtime at 10 p.m.!

Most of us in the club had been children together. The ones evacuated had been scattered and so we did not know each other as teenagers any better than we knew those who had stayed behind. The club represented a new beginning in our life on the island and we were encouraged by the stalwart support of 'old stagers' like Mr. Theo Allez and Mr. Tom Lainé, whose face seemed permanently composed into the gratitude of his prayers. In these struggling beginnings, the church was affirming that young people mattered.

As I squashed the tiny little red insects which crawled so profusely over the church pews, warmed by the day's sun, I was aware that even in rote words of praise and the amateurish sermon, there was a genuine and deep sense of thanksgiving. I found no overt bitterness or desire for revenge on the Germans. We had all come through and wherever we had been, we were now a people together, tired perhaps and faced with problems, but on pilgrimage. In those bonds of solidarity, there was a growing trust in God's purposes and in His grace. The whole of life could be lived as a prayer.

As the evening light faded at the close of the service, the preacher turned to the well-loved hymn, 'The day Thou gavest, Lord, is ended'. . . .

> *So be it, Lord; thy throne shall never*
> *Like earth's proud empires, pass away.*
> *Thy kingdom stands and grows for ever,*
> *Till all thy creatures own thy sway.*

In my short life span, the power bases in the international arena had shifted dramatically. In my particular patch also, authority had been assumed by this person or that, since it could not be accorded by inaccessible parents. In elusive ways, my mentors had balanced their sense of responsibility for me, relative to each other. For most of us, there were muddles and uncertainties and some distress, but overriding all, were the benefits of the goodwill and kindness which we experienced, and we generated our own vitality.

There was enough continuity with our home background to preclude breakdown and the links with the familiar helped us survive the initial shock of disconnection and fragmentation. Most of us received enough encouragement and nurture to grow and develop and to get over the feelings of loss and deprivation and the loneliness of having no one close to confide in. There were some who forged ahead more confidently than their own restricted upbringing at home might have allowed.

Looking back, I see now, that like any other slice of life, this one had everything life is. The variations are endless in their fascination, but

*plus ça change, plus c'est la même chose.*

This story, in many ways, exemplifies the emotional, social and cultural changes and realignments experienced by Guernsey people in this period. Wherever we were and whatever we were doing, we were involved and played our part in this process.

It would need a closer scrutiny of those times and of my subsequent development to see why four main strands run through the texture of this presentation. In the writing, they seem to have emerged by a process of self-selection, each distinct, but interwoven:

–   how authority, power and responsibility were exercised
–   how continuity and change were experienced in relation to each other
–   how personal communication and relationships evolved
–   how life was viewed as a prayer, where grace was given and received.

Their evolving pattern in my life influenced the shaping of my sense of identity and set me on my course. In trying to understand where I belonged, how I related to others and what I hoped for, I came to find myself. Everything that happened then or since is even now being distilled and transmuted into that living whole, which is 'the hope of glory'.

By the end of the summer of 1946, the conversation at home had turned to packing and my moving on to London. My parents by now had realised more clearly that what had happened could not be undone and we had much to build on. There was more to my life than being part of theirs.

News of others who had gone away was reassuring. Ruth was working successfully as a nurse, for instance. This time, my leaving would not be such a devastating break and I would be in contact.

Sometimes, I felt, they must be pleased with all my hopes and plans, for there was a burst of practical support. Knowing that Aunty Am was never one to splurge out on dress, my mother asked her if she could spare a few clothing coupons. I did not have enough to replace my worn pyjamas. The wooden hay-box which had cooked so many a wartime meal was scrubbed and earmarked for my books. It would supplement the case which had stood me in good stead and held the symbols of the things I valued. Where that case was, there was my home also.

And now, a rugged path led me over the cliffs from Petit Bôt towards le Gouffre, where small fishing boats bobbed on the deep blueness of unfathomable water.

High up, time-worn in huge formations, protruding rocks emerged through creeping strands of tiny flowerets, their surface flattened by long centuries of wind and rain. I found a cradling niche, where I could sit in armchair comfort and hear the crash of waves, which splintered on the rocks below and splayed with whitening froth into black gullies. The sunlit slopes still bore brow-beaten signs of the denuded. For near defensive installations, close vigilance had kept the bracken low.

But soon, the gorse would spring again from yesterday's dried furze. In time, its hopeful flame would blaze again in yellow glory.

I knew that, come what may, I would return for deep reflection. Those tides would break upon my shores long after I had reached the end of my last journey.